ROUSSEAU ON

WOMEN, LOVE, AND FAMILY

JEAN-JACQUES ROUSSEAU

On Women, Love, and Family

Edited by
CHRISTOPHER KELLY AND
EVE GRACE

DARTMOUTH COLLEGE PRESS
Hanover, New Hampshire

PUBLISHED BY UNIVERSITY PRESS OF NEW ENGLAND
HANOVER AND LONDON

Dartmouth College Press
Published by University Press of New England,
One Court Street, Lebanon, NH 03766
www.upne.com
© 2009 by the Trustees of Dartmouth College
Printed in the United States of America
5 4 3 2 1

Library of Congress Cataloging-in-Publication Data

Rousseau, Jean-Jacques, 1712–1778.
[Selections. 2009]
Rousseau on women, love, and family / edited by
Christopher Kelly and Eve Grace.
p.   cm.
Includes bibliographical references.
ISBN 978-1-58465-750-7 (pbk. : alk. paper)
1. Women. 2. Love. 3. Family. 4. Philosophy, French—18th century.
I. Kelly, Christopher, 1950– II. Grace, Eve. III. Title.
B2132.E5   2009
194—dc22   2008054083

Frontis illustration: The inoculation of love,
Beinecke Rare Book and Manuscript Library, Yale University

 University Press of New England is a member of the Green Press Initiative. The
paper used in this book meets their minimum requirement for recycled paper.

Contents

III. Women and Politics

IV. Love

V. Family

Preface

The majority of the works included in this volume are taken from *The Collected Writings of Rousseau*. Some changes have been made in the translations, and endnotes have been reduced. New translations have been made of material taken from *Emile*, the *Second Discourse*, and the *Letter to d'Alembert*. In addition, new translations have been done of *Emile and Sophie; or, The Solitaries* and the letters to "Henriette." We have consulted the critical editions of *Le Lévite d'Éphraïm* (Paris: Honoré Champion, 1999) and *Émile et Sophie, ou les Solitaires* (Paris: Honoré Champion, 2007), both edited by Frédéric S. Eigeldinger.

We would like to thank Randall Hendrickson for his assistance on the bibliography and Joel McCrum for his technical assistance in the preparation of the manuscript. Eve Grace would like to express her gratitude to the Earhart Foundation for its generous support of the labors that went into this volume. We thank the Beinecke Rare Book and Manuscript Library for supplying the illustrations from the first edition of *Julie*, used as the cover and frontispiece of this volume. Finally, we thank Jonathan Pidlueny for his work on the index.

Chronology

1712

June 28: Rousseau is born in Geneva.

1728

March 14: Rousseau decides to run away from Geneva.

1737–1740

While living in Chambéry, Rousseau writes *Narcissus*.

1746–1751

Rousseau works as a secretary for the Dupin family. Probable date of "On Women," *Essay on the Important Events of Which Women Have Been the Secret Cause*, and "Household on rue St. Denis."

1752

December 18: Premiere of *Narcissus*.

1753

January or February: Publication of *Narcissus* along with its important "Preface."

1754

Summer: During a visit to Geneva, Rousseau forms his plan to write *The Death of Lucretia*.

1756

Rousseau mentions in a letter that he has finished *Queen Whimsical*.

1757

October 10: Publication of Volume VII of the *Encyclopédie*, containing d'Alembert's article on Geneva.

1758

August: Publication of the *Letter to d'Alembert*.

1761

January: *Julie* goes on sale in Paris one month after going on sale in London.

1762

Possible date of *Letters to Sara*.

May: Publication of *Emile*.

June 9: A warrant is issued for Rousseau's arrest and he flees France, composing *The Levite of Ephraïm* on his trip.

Earliest references to *Emile and Sophie; or, The Solitaries*.

November: Rousseau works on *Pygmalion*.

1764

May 7: First of the letters to "Henriette."

November 4: Second letter to "Henriette."

1766

January 13: Rousseau arrives in London, accompanied by David Hume.

1770

April: Rousseau composes some of the music for *Pygmalion*. It is performed in Lyon.

1778

July 2: Rousseau dies at Ermenonville.

Introduction

This volume gathers writings, both short works given in their entirety and excerpts from longer works, in all of which Jean-Jacques Rousseau explores human sexuality. Rousseau is most famous for his fiery denunciations of the rapacity of the powerful and the plight of the weak, for his clarion call to freedom, humaneness, and equality. The new prophet of a benevolent Nature, Rousseau attacked the social and economic relations in which we are enmeshed as forcing us, against ourselves, to become the hypocritical, callous, petty, and unhappy beings we decry. Modern commentators on the condition of women, moved by a moral animus consistent with the thrust of Rousseau's critique of society, have decried the inequalities in political and economic power between women and men that lock women in a cage of stultifying traditional gender roles. Since Rousseau is so often regarded as a founder of the modern left and would therefore seem to be a kindred spirit, it comes as a disappointment to those concerned with women's issues to find that Rousseau does not adopt the account of sexual politics that would seem to these commentators to flow naturally from what they take to be his primary concerns. What follows are attempts to introduce Rousseau's complex, nuanced, and controversial account of women, love, and the family within the broader context of some of these primary concerns.

The disappointment of contemporary feminists does not stem from any sense that Rousseau ignored the issues that concern them. Indeed, perhaps no major political philosopher has devoted so much attention to issues involving women. Rousseau not only agrees but even insists that sexuality and the relations that develop with it have profound consequences for human life, both private and public. In his view, the ideals we hold of what is attractive or lovable lead us toward, or away from, the greatest of private joys. The way in which we experience both desire for others, and our own potential attractiveness to them, profoundly shape the character of our passions, our attachments, even our capacity for humaneness. The desire to be loved by one's beloved can sculpt mind, passions, and even flesh in the image of what we imagine our beloved imagines of us. In Rousseau's view, in fact, the opinions and expectations men and women have of one another play a decisive role in shaping the morals that are the keystone of a sound political order, or of the best possible existence on the margins of a corrupt one.

For Rousseau, the core of human health or happiness is a vigorous, even ferocious, independence. The measure of any social arrangement, then, would be the degree to which it fosters that independence. Yet Rousseau contends that social relations enslave us and put us into contradiction with ourselves; the more developed the society, the more harmful we become both for ourselves and others. If the relations between the sexes inevitably become part of the disease, however, they also hold out the best hope for a palliative, if not for a cure. Rousseau takes love so seriously, then, because love is fundamentally connected to liberty, and so to happiness.

Since Wollstonecraft, however, critics have charged that even if Rousseau's characterization of vigor and independence as the peak of human health applies to human beings simply, and not only to men, Rousseau seeks to cultivate it only in men.[1] The eponymous hero of his philosophical novel on education, *Emile*, is reared in every way to remain as much as possible his own master within society, a being who is ruled by his own reason and will. The education of Sophie, who is to become his wife, on the other hand, seems to be designed to make her nothing if not subject to opinion, a frivolous being concerned with appearance rather than strength who is submissive toward her husband and whose activities are limited to that of wife and mother. Rousseau is further charged with adding insult to injury by arguing that women are thereby fulfilling their natures.[2] Rousseau, then, seems to buy the independence of boys and men at the expense of physical and moral dependency in girls and women.[3]

For some commentators, then, Rousseau clearly falls back in this instance into the same "traditional" or "patriarchal" understanding that has so often been used to excuse the subjection of women. His work is therefore nothing if not a case in point of the depth of the alleged ingrained sexism of so many famous philosophers.[4] Rousseau's failure to demand the same equality and freedom for women as he does for men is in striking contrast to a number of his predecessors and contemporaries, who carried the torch of Enlightenment into this sphere as well, arguing that women should be emancipated from the legal and social restrictions that were imposed upon them.[5] It is less well known that early in his life, Rousseau's views seemed to have been more in harmony with theirs. In extant fragments of his early work, he deplored the inequality of conditions that prevented women from exercising and displaying their talents, and sketched a grim picture of a wife's brutal treatment at the hands of her husband.[6] During the period he wrote these passages, when he was employed as a secretary and research assistant in a wealthy family, Rousseau also engaged in extensive historical research on the political role women had played throughout history.

This work was undertaken, however, prior to the radical turn in his thought that began with his *Discourse on the Sciences and the Arts*, or *First Discourse*. While his later works do not simply abandon the conclusions of his earlier work—consider, for example, the mockery of the idea of male supremacy within a monarchy in *Queen Whimsical*[7]—the general tone is far different. With the *First Discourse* Rousseau ignited a controversy over the worth of civilization and progress that continues to this day. The "crowning achievement" of Enlightenment thought, allegedly, was to have discovered how to emancipate human beings from the ignorance, penury, and violence to which they were subject by nature, by binding them irretrievably to a civilization dedicated to scientific and material progress. A clear understanding of the inalienable appetite for comfortable self-preservation that drives human reason, a spirited defense of the individual's prudent reason as the only source of legitimate authority, and a sober adherence to the rules necessary to enable each to pursue the way toward satisfaction, provide the true and stable foundation for society governed by the universal and effective rule of law that nature fails to provide.[8]

Enlightenment thinkers claimed they had discovered an effectual morality: by constructing both political and private relations on the model of commercial contracts, duty can be made almost fully rational by transforming it into the handmaid of an unleashed and unabashed self-interest. Careful inference from our passions, as well as reflection on the behavior of human beings whenever the easy flow of security and goods is threatened, reveal us to be fundamentally anxious, and therefore aggressive, beings who are driven to struggle in a relentless competition for power after power, if only to secure a temporarily stable footing.[9] Human beings are therefore profoundly individual, for the goods they seek cannot really be shared, and their welfare demands that they enter any relation with others fully aware of this fundamental fact about themselves. It followed from this understanding that marriage and family too must be understood as a temporary contract between two rational individuals of equal freedom or power, to be terminated at the pleasure of the parties once the little corporation of raising children had achieved its objective.[10]

The way to lasting peace and prosperity, to ever greater freedom and equality, seemed open. Standing at the cradle of liberal democratic free market societies, however, Rousseau pronounced these hopes to be stillborn. His declaration of war against the philosophical and political doctrines with which the modern realists sought to transform the world was accompanied by a ferocious attack on their rationally self-interested individual, always on the lookout for the best deal, whom they sought to promote as an ideal human type. The radical change that took place in Rousseau's account of the optimal relations between the sexes, in his views on love, family, and the role of women within societies, then, is inseparably connected to his profound doubts that the child of the Enlightenment would grow up to enjoy freedom and equality in any real sense within modern liberal commercial societies. The same reservations applied in spades to the modern "enlightened" absolute monarchies favored by many of Rousseau's contemporaries.

Rousseau's turn against the Enlightenment, however, was decidedly not a conservative or reactionary one. In the second of his three central works, the *Discourse on the Origin and Foundations of Inequality Among Men*, he showed himself to be in fundamental agreement with the reductionist account of human nature, according to which our nature must be understood in terms of subrational inclinations, and our reason conceived as only the "scout and spy" of the passions. He had no quarrel with liberal or early modern thinkers over the claim that reason reveals us to be an "ingenious machine" driven solely by self-love. The *Second Discourse* not only shares, but deepens, the understanding of human beings as radically asocial or individual, bereft of any authority or guidance independent of the pressure of their basic drives.[11]

Rousseau does, however, disagree on two fundamental points. First, he doubts whether the rational account of nature according to which we are more clever animals is in the end compatible with the needs of political societies. His contemporaries were, in his view, too idealistic about the benefits to be derived from the widespread adoption of enlightened rationalism. "Your system is very good for the men of Utopia; it is worth nothing for the children of Adam."[12] For the golden rule of doing unto others as we would have done unto us cannot be founded upon a calculation of self-interest, and least of all when it is properly understood. No binding obligation to respect the rights of others can be constructed from self-interest alone, for the very selfishness that leads us to make promises of mutual aid in order to obtain what we wish will lead us to see that exploiting or abandoning those promises is at times far more profitable. If no common good exists that transcends the temporary alliance of the private interests of each, then each reasonably comes to perceive that "social laws are a yoke that each wants to impose on the other without having to bear himself."[13] Indeed, using others as a means to our interest, and at the expense of theirs may not only be more profitable but, in the end, according to the Enlightenment argument itself, is entirely justified.

The more human beings understand themselves as individuals in competition with one another, then, the more their relations will become a covert state of war. Among the casualties of such a state will be the only bonds that actually and effectively restrain human beings, the bonds of sentiment and affection.[14] While commercial liberal societies will aim shrewdly to manage this cold war, one in which the "spirit of party and faction" regulates "the necessary and ordinary operations of government," Rousseau predicts that we will merely abandon force for fraud. Modern societies will be clothed with the "appearance of right," under which they will inevitably if secretly succumb to the iron law of oligarchy.[15]

In Rousseau's view, Enlightenment thinkers were not only, in the long run, subverting the very moral laws they had hoped effectively to create for the first time. They were much too superficial in their account of human nature, an account that they claimed justified the explicit narrowing of the political horizons of human beings to security of life and the pursuit of comfort, power, and pleasure. In their view, we are forced to take our bearings from the most basic self-interest, because no principle of reason or morality has any independent authority or power over our self-regard. Rousseau responded to this claim by questioning the naturalness of the power-hungry passions that so informed his contemporaries' understanding of what is human.

He did so in the *Second Discourse* by taking the reductionist account of nature to its logical conclusion. Once we dismantle the view that human beings are governed by "soul" (that is, ends shown to us by reason that transcend the satisfaction of "appetite"), once we argue that reason is only an instrument of the passions, we are compelled to reach the conclusion that all passions based on opinions—that is, all the human passions mistakenly imputed to nature—must have developed historically. The necessarily competitive passions that early modern thinkers had imputed to nature, and that put us in a natural state of conflict, may or may not arise depending on the development of our thinking, and on the kind of society in which we find ourselves. Societies in turn will differ according to historical epoch. While Locke and Hobbes may accurately describe the Europeans of their day, they do not account for very different human types in different epochs, who had lived without the needs and therefore the passions that his fellow moderns had deemed necessary or natural to them. Rousseau concludes, then, that human beings must have "evolved." He thereby eviscerated the "state of nature" teaching that grounded the legitimacy of liberal commercial societies, and that had already gained prominence in Europe and elsewhere.

Strictly speaking, the only inclinations that are truly natural to human beings are the necessary or physical impulsions that drive human beings directly whether they think of them or not; for example, hunger or the desire for rest. Before we develop ideas of more sophisticated ways to satisfy these desires, ideas that lead us to imagine and develop other and greater desires, these minimal needs are easily satisfied. Furthermore, natural self-love is tempered by our capacity to commiserate with the ills of others and to stay our hand when we can find our own good elsewhere. Originally, then, human animals are "naturally good": because their natural passions are limited, they are self-sufficient and free, and they neither want to serve others nor to dominate them.[16]

This natural freedom and equality is true of both the male and female human animal. For if we understand procreation and nurture in a strictly natural or physical sense, as it existed prior to the development of reasoning and continues to exist among other animals, there is no significant gender differentiation apart from the basic procreative division of labor. Without the long period of tutelage and dependence required to produce a thinking being, Rousseau argues, pregnancy and nursing would not fundamentally affect the female animal's independence. She had ties to her cubs for a time as a female bear does to hers, and like the female bear, kept her strength and independence.[17]

Moreover, self-love, our primary natural inclination, is originally independently and effortlessly satisfied; our fulfillment lies simply in ourselves, in our existing. The pleasure we take in the sentiment of our existence, the delight we take in our own vitality, lies, according to Rousseau, at the core of self-love. This sentiment, however, is intensified by the increased vigor with which one exercises one's will. As society begins to develop and human faculties to unfurl, the human species reaches "the veritable youth of the world" in "savage" or wild tribes. At this point, human beings have attained the greatest development of their faculties, intensity of passion, and proud self-consciousness, while still enjoying natural equality and independence. The sweet sentiment of existence is not only magnified through their splendid vigor and ferocious love of freedom, but supplemented by attachments to others—nation, children, wives and husbands, friends—that produce the "sweetest sentiments" felt by human beings.[18]

the turn of the conversation becomes less polite, reasons take on more weight; one does not content oneself with pleasantry or formulas of politeness. One does not get out of trouble by means of witticisms. One does not take it easy in disputation; each, feeling himself attacked by all of his adversary's strength, is obliged to use all of his own in order to defend himself, and this is the way that the mind acquires precision and vigor. If some licentious remarks get mixed up in all that, one must not be too alarmed by it: the less coarse are not always the most decent, and this language, which is a little bumpkinish, is still preferable to that more refined style, in which the two sexes seduce each other and decently familiarize themselves with vice. The manner of living, more in conformity to man's inclinations, also matches his temperament better. One does not remain all day long settled in a chair. One indulges oneself in games involving exercise; one goes, one comes, numerous circles are held in the country; others go there. One has gardens for walking, spacious grounds for exercising, a large lake for swimming, the entire country open for hunting, and one must not believe that this hunt is done so conveniently as in the environs of Paris where one finds game under one's feet, and where one shoots on horseback. In sum, these decent and innocent institutions gather together everything that can contribute to forming in the same men friends, citizens, soldiers, and consequently everything that best suits a free people.

The women's societies are accused of one defect; which is that of making them into scandal-mongers and satirists. Indeed, one can well understand that the anecdotes of a small town do not escape these feminine comitia; one also can well imagine that the absent husbands are not spared very much, and that every woman who is pretty and admired does not find it easy in her neighbor's circle. But perhaps there is more good than harm in this inconvenience, and it is still incontestably less than the ones that it replaces. For which is better: that with her friends a woman says some evil about her husband, or that, tête-à-tête with a man, she does some evil to him, that she criticizes her neighbor's dissoluteness, or that she imitates it? Although the Genevan women say what they know rather freely, and sometimes what they conjecture, they have a genuine horror of calumny, and one will never hear them bring up against someone else accusations that they believe to be false; while in other countries women, equally guilty by their silence and by their speeches, out of fear of reprisals, hide the evil that they know, and out of vengeance make public that which they have invented.

How many public scandals does the fear of these severe observers hold back? In our City they almost function as Censors. This is the way that in the fine times of Rome, the Citizens, keeping watch over one another, accused each other publicly out of zeal for justice. But when Rome was corrupted and there was nothing left to do for good morals but to hide the bad ones, the hatred of vices that unmasked them became a vice. To zealous citizens succeeded despicable informers; and rather than as previously the good accused the wicked, they were accused by them in their turn. Thank Heaven, we are far from such a fatal conclusion. We are not reduced to hiding ourselves from our own eyes, out of fear of horrifying ourselves. As for me, I shall not have a better opinion of women if they will be more circumspect: one will spare oneself more when one will have more reasons for sparing oneself, and when each will need for herself the discretion the example of which she will set for others.

Let us not be so alarmed, then, about the cackling of women's societies. Let them monger scandal as much as they want, provided that they monger it among themselves. Genuinely corrupt women could not bear this manner of living for very long, and however dear scandalmongering might be to them, they would like to do it with men. Whatever one might have said to me in this regard, I have never seen any of these societies, without a secret impulse of esteem and of respect for those who compose it. "Such is," I tell myself, "the destination of nature, which gives different tastes to the two Sexes, so that they might live separately and each in its manner.* These lovable persons pass their days this way given over to the occupations that suit them, or to innocent and simple amusements, very proper for touching a decent heart and for giving a good opinion of them. I do not know what they have said, but they have lived together: they might have talked about men, but they have done without them; and, while they were so severely criticizing other people's behavior, at least their own was irreproachable."

---

*This principle, upon which all good morals depend, is developed in a clearer and more extended manner in a manuscript of which I am the depositary, and that I am proposing to publish, if I have enough time left to do so, although that announcement is hardly suited to win over the favor of the Ladies in advance. One will easily understand that the Manuscript about which I was speaking in this note was that of the New Héloïse, which appeared two years after this work.[4]

CHAPTER EIGHT

Letters to "Henriette"

[*Particularly after the publication of* Julie *in 1761 and* Emile *in 1762, Rousseau received many letters from admiring readers, many of whom asked him for advice about their personal lives. The identity of the woman who called herself "Henriette" is not known and, at first, Rousseau assumed that his correspondent was Suzanne Curchod, a young woman from Geneva who was at one time engaged to Edward Gibbon and later married the financier Necker. "Henriette" wrote to Rousseau saying that, as a woman who was no longer young, not beautiful, and without a great fortune, she sought her happiness through the pursuit of knowledge that would satisfy her and be a resource for attracting friends. She asked for Rousseau's advice about how she should go about seeking the tranquillity of heart she desired and urged him to reconsider his reservations about women who pursued learning.*]

May 7, 1764

I am not hoodwinked, Henriette, about the object of your letter, nor about your dating it from Paris either. You are looking less for my opinion about the decision you have to make than for my approval for the one that you have made. On each of your lines I read these words written in large characters: *Let us see whether you will have the audacity to condemn someone who thinks and writes this way to no longer thinking or reading.* This interpretation is assuredly not a reproach and I can only be grateful to you for putting me in the number of those whose judgments matter to you. But while flattering me you are not requiring me, I believe, to flatter you, and to disguise my sentiment from you, when it pertains to your life's happiness, would be to respond badly to the honor you have done me.

Let us begin by setting aside useless deliberations. It is no longer a question of reducing yourself to sewing and embroidering. Henriette, one does not take off one's head like one's bonnet, and one does not return to simplicity any more than to childhood. Once it is in effervescence the mind always remains that way, and anyone who has thought will think for his whole life. That is the greatest misfortune of the condition of reflection: the more one feels its ills, the more one increases them, and all our efforts to leave it do nothing but bog us down more deeply in it.

Let us not speak about changing condition then, but of the advantage you can draw from yours. This condition is unfortunate; it must always be so. Your ills are great and without remedy. You feel it, you groan at it. And in order to make them bearable, you are seeking at least a palliative for them. Isn't that the object that you are proposing for yourself in your plans of studies and occupations?

Your means can be good for another purpose, but it is your end that is deceiving you: not seeing the genuine source of your ills, you are seeking that alleviation for them in the cause that gave birth to them. You are looking for them in your situation, whereas they are your work. How many people of merit, born into well-being and fallen into indigence, have borne it with less success and happiness than you have and nevertheless do not have those sad and cruel awakenings whose horror you describe with so much energy. Why so? Doubtless, you will say, they do not have so sensitive a soul. I have not seen anyone in my life who would not have said the same thing. But in the end what is that so vaunted sensitivity? Do you want to know, Henriette? In the final analysis it is an amour-propre that compares itself. I have put my finger on the seat of the illness.

All your miseries come and will come from having displayed yourself. By that manner of seeking happiness it is impossible for one to find it, for it is impossible ever to obtain the place one lays claim to in other people's opinion. If they grant it to us in some respect they refuse it to us in a thousand others and a single exclusion torments more than a hundred preferences flatter. It is much worse in a woman who, wanting to make herself into a man, to begin with puts all her own sex against her and is never taken at her word by ours, so that her pride is often as mortified by the honors that are given to her as by those that are refused to her. She never has precisely what she wants, because she wants contradictory things, and because, by usurping the rights of one sex without wanting to renounce those of the other, she fully possesses neither.

But the great misfortune of a woman who displays herself is to attract, to see only people who act as she does and to turn away the solid and modest merit that does not display itself at all and that does not run to where the crowd is assembled. No one judges men so badly and so falsely as people with pretensions; for they judge them only after themselves and what resembles them, and that is certainly not to see the human race by its beautiful side. You are dissatisfied with all your societies, I can well believe it. Those in which you have lived were the least suited to making you happy. You found no one in them in whom you could take that confidence that soothes. How would you have found it among people solely preoccupied with themselves alone, whom you asked for the foremost place in their hearts, and who do not even have a second place to give? You wanted to shine, you wanted to take precedence, and you wanted to be loved. These are incompatible things. You must choose. There is no friendship at all without equality, and there is never any equality recognized between people with pretensions. It is not enough to need a friend in order to find one; one must also have something to provide for someone else's needs. Among the provisions that you have made, you have forgotten that one.

The proceeding by which you acquired acquaintances does not justify either its object or its employment. You wanted to appear to be a philosopher; that was to renounce being one, and it was much better to have the air of a girl who is waiting for a husband than of a wise man who is waiting for incense. Far from finding happiness in the effect of the efforts that you have given to appearance alone, you have found in it only apparent goods and genuine ills. The condition of reflection into which you have thrown yourself has caused you incessantly to make painful returns upon yourself and you nevertheless want to banish these ideas by the same sort of occupation that gave them to you.

You see the error of the path you have been taking, and, believing you are changing it by means of your plan you are still proceeding toward the same goal by means of a detour. It is not at all for yourself that you want to return to studying; it is still for others. You want to make provisions of knowledge to take the place of looks at another age: you want to substitute the empire of knowledge for that of charms.

You do not want to become the indulgent companion of another woman, but you want to have indulgent male companions. You want to have friends, that is to say, a court. For the friends of a young or old woman are always her courtiers. They serve her or leave her; and you are taking from afar measures for holding onto them so as always to be the center of a sphere, small or large. Without that I believe that the provisions that you want to make would be the most useless thing for the object that you believe in good faith you are proposing for yourself. You want, you say, to put yourself in a condition to understand others.

Do you need a new competence for that? I do not know, in truth, what opinion you have of your present intelligence but were you to have Oedipuses for friends, I hardly believe that you very much want to understand the people whom you cannot understand now. Why, then, so many efforts to obtain what you already have? No, Henriette, that is not it; but when you will be a sibyl you want to proclaim oracles, your true plan is not so much to listen to others as to have auditors yourself. Under the pretext of laboring for independence you are still laboring for domination. It is thus that, far from alleviating the weight of opinion that is making you unhappy, you want to aggravate its yoke. This is not the way to procure more peaceful awakenings for yourself.

You believe that the only relief from the painful feeling that is tormenting you is to distance yourself from yourself. I, completely to the contrary, I believe that it is to bring you closer to yourself.

Your entire letter is full of proofs that until now the sole goal of your behavior has been to put yourself under other people's eyes in an advantageous manner. How, having succeeded in public as much as anyone and taking away from it so little internal satisfaction, have you not felt that the happiness you need is not there and that it was time to change plans? Yours might be good for glory but it is bad for felicity. One must not at all seek to distance oneself from oneself because that is not possible and because everything leads us back there however reluctantly. You agree that you passed some very sweet hours in writing to me and speaking to me about yourself. It is surprising that this experience does not put you on the way and does not teach you where you should seek, if not happiness, at least peace.

Nevertheless, although my ideas in this differ very much from yours, we are just about in agreement about what you should do. Henceforth study is the lance of Achilles that must cure the wound that it has made.[1] But you want only to quell the pain, and I would like to remove the cause of the illness. You want to distract yourself from yourself by means of philosophy. I, I would like it to detach you from everything, and return you to yourself. Be certain that you will be content with others only when you do not need them any longer, and that society will become agreeable to you only when it ceases to be necessary for you. Never having to complain about those from whom you will require nothing, it is then that you will be necessary for them, and feeling that you suffice to yourself, they will be grateful to you for the merit that you are willing to put in common. They will no longer believe that they are doing you a favor, they will always be receiving it; the pleasures of life will seek you out by the mere fact that you will not be seeking them out, and it is then that, satisfied with yourself without being able to be dissatisfied with others, you will have a peaceful sleep and a delightful awakening.

It is true that studies made with such contrary intentions must not resemble one another very much and there is certainly a difference between the cultivation that adorns the mind and the one that nourishes the soul. If you had the courage to savor a project whose execution will be very painful to you at first, it would be necessary to change your directions a great deal. That would require thinking about it well before beginning the work. I am sick, occupied, dejected, I have a slow mind, painful efforts are necessary for me to depart from the small circle of ideas that are familiar to me, and nothing is more distant from them than your situation. It is not just for me to tire myself out for nothing, for I can hardly believe that you would want to undertake to recast, so to speak, your entire moral constitution. You have too much philosophy not to see this undertaking with fright. I would despair of you if you set yourself to it easily. Thus let us not go any farther at present. It is enough that your principal question has been resolved. Follow the career of letters. No other is any longer left for you to chose.

These lines, that I am writing to you in haste, absentminded and suffering, perhaps do not say anything of what needs to be said: But the errors that my precipitation might have caused me to make are not irreparable. What was necessary before everything was to make you feel how much you interest me and I believe that you will not doubt it upon reading this letter. Up until now I regarded you only as a beautiful thinker who, if she had received a character from nature, had taken care to stifle it, to annihilate it under the exterior—like one of those masterpieces cast in bronze that one admires from the outside and whose inside is empty. But if you still can weep over your condition it is not without recourse; as long as a little substance is left in the heart, one must not despair of anything.

Motiers, November 4, 1764

If your situation, Mademoiselle, barely leaves you time to write to me, you must conceive that mine leaves me even less to answer you. You are only subjected to your business and the people you are dependent on and I, I am subjected to that of every piece of business and everyone because, judging me to be free, everyone wants to dispose of me by right of first occupant. Furthermore, always harassed, always suffering, overwhelmed with troubles and in a condition worse than yours, I use the few moments they leave me in breathing. I am too occupied not to be lazy. For a month I have been seeking a moment to write to you at my ease: this moment does not come, thus I must steal the time to write to you, for you interest me too much to leave you without an answer. I know few people who attach me more and no one who astonishes me as much as you do.

If you have found in my letter many things that did not square with yours: that is because it was written for someone other than you. In your situation there are such striking relations with that of another person who precisely was at Neufchâtel when I received your letter that I did not at all doubt that that letter came from her, and I was thrown off the scent with the idea that someone was trying to put me off it. Thus I spoke to you less based on what you told me about your character, than based on what was known to me about hers. I believed I found the reason for the internal malaise whose detailed account you were giving me in her mania for displaying herself, for she is a certified learned woman and fine wit. I began by attacking that mania as if it were yours, and I did not doubt at all that by leading you back to yourself I would be returning you to the repose from which, according to me, nothing is farther than the condition of a woman who displays herself.

A letter written on such a case of mistaken identity must contain many doltish remarks. Nevertheless in my error there was this good thing: it gave me the key of the moral condition of the person to whom I thought I was writing, and based on that assumed condition I believed I glimpsed a plan to follow to draw you away from the anguish that you were describing to me, without having recourse to distractions that, according to you, are the only remedy for it, and that, according to me, are not even a palliative. You inform me that I deceived myself, and that I saw nothing of what I believed I saw. How would I find a remedy for your condition, as this condition is inconceivable to me? You are a distressing and humiliating enigma to me. I believed I knew the human heart and I know nothing about yours. You are suffering, and I cannot relieve you.

What, because nothing foreign to you satisfies you, you want to flee yourself, and because you have cause to complain of others, because you despise them, because they have given you the right to do so, because you feel inside yourself a soul worthy of esteem, you do not want to console yourself with it for the disdain that those who do not resemble it inspire in you? No I do not understand anything about this strangeness; it is beyond me.

Shouldn't this sensitivity that makes you dissatisfied with everything have turned in on itself? Shouldn't it have nourished your heart with a sublime and delightful sentiment of amour-propre? Doesn't one always have in it the recourse against injustice and the compensation for insensitivity? It is so rare, you say, to meet a soul; that is true, but how can one have one, and not take pleasure in it; if upon probing one feels the souls of others to be limited and narrowed, one loses enthusiasm for them, one detaches oneself from them—but after having been so uncomfortable in someone else's house, how pleasant it is to return to one's own house. I know how much the need for attachment distresses sensitive hearts with the impossibility of forming them. I know how sad that condition is but I know that it nevertheless has some sweet pleasures, it causes streams of tears to be shed, it gives a melancholy that bears witness to us of ourselves, and that one would not want not to have. It causes solitude to be sought out as the only refuge in which one finds oneself with everything that one has reason to love. I cannot say it to you again too many times: I know neither happiness nor peace in distance from oneself; on the contrary, I sense more every day that one can be happy on the earth only in proportion as one removes oneself from things and one draws near to oneself. If there is some feeling sweeter than esteem for oneself, if there is some occupation more lovable than that of increasing this feeling, I might be wrong. But that is how I think; judge based on that whether it is possible for me to enter into your perspective, and even to conceive your condition.

I cannot keep myself from still hoping that you are deceiving yourself about the principle of your malaise, and that instead of coming from the sentiment that reflects upon yourself, it comes, on the contrary, from the one that still ties you, unbeknownst to you, to the things from which you believe you are detached and that perhaps you only despair of enjoying. I would like that to be so; I would see a foothold for acting, but if your account is exact I do not see any at all. If I had your first letter under my eyes at present and more leisure to reflect on it, perhaps I would succeed in understanding you and I would not spare my effort, for you genuinely worry me. But that letter is lost in heaps of papers; to find it again would take me more time than is left me, and I am forced to put back this search to other moments. If the uselessness of our correspondence did not make you lose enthusiasm for writing to me it is likely that this would be a means for understanding you in the end. But I cannot promise you any more exactitude in my answers than I am in a condition to put into them. What I do promise you, and which I shall keep very well, is to occupy myself with you very much, and not to forget you during my life. Your last letter, full of flashes of wit and deep feelings, affects me even more than the preceding one. Whatever you might say about it, I shall always believe that it depends only on the person who wrote it to be pleased with herself and to compensate herself that way for the rigors of her fate.

III

WOMEN AND POLITICS

CHAPTER NINE

The Death of Lucretia

Tragedy

[*Rousseau began to write this play while he was visiting Geneva shortly after he completed the* Second Discourse, *His goal in it was to provide a portrait of republican female virtue that could be successful in the monarchic French theater. He abandoned the work before completing it and soon turned his attention to his novel,* Julie. *In addition to the completed portion given below, numerous fragments of the continuation survive.*]

CHARACTERS

LUCRETIA
COLLATINUS, HUSBAND OF LUCRETIA.
LUCRETIUS, FATHER OF LUCRETIA.
SEXTUS, SON OF TARQUIN.
BRUTUS.
PAULINE, LUCRETIA'S CONFIDANT.
SULPITIUS, SEXTUS'S CONFIDANT.

The setting is Rome.

[ACT I.

SCENE I.
LUCRETIA, PAULINE.]

LUCRETIA.

Day is about to break; go, Pauline, prepare the purple dye and the linen so we can get back to work.

SOURCE: Jean-Jacques Rousseau, *Letter to d'Alembert, and Writings for the Theater. Collected Writings of Rousseau* X, trans. and ed. Allan Bloom, Charles Butterworth, and Christopher Kelly (Hanover, N.H.: University Press of New England, 2004).

PAULINE.

But Madam, in your exhausted condition you need rest more than work; and I don't know what to think of the extraordinary agitation I've seen you in for the last two days.

LUCRETIA.

I admit to you that I feel tormented by a hidden anxiety whose cause is unknown to me. A somber terror frightens me; sleep eludes me; and when my eyes become heavy, dreadful dreams jolt me awake and plunge me back into my fear. I don't know if it is my health declining; I don't know if it is forebodings that threaten me and, without being guilty, I believe I would feel remorse were my whole consolation not to be to turn inward to the depths of my heart.

PAULINE.

Lucretia, remorse! If an excess of the most severe virtue could give it, you would doubtless have it.

LUCRETIA.

Believe me, Pauline, virtues never have excesses, and anyone who had them all would never be accused of having too many.

PAULINE.

What name might I give this excessive reserve, this austere humor, that imprisons you in your house, that, in order to keep dangerous company from you, deprives you of that of decent people and that, in a word, deprives the Roman people of the example of your virtues, and your attractions of the homage of all hearts?

LUCRETIA.

Do you call the pleasure of living peacefully in the bosom of one's family a prison? As for me, I shall never need any other company for my happiness nor any other esteem for my glory than that of my Spouse, my Father, and my Children.

PAULINE.

But in hiding thus your charms and virtues, you lose the means of extending their rights; and you forget that it pertains to the graces to teach wisdom with profit.

LUCRETIA.

If my friendship means anything to you, drop this tone that will eventually deprive you of it. I've told you a hundred times, my first duty is toward myself; the only lesson suitable for me to give is the example of a decent life, and I have always believed that the woman most worthy of esteem is the one least spoken of, even were it to be praised. May the Gods keep my name from ever becoming famous: this grievous splendor is purchased by our sex only at the expense of happiness or innocence.

PAULINE.

If my zeal has possibly displeased you, at least do not blame its motives. I would like to see you live in a more pleasant fashion. By means of a little company, fun, and relaxation, I would like to bring back your health, prey to a sudden melancholy; and, if I dare say so, your glory itself would only be improved.

LUCRETIA.

My glory? Explain yourself; I do not understand you at all.

PAULINE.

Will you forgive me for a sincerity that I owe you? Rome beheld with approval your first intended. All the wishes of the People, as well as Tarquinius's choice, united you to his successor. Who other, they said, than the heir to the Crown would be worthy of possessing Lucretia? Let her occupy a Throne she will make honorable; she must bring about Sextus's happiness so that he learns from her to bring about that of the Romans. Everything changed, to the Prince's great despair, against the King's will, the People's, and it would be to offend reason to doubt that it were not also against yours. The unyielding Lucretius broke off a marriage which should have been among his most ardent wishes. A Roman of the Middle Classes obtained the prize to which he who is to be its sovereign hardly dared aspire. I abandon a comparison which might offend your scruples, but it is impossible that in spite of yourself you not feel which one most deserved to please you.

LUCRETIA.

Be mindful that you are speaking to the wife of Collatinus, and that since he is my Spouse, he was the one most worthy of being so.

PAULINE.

I ought to think on that point only what you prescribe to me; but the public, jealous of the only freedom it still has and whose judgments are feared by its very masters, has not given the same approval to Lucretius's choice as you. How can one not be difficult about the merit of anyone who would dare to aspire to Lucretia? In all respects, Collatinus was found less pardonable in doing so than Sextus, and the people believes itself too good a judge of true merit to doubt that you think differently than it does on this point.

LUCRETIA.

How badly the People consults its true interests in meting out its esteem and its scorn! The Romans admire in Sextus the brilliant qualities that will one day cause them misfortunes and disdain in Collatinus the humanity and the sweet and moderate passions that would have made of a vulgar court attendant, instead of the son of Tarquinius, the best of all Princes. As for me, it is certain that the constant and peaceful love of Collatinus makes me happy and that the tempestuous fits of Sextus would never have made him anything but a bad Husband. But what do all these discourses have to do with my taste for seclusion?

PAULINE.

Very well, Madam, since I must conclude, I fear that the purity of your glory will suffer more from this excessive reserve than it would from the contrary excess, and that if this desire for such a secluded life is not attributed more to sorrow for the spouse you have lost than to love for the one you possess, it will at least be regarded as a precaution that is more injurious to your heart than necessary to your virtue.

LUCRETIA.

Do you think that, were these suspicions to exist, a reasonable and well-behaved woman should regulate her conduct according to the vain discourses of the People and that according to such chimerical interpretations. . . . I see a stranger! . . . By the Gods, what do I see?

PAULINE.

It is Sulpitius, one of the prince's freedmen.

LUCRETIA.

Sextus's! What does this man come to do here?

SCENE II.
[LUCRETIA, PAULINE, SULPITIUS.]

SULPITIUS.

To alert you, Madam, to the impending arrival of the Prince and your Spouse and to give you a Letter from him.

LUCRETIA.
    From whom?

SULPITIUS.
    From Collatinus.

LUCRETIA.
    Give, right away.

                                                                (Aside, after having read.)
    By the Gods! (*To Pauline.*) Read.

PAULINE, *reads.*
    The King has just left on a twenty-four-hour unexpected trip, which
leaves me the leisure to come see you; it is not necessary to add that I
am taking advantage of it, but it is necessary to alert you that the Prince
wished to accompany me. So have a suitable lodging prepared for him
and be mindful in receiving the heir of the Crown that upon him the
fortune of your Spouse depends.

LUCRETIA, *to Pauline.*
    Do what is necessary to receive the Prince; you will tell Collatinus it is
with regret that I do not better second his intentions and, in speaking to
him of the exhaustion you have seen me in for the last two days, add
that my disturbed health leaves me no strength to obey his orders myself
or to see anyone but him.[1]

SCENE III.
[PAULINE, SULPITIUS.]

SULPITIUS.
    Well, now, Pauline! What do you make of Lucretia's dismay over the
news of the Prince's arrival and whence do you think so much trepida-
tion would come to her if not from her own heart?

PAULINE.
    I greatly fear we have been too eager to judge Lucretia. Ah, believe
me, Sulpitius, this is not a soul to be measured according to ours. You
know that when I entered her service, I thought like you with respect to
her secret inclinations and that in harmony with her own heart, as I
hoped, I was confident I could easily favor the Prince's desires. Looking
at it more closely, I have quite changed my opinion. Since having become

acquainted with this sweet and sensitive, but virtuous and steadfast, character I have become convinced that Lucretia, fully the mistress of her heart and passions, is capable of loving nothing but her spouse and duty.

SULPITIUS.

Will you always be the dupe of these lofty words and never understand that duty and virtue are terms void of meaning in which no one believes, but in which each one would have the rest of the world believe? Think: whatever Lucretia may show you, she would never be able to love her duty more than she loves her happiness; and I am quite deceived if she can ever find it other than in fulfilling that of Sextus.

PAULINE.

I believe I know something about feelings and you, more than anyone, can accord me justice in this regard. I have plumbed hers with a care proportionate to the interest taken in this by the Prince who employs us and with all the skill necessary so as not to become suspected in any way by Lucretia. I have exposed her heart to the surest tests, against which the most dissimulated reserve is least guarded; sometimes, I pitied her for what she had lost; other times, I praised her for what she had preferred; sometimes flattering her vanity, at others offending her amour-propre, I tried to arouse her jealousy, her tenderness, or at least her curiosity. And whenever it has been a question of Sextus I have always found her as tranquil as about any other subject and always equally ready to continue or end the conversation without any appearance of pleasure or pain.

SULPITIUS.

Then, in spite of all the tenderness with which you favor me, my heart must know more about love than yours: for I have seen more of it in the instant in which I just observed Lucretia than you during the six months you have been in her service, and the emotion the mere name of Sextus arouses in her lets me judge the one his appearance must arouse in her.

PAULINE.

Her health has been so altered for the last two days that her Mind is affected, and her very listlessness may well have produced the effect you attribute to Collatinus's Letter. Too much credulity may deceive me, I admit; but, then, might not too much insight deceive you?

SULPITIUS.

We ought at least desire that my eyes be better than yours and foment and ignite a love on which the happiness of the one who is to unite us depends. You know that the Prince's promises are at the price of the success of our efforts; moreover, you are not unaware that in our condition the vices of our masters serve us as steps for arriving at fortune and that it is in arousing their passions that we manage to satisfy our own. We would be lost if they were wise enough to get along without the secret services by which we ensnare them. Thus it is that in turn one makes oneself necessary to those upon whom one depends, and the greatest misfortune that could befall an ambitious Courtier would be to serve a reasonable and just prince who loved only his duty.

PAULINE.

I agree with all that,[2] but the interest we have in profiting from the error of others in no way disposes us to deceive ourselves; and the advantage we shall derive from Lucretia's faults is no reason to hope she commits them. Besides, I shall admit to you that after having seen this lovable and virtuous woman up close, I find myself less suited than I thought for seconding the Prince's designs. I believed I had only to combat a ferocious virtue that I detested from the outset; but her sweetness so excuses her good behavior that, after having discerned the charms of her character, one forgives those of her person and loses the courage and the will to sully so pure a soul.

SULPITIUS.

Given our situation, this studied language is not very suitable to me: our interests are too linked for us to need to resort to ruses with one another. The Prince asks you for a secret meeting, and you will soon be able to employ with him the tricks that appear to you most suited for making him value your services; but I who know your heart and who am content to possess it such as it is, I do not approve that in a matter like this, upon which both of our fates depend, you affect to display at a rather inopportune time more delicateness than reason.

PAULINE.

How unjust your reproaches are and how badly you have understood me! The more I cherish the hand you offer me, the less I want the honor of obtaining it to cost me that of deserving it. But you can believe that I in no way seek to vaunt myself and that if I dissimulate anything from you, it is rather my scruples than my hopes. I shall continue to serve Sextus as you insist and it will not be my fault if it is not successfully. But would not promising you more of an outcome from all of my efforts than I expect, myself, be to deceive you? Farewell; time flies; I must go carry out the orders I have just received. When the Prince has come, I shall be sure to alert you the first instant when I can see him in secret.

SCENE IV.

SULPITIUS.

How I hate these indecisive characters who never know how to direct themselves by reason and are good or bad only because they are weak! Her pusillanimous mind is as removed from the maxims that lead to great things as her rank and fortune are beneath my pretensions and my hopes. But I must flatter her with a chimerical union until, with her help, Lucretia seduced and Sextus satisfied, leave, so to speak, at my discretion the choice of my rewards. . . . I hear the noise of Horses! . . . Would it be the Prince already? . . . By the Gods! What do I see? Lucretia's Father and Brutus? Let me run to head off my Master and alert him to this Setback.

SCENE V.
BRUTUS, LUCRETIUS.

BRUTUS.

Do you know who that man is we just passed?

LUCRETIUS.

His face is not unknown to me.

BRUTUS.

He is one of Sextus's freedmen.

LUCRETIUS.

Sextus's! What does he come to do in this castle?

BRUTUS.

You are not unaware either of the former attachment his master had for your daughter, nor of the ties he seeks to form with her Spouse; you know, moreover, that he is the King's son, and you ask what he wants?

LUCRETIUS.

To bring the crimes of his Household into my family? Oh Brutus! . . .

BRUTUS.

I can tell you more, for it is now time to hide nothing from you. Namely Lucretia loves Sextus.

LUCRETIUS.

Him! My daughter? What are you saying, unfortunate one!

BRUTUS.

Calm yourself, worthy and blessed Father, and recognize the Treasure the Gods have given you. Yes, the son of Tarquinius is adored by your daughter; but do you know that this hidden sentiment, discerned by me alone, is no less unknown to the one who is experiencing it than to the Tyrant who is its object; do you know that the discovery of this fatal secret would cost this chaste and respectable woman her life; do you know what prodigies of strength and virtue this involuntary love, subjugated without being known, can produce in her great soul? Learn that passions to be conquered are a more powerful spur to heroic Souls than cold lessons of wisdom which, finding no obstacle, acquire no strength through resistance; learn, you, whose virtue has never been altered by anything, that from the bosom of our repressed desires arises this generous pride that teaches us to scorn the weaknesses of others after having triumphed over our own. It is by this very aspect that alarms you that your daughter is most worthy of all our trust; let us dare to declare our plans to her and the Tarquinians are lost, for Sextus is loved.

LUCRETIUS.

Brutus, let us speak softly and in no way expose these great secrets to indiscreet ears. We shall finish this conversation when we have leisure. I shall go in to my daughter and tell her only what is necessary. You, go head off Collatinus and prepare his mind for the great things that we have to say to him.

SCENE VI.

BRUTUS.

Tutelary Gods of Rome! the moment draws near in which your auspices are going to be justified. It is too much to bear that Tyrants dare usurp your rights and dishonor your finest work. It is time to show servile nations a People of men: it is time to teach the universe what the love of liberty can do with generous souls for the progress of Virtue!

END OF THE FIRST ACT.

ACT II.

SCENE I.
[SULPITIUS, SEXTUS.]

SULPITIUS.

There, My Lord, is the entrance to Lucretia's apartment; this door leads to Pauline's quarters, and it is here that she is to alert me the first moment she can speak with you secretly.

SEXTUS.

Here, then, is the blessed abode of all that Rome and the world contain of charm and virtue. How my agitation redoubles as I approach her dwelling! I would approach that of the Gods with more assurance, and I cannot understand, in comparing my rapture with my fright, how the same heart can bring together such burning desire with such timidity.

SULPITIUS.

The explanation is not difficult: doubt of success alone causes all your terror, and you would soon cease to fear Lucretia were you willing to entrust yourself a little more to Sulpitius.

SEXTUS.

Friend, how poorly you read in this heart you want to reassure. See whether I recognize your zeal; see how far I am able to let my confidence in you extend. On your word, I undertake the seduction of the most chaste woman; I prefer to believe that Lucretia lacks virtue than suspect you of fooling me with vain hopes. Alas, so as not to die of despair, I must indeed flatter myself with these chimeras. But acquaint yourself with all the derangement of your unfortunate friend. Think of the promptings of shame and horror that arise in me when I think that Sextus's worthiest exploit will be to corrupt by tricks an innocent and pure soul he could not reach by attentiveness. Think of the scorn this unfortunate woman will have for me when she knows of the shameful means I have used to seduce her. Think of the eternal tears the loss of her innocence will perhaps cost her, of the just curses she will one day heap upon the one who ravished it from her. Think of the wretched misery that will follow the transitory happiness your pity prepares for me. An idolater of Lucretia, I wanted to have all of her soul. Love, esteem, confidence, friendship—her heart is not susceptible of a sentiment mine is not furiously jealous of. Alas, in possessing her how far shall I still be from the supreme happiness I formed a ravishing idea of for myself. Ah, Sulpitius, when you have given me Lucretia, tell me, what will you do to make me happy?

SULPITIUS.

Sire, if you love her, what more do you need than to be loved by her? Allow me to say it: this language is not yet appropriate; in your discourse, I find the jealous worries of a favored lover rather than the ardent desires of a heart that aspires to be so; and all these refined sentiments are hardly to be imagined in the rapture of genuine passion.

SEXTUS.

Imprudent man, were you acquainted with my passion, you would keep yourself from using this language with me. Ah, if the hope you flatter me with were ever to be extinguished, fear learning what fury my heart is capable of, fear lest your days and mine be the least sacrifice my disappointed arm could make to my rage.

SULPITIUS.

Calm this transport of rage and bear in mind where you are. I repeat: you will be happy if you want to be so; but Lucretia's heart is the least obstacle you have to overcome. Her pride, which will defend her against you and herself, is not yet your most dangerous enemy. You must be most wary of yourself, of these indiscreet transports that can escape you; only in covering your plans with the deepest mystery can you hope to get her to approve them. With a woman so sensitive to honor, all of your delicateness must be in bending hers; and if she is ever sure of secrecy, you will soon be sure of her heart.

SEXTUS.

Friend, take pity on my derangement and forgive my foolish speeches, but count upon my docility toward all of your advice; you see me inebriated with love to the point that I am no longer capable of guiding myself. Lucretia is always at the bottom of my heart and before my eyes; I hear her sweet voice; her heavenly glance is turned upon me; mine can see only her; my existence is entirely and solely in her; I live only to adore her and all the powers of my soul alienated from every other object hardly suffice for the feelings that consume me. So make up for this self-forgetfulness; guide your blind master's steps and act so that with my happiness I owe you the return of my lost reason.

SULPITIUS.

Be mindful that we have more than one sort of precaution to take here and that the arrival of Lucretia's Father ought to make us even more circumspect. Again, I suspect this voyage with Brutus covers over some mystery; and from the way they were watching us, I believe I saw that they feared being watched themselves. I do not know what is being secretly concocted, but Lucretius looks unkindly upon us and I admit to you that this Brutus has always displeased me.[3]

SEXTUS.

Ah, what do we have to fear from the vain mutterings of an old man and the plans of a fool?

SULPITIUS.

This fool knows, nonetheless, how to make himself the darling of the Romans and to hold his own at the court, while this old man is the governor of Rome and—what is more—the Father of Lucretia.

SCENE II.
A SLAVE, SEXTUS, SULPITIUS.

THE SLAVE.

Sire, Pauline is waiting for you.

SEXTUS.

Let us go learn if I am permitted to live.

SULPITIUS.

I see Brutus and Lucretius; let us avoid being noticed by them.

SCENE III.
BRUTUS, LUCRETIUS.

LUCRETIUS.

Did I not just see two men quickly slip into Pauline's quarters?

BRUTUS.

I saw them just as you did. It is the Tyrant and his satellite.

LUCRETIUS.

What, even under my eyes . . .

BRUTUS.
Let them rush to their ruin, and be mindful of Collatinus who follows us.

SCENE IV.
LUCRETIUS, BRUTUS, COLLATINUS.

LUCRETIUS.
Stop, Collatinus; you will see your Spouse in due time, but it will not always be the moment to avenge your affronts and hers.

COLLATINUS.
Our affronts! what am I to understand . . . ?

LUCRETIUS.
What, had you a more sensitive heart or a less blind ambition, you would not have been unaware of for such a long while.

COLLATINUS.
I still do not understand you at all.

LUCRETIUS.
Imprudent man: with what design do you think an impetuous man feigns to knit with you a friendship his equals have never known? Imagine, if you can, the indignation that seizes me when I see my daughter's spouse himself bring into his house the enemy who wants to dishonor her.

COLLATINUS.
I cannot suspect the Prince of forming foolish plans and, were he to form them, who ought to scorn them more than I? May the Heavens keep me from so offending the wife the Gods and you have given me as to believe that I must add the cares of my prudence to those of her virtue! It is enough for me to know Lucretia; what do Sextus's feelings matter to me.

LUCRETIUS.
What do they matter to you? Do not deceive yourself, Collatinus. The very respect you owe your Spouse obliges you to avenge or forestall any sentiment that offends her. Learn that a chaste woman ought to hear only the discourse of which she can approve and that with respect to her a planned undertaking is necessarily an affront received.

COLLATINUS

Tell me, then, what I ought to do to become acquainted with, stop, or punish the designs of Sextus?

BRUTUS.

Oh, Collatinus! Tyrants punish as soon as they suspect; they are therefore guilty as soon as they are suspect. Lucretia's Beauty; Sextus's former love [for her]; his poorly disguised vices; and, above all, the maxims of his equals are, along with his trip here, proofs of his criminal intentions which will soon furnish you more evident ones if you want to look for them. At this very instant Sextus is in Pauline's quarters; I shall let you imagine for yourself the purpose of their secret conversation. As for the remedy, it is sure, unique, and depends on a single word. Do you know how to be a man and would you know how to die?

COLLATINUS.

Yes, without doubt, I shall know how to die; but in consulting wisdom and in following my duty.

LUCRETIUS.

Well, then, let yourself be led by a tender Father who loves you and by his friend who wants to hold you in esteem. You will do your duty, for you are a Roman; and you will act wisely in seeing to your safety, for as concerns the husband of a woman a Tyrant loves, there never is any. Often, so as better to preserve one's life, one must know how to brave death.

COLLATINUS.

Hurry up and explain yourself.

BRUTUS.

Listen. The Gods wanted Rome to bear the yoke of servitude once so as to learn to recognize it and consequently to detest it. Our trial suffices henceforth; we abhor our chains as much as is possible; thus, it is time to break them. All of Rome speaks to you here through my mouth: either we shall all perish or we shall destroy the monster who devours us. But the measures we have taken are so certain that instead of the risk of the undertaking all that remains for you is to share in the glory of success. So choose either to see yourself scorned by the Tyrant, dishonored by his son, a slave of the one and the other, and a companion of their unhappiness; or, with us, to avenge your fatherland, your spouse, yourself—to be virtuous, free, and, to say it all in a word, a worthy spouse of Lucretia, a worthy son of her virtuous Father, a friend of Brutus, and a citizen of Rome.

COLLATINUS.

You astonish me, without frightening me; but before I decide, let me ask you to shed some needed light. In designing such a great undertaking, you must have foreseen all the difficulties. Therefore, I want to believe that in spite of so many obstacles, in spite of Tarquinius's vigilance, and in spite of the terrifying power of whoever disposes of the public forces you will overthrow the usurper and destroy arbitrary power. But what will you do afterward for Rome and for us? Shall we leave our fellow citizens prey to anarchy, shall we sacrifice the Fatherland to revenge? Or, delivered from a Master whose power we share, shall we, as the prize for our good deeds, become slaves of the Multitude?

LUCRETIUS.

I understand you; you prefer slavery to equality, and for you to serve tyrants is less harsh than ruling over the People is appealing. Son, renounce this puerile ambition, which offers you only a doubtful authority in exchange for certain chains. Do you not see that if the reputation of great people makes them apparently share absolute power, its weight is really heavier for them than for the small people? Only taxes are requested of the People; except for that, it is free: but the freedom, fortune, and life of all those who draw near to the Tyrant are constantly in peril. The ferocity of his caprices falls mainly upon what catches his eye; were you today his most cherished favorite, tomorrow you might perhaps be his least slave.

COLLATINUS.

I am grateful for your confidence and touched by your tenderness; but in thinking of ourselves alone, do you mean to forget the Fatherland? Be mindful of the horrors of civil Wars, of the danger of being without a leader, of the license of an enraged populace. Rome will perish by its independence or will only change masters; and without softening her fate you will cause her more evil in a single moment than Tyranny would have been able to do in a great number of years.

BRUTUS.

Young man, abandon this error. Rome's constitution, stronger than its Tyrants, has made it free from its birth on. We have the Comitia,[4] a senate and Laws that draw their authority from themselves. Our government is ready-made, formed, and to make it wise it is necessary only to take away what it has too much of. Thank heaven we are not like those effeminate people for whom, everything existing only by the will of Kings, everything perishes as soon as they are no longer, for lack of a legitimate and independent authority. Were the Tyrant to fall today, tomorrow Rome would be tranquil, submitted to laws, and will only have lost an enemy. Friends, time presses, and discussions are untimely when there are not two sides to choose from. We have consulted as to her needs and our hearts; reason has confirmed it, and the event is sure. It is not in any way for ourselves but for you that we are speaking here. Know that perhaps tomorrow she will number among her children only liberators or those who have been banished.

COLLATINUS.

Oh, Brutus, your voice stirs my soul and I feel pierced through by the celestial fire that shines in your eyes. Yes, let Rome be free! What power can resist your zeal and what cowardly heart would hesitate to share in it? But, Friend, see the bottom of my own. Must one renounce . . .

BRUTUS, *taking his hand and shaking it.*

Believe me, Collatinus, believe in Brutus's soul—one at least as proud as your own. It is greater and finer to be counted among free men, even in the last rank, than to be first in Tarquinius's court.

COLLATINUS.

Ah, what a difference between us. Your greatness is entirely in the depths of your soul and I need to seek mine in fortune.

LUCRETIUS.

Well, now, do we not need leaders? Son, you will command Romans, you will ensure that the laws reign, and in the end you will raise yourself to the point of knowing how to obey and to become our equal.

COLLATINUS.

I give in and want only to obey you.

BRUTUS.

That is enough. Rome has your faith. We shall come back to this conversation at greater leisure. (*Softly, to Lucretius*) Your son-in-law is ambitious, weak, and not very clever. We are lost if you let him out of your sight. Follow him and leave the rest up to me.[5]

CHAPTER TEN

Essay on the Important Events of Which Women Have Been the Secret Cause[1]

Roman History, Catrou and Rouillé, Tome 4, p. 169[2]

I am not claiming to speak here about all the affairs that women have managed by themselves, either by virtue of their birth, or even by virtue of the posts to which their merit and their talents had raised them; it is a subject which as a result of repetition is now beginning to become threadbare. I shall limit myself solely to giving some idea of the memorable events the production of which peoples have attributed to the most sublime causes and that nevertheless owed their origin only to the secret instigation of women. This is what my title proclaims, and that is simply what I shall limit myself to, well satisfied to give some general perspectives on a completely new subject that the abundance and attractiveness of the matter will doubtless engage someone to push farther afterward.

I am even sorry in good faith at not having been anticipated and that some delicate pen has not caught a fancy for treating the subject I am undertaking; from it someone would have written a seductive book for every reader who is not a fool. As for me, I frankly admit that I have only precisely the amount of genius that is necessary to feel perfectly all the attractiveness that my matter would provide in the hands of an intelligent man.

One does too much honor to men, or perhaps sometimes not enough, by attributing solely to their ambition, their courage, their love for glory, their vengeance, or their generosity the majority of the striking actions that have made a commotion in history, and that often have no other principles than the passions that, for being less clamorous on the exterior, only more securely produce the most prodigious effects, and

SOURCE: Jean-Jacques Rousseau, *Autobiographical, Scientific, Religious, Moral, and Literary Writings. Collected Writings of Rousseau* XII, trans. and ed. Christopher Kelly (Hanover, N.H.: University Press of New England, 2007).

that the vulgar certainly do not suspect to have so much ascendancy over great men as they have in fact.

It is easy to understand what I am driving at.

I shall give rise to the idea. It will be the fault of private individuals, perhaps that of the public, if no one undertakes to execute it. Moreover, it must not be believed that intelligence is enough to fulfill such a project well. I dare to say that knowledge added to intelligence is not enough. How many people are there who imagine themselves to be well informed about the intrigues of courts, the plans of Princes, the motives that make them act—in a word, about history, politics, and negotiations and who hardly know any more about them than what they read in the gazette? It is the same for the past. I would very much like someone to tell me whether ninety percent of our historians have been adequately informed to fulfill the task they have imposed on themselves: what posts have they filled, what negotiations have they handled, what mistresses have they had who might have unveiled these great mysteries to them, these primitive springs—always hidden, sometimes very frivolous—that are the motive forces of almost all the proceedings of the great and consequently of the events that depend on them, and in the circle of which almost the entire history of the human Theater is restricted. It is so little true that it is enough to be a man of letters, an intelligent man, a scholar in order to be in a condition to write history well, as I am conceiving it, that even a Prime Minister would sometimes not be too good to succeed in it. But let a favorite, retired from the Court and who stayed in a position for a long time, occupy his leisure by describing what he has seen and the business of his time; purchase his memoirs, have them recast by a skillful hand who knows how to put them into order and to fill their gaps with the particulars of events that he did not deign to insert there because they were too common—that is a history.

But they propose only to write the history of what has come into the public's knowledge; let us therefore no longer vaunt the advantages of history and let us admit that it is only a history of pretexts and specious appearances with which one is dazzling the public.

The public events that I do not want to mention here. The taking of Troy. The Burning of the Palace at Persepolis. The Establishment of the Roman republic. The deliverance of Rome by Coriolanus's mother. The changing of England under Henry VIII, etc.

Division of the work

In 3 Books. The first will contain the great events in Ancient history caused by women.

The establishment of a Plebian consulate, etc.

The second in modern history. Charles VII recovering France, etc.

The third, some observations on the great men who let themselves be governed by women. Themistocles. Antony, etc.

Fulvia, the wife of Antony, stirs up war for not having been capable of being loved by Caesar.

CHAPTER ELEVEN

The Levite of Ephraïm

[First Draft Preface]

As for the third [piece],[1] which is merely a kind of short poem in prose, paraphrase of the last three chapters of *Judges*,[2] I admit that it will always be precious to me and that I never reread it without an inner satisfaction, not from some stupid vanity of an author, whose ineptness on this point would be inexcusable, but from a more decent feeling and one about which I even dare boast. It is enough to make myself understood to say that this writing was done en route the tenth, the eleventh, and the twelfth of June 1762.[3] This is what I occupied myself with during the cruelest moments of my life, overcome with miseries for which an honorable man is not even allowed to prepare himself. Plunged into a sea of misfortune, overcome with evils from my ungrateful and barbarous contemporaries, a single one from which I escape in spite of them and which remains to them for my vengeance is that of hatred.

This is with what that unfortunate defender of truth occupied himself during those instants of peril and of turmoil in which anger and indignation should have been devouring his heart. My enemies might well burden me with all the evils their rage [could] think of devising. There is one that remains to them for my vengeance and that I defy them to make me ever experience. That is the torment of hate.

from enemies whom I don't even know, to whom I have never done nor wished the least ill.

. . . and who think that one always loves

. . . hate me only due to the one they have done me

* * *

SOURCE: Jean-Jacques Rousseau, *Essay on the Origin of Languages and Writings Related to Music. Collected Writings of Rousseau* VII, trans. and ed. John T. Scott (Hanover, N.H.: University Press of New England, 1998).

This epoch unhappily too celebrated says enough about it to excuse the mediocrity of the work and to portray [something ?] of the author. If ever some equitable man deigns to take up my defense in compensation for so many outrages and libels, I wish only these words for praise: In the cruelest moments of his life, he wrote *The Levite of Ephraïm*.

As for me, I console myself. The sole praise that I desire and that I accord myself without shame because it is due to me. In the cruelest moments of his life he wrote *The Levite of Ephraïm*.

[Second Draft Preface]

I left Paris my heart pained with distress after the Parlement's warrant.[4] It seemed to me that having asked no other favor from men than that of not doing me any evil, I would have well merited having obtained it. Even while assuming in me the most dangerous errors, weren't my intentions pure enough and clear enough to merit some indulgence? What, then, is this much-vaunted society that never recompenses good, that often dissimulates evil and always punishes it less severely than its appearance? This is what I said to myself in the bitterest suffering, while rendering to myself the testimony that no man of good sense and of good faith could refuse me. These sad ideas followed me in spite of myself, and made my voyage disagreeable. I chased them away with all my power; there wasn't one with which my heart was occupied less voluntarily than that of the wrongs that could have been done me, and I get much more angry about the injustices that I witness than those of which I am the victim. I thought of diverting my reverie by occupying myself with some subject; this one came to mind, and I found it suited enough to my views. It offered me a type of intermediary between the condition I was in and that into which I wished to pass, I could from time to time abandon myself to my somber mood, then substitute the sweetest objects for it and, as soon as my subject permitted it, I imitated it, but . . . the delightful images of M. Gessner.[5] In this fashion I almost fulfilled my goal and pleasantly completed my voyage. This bagatelle was for a long time forgotten. I took it up and touched it up on a somewhat similar occasion and with the same success. I would hope that readers take some of the pleasure in reading it that I took in imagining it. It would be harsh to judge it very severely, given the occasion on which it was written. But it has an aspect for which decent men will applaud it, I am sure of it, and they will feel that a man who occupies himself in this way when he was tormented is not a very dangerous enemy.

The Levite of Ephraïm

FIRST CANTO

Sacred anger of virtue, come animate my voice. I shall tell of the crimes of Benjamin and the vengeance of Israel; I shall speak of unprecedented infamies and of still more terrible punishments. Mortals, respect beauty, morals, hospitality. Be just without cruelty, merciful without weakness. And know how to pardon the guilty rather than punish the innocent.

O you, easygoing men, enemies of every inhumanity; you who for fear of contemplating the crimes of your brothers, prefer to let them go unpunished, what picture am I going to offer to your eyes? The body of a woman cut into pieces, her torn and palpitating limbs sent to the twelve Tribes; the whole people, seized with horror, raising a unanimous protest to the Heavens, and crying out together: No, nothing like it has been done in Israel since the day our fathers left Egypt until this day. Sacred people, assemble yourself; pronounce on this horrible act and discern the price it has merited. He who averts his glance from such infamies is a coward, a deserter from justice; genuine humanity contemplates it in order to know it, to judge it, to detest it. Let us dare enter into these details and go back to the source of the civil wars that caused one of the Tribes to perish and cost the others so much blood. Benjamin, sad child of grief, who brought death to your mother,[6] it is from your bosom that came the crime that has ruined you; it is your impious race that could commit it and that had to atone for it too much.

In the days of freedom in which no one reigned over the people of the Lord, there was a time of license in which each, without recognizing either magistrate or judge, was alone his own master and did all that seemed to him good. Israel, then scattered in the fields, had few great cities, and the simplicity of its morals rendered superfluous the empire of laws. But all hearts were not equally pure, and the wicked found the impunity of vice in the security of virtue.[7]

During one of those short intervals of calm and equality that remain in oblivion because no one commands others and no evil at all is done, a Levite of the mountains of Ephraïm saw in Bethlehem a young girl who pleased him. He said to her: Daughter of Judah, you are not of my Tribe, you have no brother; you are like the daughters of Salphaad, and I cannot marry you according to the law of the Lord.* But my heart is

---

* Numbers, 36:8. I know that the children of Levi could marry in all the Tribes, but not in the case supposed.[8]

yours; come with me, let us live together; we shall be united and free; you will make my happiness, and I shall make yours. The Levite was young and handsome; the young woman smiled; they were united, then he took her into his mountains.

There, passing a sweet life, so dear to tender and simple hearts, in his retreat he tasted the charms of a shared love; there, on a sistrum of gold made to sing the praises of the Almighty, he often sang of the charms of his young wife. How many times did the slopes of mount Hebal ring with his lovely songs? How many times did he lead her into the shade, into the valleys of Sichem, to cut the country roses and to taste the freshness on the banks of the streams? Sometimes he sought in the hollows of the rocks the combs of a golden honey in which she took delight; sometimes in the foliage of the olive trees he set deceptive traps for birds and he carried to her a fearful turtledove that she kissed while stroking it. Then, closing it up in her bosom, she shivered with joy feeling it struggle and beat. Daughter of Bethlehem, he said to her, why do you always weep for your family and your country? Do the children of Ephraïm not also have feasts, are the daughters of smiling Sichem without grace and without gaiety, do the inhabitants of ancient Atharot lack strength and deftness? Come see their games and embellish them. Give me pleasures, O my beloved; are there for me any others than yours?

However the young girl grew bored with the Levite, perhaps because he left nothing for her to desire. She slips away and flees to her father, to her tender mother, to her frolicsome sisters. She believes she will find again there the innocent pleasures of her childhood, as if she bore the same age and the same heart.

But the abandoned Levite could not forget his fickle wife. Everything in his solitude recalled for him the happy days he had passed near her, their games, their pleasures, their quarrels, their tender reconciliations. Whether the rising sun gilded the summit of the mountains of Gelboe, or a sea breeze came in the evening to refresh their burning rocks, he wandered sighing in the places the unfaithful one had loved, and at night, alone in his nuptial bed, he watered his bed with his tears.

After having drifted four months between regret and vexation—like a child who, being chased away from a game by others, feigns no longer wanting to continue while burning to start again, then finally, tearfully, asks to get back in—the Levite, driven by his love, takes his mount and, followed by his servant with two donkeys of Epha loaded with his provisions and gifts for the relatives of the young girl, he returns to Bethlehem to be reconciled with her and to try to bring her back.

The young woman, perceiving him from far off, starts, runs to meet him, and greeting him with caresses, introduces him into the house of her father, who, learning of his arrival, runs up also full of joy, embraces him, receives him—him, his servant, his baggage—and hastens to treat him well. But the Levite, his heart constricted with emotion, could not speak; nevertheless, moved by the good welcome of the family, he raised his eyes to his young wife and said to her, Daughter of Israel, why do you flee me? What evil have I done to you? The young woman began to cry, covering her face. Then he said to the father: Give me back my companion; give her to me for love of her; why would she live alone and abandoned? Who other than I can honor as his wife the one whom I received a virgin?

The father looked at his daughter, and the daughter's heart was touched by the return of her husband. The father therefore said to his son-in-law: My son, give me three days; let us pass these three days in joy, and on the fourth day, you and my daughter will leave in peace. The Levite therefore remained three days with his father-in-law and all his family, eating and drinking familiarly with them; and on the night of the fourth day, rising before the sun, he wanted to leave. But his father-in-law, catching hold of him by the hand, said to him: What! You want to leave on an empty stomach? Come fortify your stomach and then you will leave. They sat down at table and, after having eaten and drunk, the father said to him: My son, I beg you to enjoy yourself further with us today. Nonetheless, the Levite, rising, wanted to leave; he believed the time he passed far from his retreat robbed him of love, was given over to others rather than to his beloved. But the father, not being able to resolve himself to be separated from her, engaged his daughter to obtain this day as well; and the daughter, caressing her husband, had him remain until the morrow.

As soon as it was morning, as he was ready to leave he was stopped yet again by his father-in-law, who forced him to seat himself at table while awaiting full daylight; and the time flowed by without them per- ceiving it. Then the young man having got up to leave with his wife and his servant, and having prepared everything: O, my son! the father said to him: You see that the day advances and that the sun is on its decline. Do not set out so late; for pity's sake, gladden my heart further the rest of this day; tomorrow at the break of day you will leave without delay. And speaking in this way, the good old man was entirely stricken; his paternal eyes welled with tears. But the Levite did not surrender, and wished to leave at that instant.

What regrets this fatal separation cost! What touching farewells were said and resumed! What tears the sisters of the young girl shed on her face! How many times they took her again by turns in their arms! How many times did her mother, in tears, holding her once again in hers, feel the pain of a new separation! But her father in embracing her did not cry; his mute clasps were doleful and convulsive; sharp sighs lifted his chest. Alas! He seemed to foresee the horrible fate of the unfortunate one! O! if he had known that she would never again see the dawn! If he had known that that day was the last of her days. . . . They finally leave followed by the tender benedictions of their whole family, and wishes worthy of being granted. Happy family, whose peaceful days flow in the most perfect union from the bosom of friendship, and that seems to have only one heart for all its members. O innocence of morals, sweetness of soul, antique simplicity, how lovable you are! How has the brutality of vice been able to find a place amidst you? How is it that the furies of barbarism did not respect your pleasures?

SECOND CANTO

The young Levite followed his route with his wife, his servant, and his baggage, transported with joy in bringing back his heart's friend, and, uneasy about the sun and the dust, like a mother who brings back her son from the nurse's and fears for him the air's ravages. Already the city of Jebus[9] was spied on the right hand, and its age-old walls offered them a refuge for the approaching night. The servant then said to his master: You see the day ready to end; before the darkness takes us unawares let us enter the city of the Jebusites, we shall seek a refuge there, and tomorrow, continuing our voyage, we can arrive at Geba.

God forbid, said the Levite, that I lodge among an infidel people and that a Canaanite give shelter to the Lord's minister.[10] No, but let us go as far as Gibeah to seek hospitality among our brothers. They thus left Jerusalem behind them, they arrived after the setting of the sun at the heights of Gibeah, which is of the Tribe of Benjamin. They turned off to pass the night there, and having entered, they went to seat themselves in the public plaza, but no one offered them a shelter, and they remained unprotected.

Men of our days, do not malign the morals of your fathers. These first times, it is true, did not abound like yours in the comforts of life; vile metals did not suffice there for everything; but man had vitals that did the rest. Hospitality was not for sale, and they did not then traffic in the virtues. The sons of Jemini[11] were not the only ones, doubtless, whose hearts of iron were hardened; but that hardness was not common. With patience brothers were found everywhere; the voyager deprived of everything did not lack anything.

After having waited a long time uselessly, the Levite was going to unfasten his baggage, in order to make the young girl a bed less hard than the naked earth, when he perceived an old man, returning late from his fields and from his rustic labors. This man was, like him, from the mountains of Ephraïm, and he had come in bygone days to establish himself in this city among the children of Benjamin.

Raising his eyes, the old man saw a man and a woman seated in the middle of the plaza, with a servant, beasts of burden, and baggage. Then drawing near he said to the Levite: Stranger, where are you from and where are you going? He answered him: We come from Bethlehem, city of Judah; we are going back to our dwelling place on the slopes of the mountain of Ephraïm, whence we have come; and now we were seeking the hospice of the Lord, but no one has wanted to lodge us. We have grain for our animals, bread, wine for me, for your servant, for the young man who follows us; we have everything that is necessary for us, we lack only shelter. The old man answered him: peace be with you, my brother; you will not remain in the plaza; if you are lacking something, let the crime be mine. Then he led them into his house, had their baggage unloaded, filled the rack for their beasts, and having had the feet of his guests washed, he made for them a feast of the Patriarchs, simple and without ostentation, but abundant.

While they were at table with their host and his daughter,* promised to a young man of the country, and while amidst the gaiety of a meal offered with joy, they relaxed agreeably, the men of this city, children of Belial,[12] without restraint, unbridled, without reserve, and braving Heaven like the Cyclops of Mount Etna, came and surrounded the house, rudely knocking at the door, and crying to the old man in a menacing tone: Deliver to us that young stranger whom you received within our walls without leave, so that his beauty may pay us the price of this shelter and so that he may atone for your temerity. For they had seen the Levite in the plaza, and, by a trace of respect for the most sacred of all rights they had not wanted to lodge him in their houses so as to do him violence, but they had plotted together to come to surprise him in the middle of the night, and having learned that the old man had given him refuge, they ran without justice and without shame to tear him from the house.

Hearing these madmen the old man was disturbed, was afraid, and said to the Levite: we are lost. These wicked men are not people to be brought round by reason and ever to reconsider what they have

---

*In the old custom the women of the house did not sit at table with their guests when they were men, but when there were women they did sit with them.

resolved upon. Nevertheless, he went out before them to try to sway them. He prostrated himself and, raising his hands, free from all plunder, to Heaven, he said to them: O my brothers! what speech have you pronounced? Ah! Do not do this evil before the Lord! Do not thus outrage nature, do not violate sacred hospitality. But seeing that they did not listen to him at all, and were ready to mistreat him, that they were going to take the house by storm, the old man, despairing, instantly made his choice. Making a sign with his hand in order to make himself heard amidst the tumult, he began again with a stronger voice: No, while I am alive such an infamy will not dishonor my guest and will not soil my house. But listen, cruel men, to the supplications of an unhappy father. I have a daughter still a virgin, promised to one among you; I am going to lead her to be sacrificed to you, but only so that your sacrilegious hands abstain from touching the Levite of the Lord. Then, without awaiting their response, he ran to seek his daughter to redeem his guest at the expense of his own blood.

But the Levite, whom terror had made immobile until that instant, awakening to this deplorable sight, forestalls the generous old man, throws himself before him, forces him to return with his daughter, and himself taking his beloved companion, without saying a single word to her, without raising his eyes to her, drags her to the door and gives her up to those cursed men. Straightaway they surround the half-dead young woman, seize her, and fight over her without pity; in their brutal fury they were like a pack of hungry wolves returning to a watering place at the foot of the icy Alps that surprises a weak heifer, throws itself on her and tears her to pieces. O wretches, who destroy your species through the pleasures destined to reproduce it, how does her dying beauty not extinguish your ferocious desires? See her eyes already closed to the light, her faded features, her dying face: the pallor of death has covered her cheeks, livid violets have chased away roses from them; she no longer has a voice to moan; her hands no longer have the force to repulse your outrages. Alas! She is already dead! Barbarians, unworthy of the name men, your howls resemble the cries of the horrible Hyena and like it you devour corpses.

The approach of the day that chases ferocious beasts back into their lairs having dispersed these brigands, the unfortunate woman uses the remainder of her force to drag herself back to the old man's abode; she falls before the door, her face against the earth and her hands extended on the threshold. Nonetheless, after having passed the night filling the house of his host with imprecations and tears, the Levite, ready to leave, opens the door and finds in this state the one whom he had loved so much. What a sight for his broken heart! He raises a plaintive cry toward Heaven avenger of crime: then, addressing the young girl: rise, he says to her, let us flee the curse that covers this earth. Come, O my companion! I am the cause of your ruin, I shall be your consolation. May the unjust and vile man who ever reproaches you for your misery perish; you are more respectable to me than before your misfortunes. The young girl does not respond at all; he is troubled, his heart, seized with fright, begins to fear worse evils. He calls her once again, he looks at, he touches her; she was no longer. O too lovable and too much loved girl! Is it then for this that I have taken you from your father's house? Here, then, is the fate that my love prepared for you? He finished these words ready to follow her, and survived her only in order to avenge her.

From that instant, occupied with the sole plan with which his soul was filled, he was deaf to every other feeling: love, regret, pity—all were changed into fury in him. Even the appearance of that body, which should have made him dissolve in tears, no longer draws from him either complaint or weeping. He contemplates it with a dry and somber eye; he no longer sees anything in it except an object of rage and despair. Aided by his servant, he loads it onto his mount and takes it into his house. There, without hesitating, without trembling, the barbarous man dares cut that body into twelve pieces; with a firm and sure hand he strikes without fear, he cuts the flesh and the bones, he separates the head and the limbs, and after having sent these frightful parcels to the Tribes, he precedes them to Mizpah, tears his clothing, covers his head with ashes, prostates himself as they arrive and demands with great cries the justice of the God of Israel.

THIRD CANTO

In the meantime, you would have seen the whole People of God be moved, assemble, leave their dwelling places, hastening from all the Tribes to Mizpah before the Lord, as a numerous swarm of bees gathers while humming around their King. They all came, they came from every part, from all the cantons, all in agreement like a single man from Dan to Beer-sheba, and from Galead to Mizpah.

Then the Levite, having presented himself dressed in mourning, was interrogated by the Elders before the assembly about the murder of the young girl, and he spoke to them thus: I entered Gibeah the city of Benjamin with my wife to pass the night there, and the people of the country surrounded the house in which I was lodged, desiring to commit an outrage against me and make me perish. I was forced to deliver my wife to their debauchery, and she died in leaving their hands. Then

I took her body, I tore it in pieces, and I sent it to you each within your boundaries. People of the Lord, I have spoken the truth; do what will seem to you just before the Almighty.

Instantly a single cry arose in all Israel, but resounding, but unanimous: Let the blood of the young woman fall back upon her murderers. Long live the Eternal One! We will not go back to our dwelling places and none of us will return beneath his roof until Gibeah is exterminated. Then the Levite cried out with a strong voice: Blessed be Israel who punishes infamy and avenges innocent blood. Daughter of Bethlehem, I carry you good news; your memory will not remain without honor. In saying these words, he fell face-forward, and died. His body was honored with public funerals. The limbs of the young woman were reassembled and put into the same sepulcher, and all Israel wept over them.

The preparations for the war they were going to undertake began with a solemn oath to put to death anyone who failed to be present. Then they numbered all the Hebrews carrying arms, and they chose ten out of a hundred, a hundred out of a thousand, and a thousand out of ten thousand, the tenth part of the entire people, from which they made up an army of forty thousand men who were to act against Gibeah, while a like number was charged with the convoys of munitions and of victuals for the provisioning of the army. Then the People came to Shiloh before the ark of the Lord, saying: which Tribe will command the others against the children of Benjamin? And the Lord answered: it is the blood of Judah that cries out for vengeance; let Judah be your chief.

But before drawing the sword against their brothers, they sent Heralds to the Tribe of Benjamin, who said to the Benjaminites: Why is this horrible thing found amidst you? Give those who have committed it over to us so that they may die, and that the evil may be removed from the bosom of Israel.

The fierce sons of Jemini, who had not been unaware of the assembly at Mizpah, nor of the resolution that had been taken there, having for their part been preparing, believed that their valor excused them from being just. They did not listen at all to the exhortation of their brothers, and, far from according them the satisfaction they owed them, they left in arms from all the villages of their portion, and rushed to Gibeah's defense without letting themselves be frightened by the number and resolved to combat alone the whole people united. The army of Benjamin had twenty-five thousand men bearing swords, aside from the inhabitants of Gibeah, of the number of seven hundred seasoned men, handling arms with both hands with the same dexterity and all such excellent slingers that they could hit a hair without the stone missing on one side or the other.

The army of Israel, having assembled and having elected its chiefs, came to set up camp before Gibeah, counting on taking that place easily. But the Benjaminites, having left in good order, attack it, break it, pursue it with fury; terror precedes them and death follows them. The routed able-bodied of Israel were seen falling by the thousands beneath their swords, and the fields of Ramah were covered with corpses, as the sands of Elath are covered with clouds of grasshoppers that a burning wind brings and kills in one day. Twenty-two thousand men of Israel's army perished in that combat, but their brothers did not grow discouraged; and having faith in their force and in their great numbers still more than in the justice of their cause, they returned the next day and ranged themselves for battle in the same place.

Nevertheless, before risking a new combat, they had gone up the previous day before the Lord, and weeping until evening in his presence, they had consulted him on the issue of this war. But he said to them: go and fight; does your duty depend on the outcome?

As they thus marched toward Gibeah, the Benjaminites made a sortie from all the doors and, falling on them with more fury than the previous day, they defied them and pursued them with such ferocity that eighteen thousand more men of war perished that day in the army of Israel. Then all the people came once again to prostrate itself and weep before the Lord, and fasting until evening, they offered oblations and sacrifices. God of Abraham, they said moaning, your people, spared so many times in your just anger, will it perish for desiring to remove the evil from its bosom? Then having presented themselves before the fearsome ark, and consulting the Lord once again through the mouth of Phineas son of Eleazar, they said to him: shall we march again against our brothers, or shall we leave Benjamin in peace? The voice of the Almighty deigned to respond to them. March, and no longer have faith in your numbers, but in the Lord who gives and takes away courage as it pleases him. Tomorrow I shall deliver Benjamin into your hands.

Instantly they already feel the effect of this promise in their hearts. A cold and sure valor succeeding to their brutal impetuosity, enlightens and leads them. They calmly prepare for combat and no longer present themselves for it as wild men, but as wise and brave men who know how to vanquish without fury and die without despair. They hide their troops behind the hillside of Gibeah and, ranging themselves for battle with the remainder of their army, they draw far off from the City the

Benjaminites, who, full of deceptive confidence because of their first successes, leave rather to kill them than to combat them; they impetuously pursue the army, which yields and purposely draws back before them; they come after it at the place where the fields of Bethel and of Gibeah join, and cry out, rousing themselves for the carnage: they are falling before us as they did the first time. Blind men, who, dazzled by a vain success, do not see the Angel of vengeance who already flies over their ranks, armed with the exterminating sword.

Nonetheless, the body of Troops hidden behind the hillside leave its ambush in good order in the number of ten thousand men, and extending around the City attack it, force it, and puts all its inhabitants to the sword, then raising a great column of smoke, it gives the army the agreed-upon signal while the furious Benjaminite rouses himself to pursue his victory.

But the able-bodied of Israel, having perceived the signal, faced the enemy in Baal-tamar. The Benjaminites, surprised to see Israel's Battalions forming, developing, extending, converging on them, began to lose courage, and turning their back, they saw with fear the whirlwinds of smoke that announced to them the disaster of Gibeah. Then, struck with terror in their turn, they knew that the arm of the Lord had reached them, and fleeing in rout toward the desert, they were surrounded, pursued, killed, trampled underfoot, while various detachments entering the cities were put to death there each in his abode.

On this day of anger and of murder, almost the whole Tribe of Benjamin in the number of twenty-six thousand men perished under Israel's sword; namely, eighteen thousand men in their first retreat from Menuhah to the east of the hillside, five thousand in the rout toward the desert, two thousand who were reached near Gidom and the rest in the places that were burned, and all of whose inhabitants, men and women, young and old, large and small, even down to beasts, were put to death, without mercy being given to any. In this way, this beautiful country, formerly so lively, so peopled, so fertile, and now reaped by flame and by iron, no longer offered anything but a frightful solitude covered with ashes and bones.

Six hundred men, the last remainder of that unhappy Tribe, alone escaped the sword of Israel and took refuge in the rocks of Rimmon, where they remained hidden four months, crying too late for the infamous deed of their brothers and the misery to which it had reduced them.

But the victorious Tribes, seeing the blood they had shed, felt the wound they had given themselves. The people came and, assembling in the house of the mighty Lord, raised an altar on which they rendered to him his homage, offering him sacrifices and thanksgiving; then, raising their voices, they wept: they wept for their victory after having wept for their defeat. God of Abraham, they cried out in their affliction, oh, where are your promises, and how has this evil happened to your people that a Tribe is extinguished in Israel? Unhappy humans who do not know what is good for you, you may well want to sanctify your passions; they always punish you for the excesses they make you commit, and it is by fulfilling your unjust vows that Heaven makes you atone for them.

FOURTH CANTO

After having bemoaned the evil they had done in their anger, the children of Israel sought some remedy in it that could reestablish the mutilated race of Jacob in its entirety. Moved with compassion for the six hundred men in refuge in the rocks of Rimmon, they said: what shall we do to preserve this last and precious remainder of one of our nearly extinguished Tribes? For they had sworn by the Lord, saying: if ever any among us gives his daughter to the son of a child of Jemini and mixes his blood with the blood of Benjamin. Then, in order to elude such a cruel oath, meditating new carnage, they took the number of the army to see whether, despite the solemn engagement, anyone of them had failed to comply, and none of the inhabitants of Jabesh-gilead was found. This branch of the children of Manasseh, looking less to the punishment of the crime than to the effusion of fraternal blood, had turned away from vengeance more atrocious than infamy without considering that perjury and desertion of the common cause are worse than cruelty. Alas! Death, barbarous death, was the price for their unjust pity. Ten thousand men detached from the army of Israel received and executed this frightful order: Go, exterminate Jabesh-gilead and all its inhabitants, men, women, children, except only the virgin girls, whom you shall lead back to camp so that they may be given in marriage to the children of Benjamin. Thus, to make amends for the desolation of so many murders, this fierce people committed still greater ones, similar in its fury to those flaming iron globes thrown by our machines, which, having fallen to the ground after their first effect, rise up with a new impetuosity and in their unexpected bounds overturn and destroy entire ranks.

During this disastrous accomplishment, Israel sent words of peace to the six hundred of Benjamin in refuge in the rocks of Rimmon, and they came back among their brothers. Their return was not at all a return of joy; they had a downcast countenance and their eyes lowered; shame and remorse covered their faces, and all Israel, dismayed, carried on their lamentations at seeing these sad remainders of one of its blessed Tribes, of which Jacob had said: "Benjamin is a devouring wolf; in the morning it will tear apart its prey, and in the evening it will share the booty."[13]

After the ten thousand men sent to Jabes had made their return, and after the young women they had led back had been numbered, only four hundred of them were found, and they were given to as many Benjaminites, like prey they had just abducted for them. What weddings for the timid young virgins, whose brothers, fathers, mothers had just been slaughtered before their eyes, and who received ties of attachment and of love from hands filthy with the blood of their near ones! A sex always slave or tyrant, that man oppresses or adores, and that nevertheless he cannot make happy nor be so himself except by letting it be equal to him.

Despite this terrible expedient, there remained two hundred men to provide for, and that people, cruel even in its pity and for whom the blood of its brothers cost so little, would perhaps have thought of making new widows for them when an old man of Lebonah, speaking to the elders, said to them: Israelite men, listen to the advice of one of your brethren. When will your hands weary of the murder of innocents? Behold the days of solemnity of the Eternal One in Shiloh. Say then to the children of Benjamin: Go, and set an ambush in the vines; then, when you see that the girls of Shiloh come out to dance with flutes, then surround them, and each abduct his woman; return to establish yourselves along with them in the country of Benjamin.

And when the fathers and the brothers of the young women come to complain to us, we shall say to them: have pity on them for love of us and of yourselves who are their brothers; because we have not been able to provide for them after this war and have not been able to give them our daughters against the oath, we shall be guilty of their loss if we leave them to perish without descendants.

The children of Benjamin then did as was told them, and when the young girls left Shiloh to dance, they sprang out and surrounded them.[14] The fearful troop fled, dispersed; terror succeeds their innocent gaiety; each calls out in loud cries for her companions, and runs with all her might. The vine stocks tear their veils, the earth is strewn with their finery, the race animates their color and the ardor of their abductors. Young beauties, where do you run? In fleeing the oppressor who pursues you, you fall into arms that enchain you. Each abducts his own and, trying to calm her, frightens her even more by his caresses than by his violence. At the tumult that arises, at the cries they make heard far off, the whole people run up: fathers and mothers push aside the crowd and want to extricate their daughters; the abductors, so authorized, defend their prey; at last, the elders make their voices heard, and the people, moved by compassion for the Benjaminites, take an interest in their behalf.

But the fathers, indignant at the outrage done to their daughters, did not cease their outcries. What? they cried vehemently, will the daughters of Israel be subjected and treated as slaves beneath the eyes of the Lord? Will Benjamin be to us as the Moabite and the Idumean? Where is the freedom of the people of God? Torn between justice and pity, the assembly at last pronounces that the captives will recover their freedom and decide their fate for themselves. The abductors, forced to cede to this judgment, released them with regret, and tried to substitute for force more powerful means over their young hearts. Immediately they escape and all flee together; they follow them, hold out their arms, and cry to them: daughters of Shiloh, will you be more happy with others? Are the remnants of Benjamin unworthy of swaying you? But several among them, already tied by secret affections, quivered with joy at having escaped their abductors. Axa, the tender Axa, among others, in throwing herself into the arms of her mother, whom she saw run up, furtively cast her eyes on young Elmacin to whom she was promised and who came full of grief and of rage to free her at the price of his blood. Elmacin sees her again, extends his arms, cries out and cannot speak; the race and emotion put him out of breath. The Benjamite perceived this transport, this glance; he divines all, he moans, and ready to withdraw, he sees Axa's father arrive.

This was the same old man, author of the counsel given to the Benjaminites. He had himself chosen Elmacin for his son-in-law, but his probity had prevented him from warning his daughter of the risk to which he exposed those of other people.

He arrives, and taking her by the hand: Axa, he says to her, you know my heart; I love Elmacin, he would have been the consolation of my old age, but the salvation of your people and the honor of your father must win out over him. Do your duty, my daughter, and save me from opprobrium among my brothers, for I have counseled everything that has been done. Axa lowers her head and sighs without responding, but finally, raising her eyes, she encounters those of her venerable father. They said more than his mouth; she makes her choice. Her weak and trembling voice scarcely pronounces, in a weak and last farewell, the name of Elmacin, at whom she dares not look, and instantly turning round half-dead, she falls into the arms of the Benjamite.

A noise arises in the assembly. But Elmacin advances and makes a sign with his hand. Then, raising his voice: hear, O Axa, he says to her, my solemn vow. Because I cannot be yours, I shall never be another's. The sole remembrance of our young years that innocence and love have embellished are enough for me. Never has the steel passed over my head, never has wine moistened my lips, my body is as pure as my heart. Priests of the living God: I dedicate myself to your service; receive the Nazarene of the Lord.

Straightaway, as by a sudden inspiration, all the young women, carried along by the example of Axa, imitate her sacrifice, and renouncing their first loves, they deliver themselves to the Benjaminites who pursued them. At this touching sight arises a cry of joy in the midst of the People. Virgins of Ephraïm, through you Benjamin is going to be reborn. Blessed be the God of our fathers! There are still virtues in Israel.

IV

LOVE

CHAPTER TWELVE

The Loves of Milord Edward Bomston[1]

[*This short work is a sort of appendix to Rousseau's novel* Julie. *It gives the details of the story, referred to in parts V and VI of the novel, of Saint Preux's English friend, Lord Edward Bomston. After befriending Julie and Saint Preux, Milord Edward travels to Italy where the following events occur. The work was not published during Rousseau's life, but appeared in the complete works edited by his friend Du Peyrou. Rousseau had given a copy of the work to the Maréchale de Luxembourg who, apparently, was offended by a presumed similarity between herself and the Marchesa.*]

The strange adventures of Milord Edward in Rome were too novelistic to be combined with Julie's without spoiling their simplicity. I will therefore limit myself to extracting and abridging here what helps to understand two or three letters where they come up.

Milord Edward, during his travels in Italy, had made the acquaintance in Rome of a Neapolitan noblewoman, with whom he soon fell deeply in love: she, for her part, conceived for him a violent passion that consumed her the rest of her life, and finally sent her to the grave. This man, rugged and uncourtly, but ardent and sensible, extreme and grand in everything, could hardly inspire or experience a mediocre attachment.

The stoical principles of the virtuous Englishman worried the Marchesa. She elected to pass herself off as a widow during her husband's absence, which was easy for her, because they were both foreigners in Rome, and because the Marchese was serving in the Emperor's troops. It was not long before the passionate Edward broached marriage; the Marchesa invoked religious difference and other pretexts.

Ultimately, they contracted an intimate and licentious relationship, until the day when Edward, having discovered that the husband was liv-

SOURCE: Jean-Jacques Rousseau, *Julie; or, The New Heloise. Collected Writings of Rousseau* VI, trans. and ed. Philip Stewart and Jean Vaché (Hanover, N.H.: University Press of New England, 1997).

ing, tried to break off with her, after heaping on her the most stinging reproaches, in a rage at finding himself guilty, without his knowledge, of a crime he held in horror.

The Marchesa, a woman without principles, but crafty and full of charms, spared nothing to hold onto him, and finally succeeded. The adulterous relationship was ended, but the relationship continued. As unworthy as she was to love, she yet did: she had to consent to seeing fruitlessly a man she adored, whom she could not otherwise keep, and with this intentional barrier stimulating love on both sides, it became the more ardent through constraint. The Marchesa did not neglect the attentions that could lead her lover to forget his resolutions: she was seductive and beautiful. All for nothing. The Englishman held firm; his great soul was being tested. His foremost passion was virtue. He would have sacrificed his life to his mistress, and his mistress to his duty. One day the seduction became too insistent; the means he was to employ in order to deliver himself from it curbed the Marchesa and made all her wiles vain. It is not because we are weak, but because we are faint-hearted that our senses always enslave us. Whoever fears death less than crime is never forced to commit a crime.

There are few of those vigorous souls which attract others and raise them to their own sphere; but there are some. Edward's was one such. The Marchesa hoped to win him over; it was he who little by little won her. When lessons of virtue took on the melody of love in his mouth, he moved her, he made her weep; its sacred flame inspired this grovelling soul; a sentiment of justice and honor brought its foreign charm into it; the truly beautiful was beginning to please her: if the wicked could change their nature, the Marchesa's heart would have done so.

Love alone took advantage of these slight emotions; as a result it gained in subtlety. She began to love in a generous manner: notwithstanding her ardent temperament, and a climate where the senses have such empire, she forsook her pleasures to attend to her lover's and, though unable to share them, she at least wanted him to take them from her. Such was on her part the favorable interpretation of a conduct in which her character and Edward's, which she understood well, could lead one to see a more insidious form of seduction.

She spared neither effort nor expense to search out anywhere in Rome a young person who was loose and dependable; she was found, not without difficulty. One evening, after a most tender conversation, she introduced her to him: Do what you will with her, she told him with a sigh; let her enjoy my love's recompense; but let her be the only one. It suffices me that when you are with her you sometimes remember the hand that gave her to you. She started to leave; Edward held her back. Stop, he said to her; if you think I am contemptible enough to take advantage of your offer in your own house, the sacrifice is not great, and I am not much worth regretting. Since you are not to be mine, I wish you to be no one's, said the Marchesa; but if love must lose its rights, suffer it at least to dispose of them. Why does my present disconcert you? Do you fear being ungrateful? Then she obliged him to take Laura's address (that was the young person's name) and made him swear that he would refrain from any other relationship. This had to move him, and it did. His gratitude was harder to contain than his love, and that was the most dangerous trap the Marchesa had set for him in his whole life.

Extreme in everything, as was her lover, she had Laura to supper, and showered attentions on her, as if to enjoy in greater pomp the greatest sacrifice love has ever made. Edward, deeply moved, yielded to his transports; his stirred and sensible soul described itself in his glances, in his gestures, he said not a word but that was an expression of the most intense passion. Laura was charming; he scarcely looked at her. She did not imitate this indifference: she looked and saw, in the true tableau of love, an object that was entirely new to her.

After supper, the Marchesa dismissed Laura, and remained alone with her lover. She had counted on the dangers of this encounter; in this she was not mistaken; but she was mistaken in counting on his succumbing; all her craft only made the triumph of virtue more resplendent and more painful for him and for her. This is the evening to which St. Preux refers, at the end of part IV of *Julie* in his admiration for his friend's strength.[2]

Edward was virtuous, but human. He had all the simplicity of genuine honor, and none of the false decorum that is put in its place, and of which worldly people make so much. After several days spent in the same transports with the Marchesa, he felt the peril increasing; and, on the point of being defeated, he preferred to offend civility rather than virtue: he went to see Laura.

She shuddered when she saw him: he found her sad, he undertook to cheer her up, and thought it would not take much effort to succeed. That was not as easy as he had thought. His caresses were ill received, his offers were rejected in a manner not characteristic of someone who is disputing what she wishes to grant.

So ridiculous a reception did not discourage him, it provoked him. Did he owe the deference of a child to this sort of whore? He proceeded brashly to exercise his rights. Laura, despite her cries, her tears, her resistance, knowing she was defeated, summoned her strength, hurled herself to the other end of the room, and cried out to him in a loud voice: Kill me if you want; you will never touch me alive. Her gestures, the look in her eyes, her tone of voice were not equivocal. Edward, astonished as one can imagine, calmed himself, took her by the hand, sat her down, sat down beside her, and, looking at her in silence, coldly awaited the outcome of this Comedy.

She remained silent; her eyes were downcast; she breathed unevenly, her heart pounded, and everything about her indicated an extraordinary agitation. Edward finally broke the silence to ask her the meaning of this strange scene. Might I have made a mistake? he asked her; could you be not Lauretta Pisana? Would to God, she said in a trembling voice. What then! he began again with a mocking smile, might you by chance have changed trades? No, said Laura, I am still the same: there is no going back on the station that is mine. He found in this turn of phrase, and the way she uttered it, something so extraordinary that he no longer knew what to think and thought this girl had gone mad. He continued: Why then, charming Laura, am I alone excluded? Tell me what makes you hate me. Hate you! she cried more sharply. I have not loved those I have received. I can stand anyone, except you alone.

But why is that? Laura, explain yourself better, I don't understand you at all. Ah! do I understand myself! All I know, is that you will never touch me. . . . No! she again exclaimed angrily, never will you touch me. Feeling your arms about me, it would occur to me that you were holding nothing but a trollop, and my rage at the thought would kill me.

She grew more overwrought as she talked. Edward saw in her eyes signs of grief and despair that moved him. He adopted less condescending manners with her, a more civil and more respectful tone. She hid her face; she avoided his eyes. He took her hand affectionately. She had hardly felt his hand than she carried it to her lips, and pressed it to them sobbing and pouring forth floods of tears.

This language, though quite clear, was imprecise. Edward brought her around only with difficulty to speaking to him more clearly. A long-dead modesty was revived by love, and Laura had never offered up her person with as much shame as she experienced when admitting she was in love.

Her love was scarcely born than it was already in full force. Laura was keen and sensible; beautiful enough to inspire a passion; tender enough to share it. But since she was sold by unworthy parents at an early age, her charms, soiled by debauchery, had lost their empire. In the midst of shameful pleasures, love fled her grasp; wicked corrupters could neither feel nor inspire it. Combustible matter does not burn of itself; but let a spark come near, and it all goes up in flames. Thus did Laura's heart take fire at the transports of Edward and the Marchesa. At this new language, she felt a delightful thrill: she lent an attentive ear; nothing escaped her avid glances. The moist flame emanating from the lover's eyes entered hers and descended into her heart; hotter blood coursed through her veins; the strains of Edward's voice excited her; sentiment seemed depicted in his every gesture; all his features animated by passion made her experience it. Thus her first vision of love caused her to love the object who had enacted it for her. If he had felt nothing for another, she perhaps would have felt nothing for him.

All this excitement followed her back home. The stirrings of budding love are always delightful. Her first impulse was to give in to this new charm; the second was to open her eyes upon herself. For the first time in her life she perceived her station; it struck her with horror. Everything that sustains the hope and desires of lovers turned to despair in her soul. Even the possession of the one she loved presented to her eyes nothing but the infamy of an abject and vile creature, on whom one lavishes contempt with his caresses; in the recompense of requited love she could see nothing but ignominious prostitution.[3] Her most unbearable sufferings thus arose from her own desires. The easier it was to satisfy them, the more awful her predicament seemed; without honor, without hope, without means, she came to know love only in time to mourn its delights. So began her long sufferings, and ended her happiness of an instant.

The budding passion that so humbled her in her own eyes raised her in Edward's. Seeing that she had the capacity for love, he no longer scorned her. But what consolations could she expect from him? What sentiment could he show her, if not the minimal interest that an honest heart that is not free can take in an object of pity that has just enough honor left to feel its shame.

He consoled her as he could, and promised to come to see her again. He said not a word about her station, not even to exhort her to renounce it. What good would it do to increase the horror she had of it, since that very horror made her despair of herself? A single word on such a subject would have been consequential, and seemed to bring her closer to him: this was what could never be. The greatest misfortune of infamous trades is that it does one no good to renounce them.

After a second visit, Edward, not forgetting English munificence, sent her a lacquered chest and several English jewels. She sent it all back with this note:

I have lost the right to refuse presents. Yet I presume to return yours; for you perhaps did not mean it as a sign of contempt. If you send it back, I must needs accept it: but yours is surely a cruel kind of generosity.

Edward was impressed by this note; he found it at once humble and proud. Without leaving the baseness of her station, Laura manifested a kind of dignity. It was almost to cancel her infamy by dint of humiliating herself. He had ceased feeling scorn for her; he began to think well of her. He continued to see her without mentioning the present; and although he felt no pride in being loved by her, he could not keep from feeling pleased with it.

He did not hide these visits from the Marchesa: he had no reason to hide them; and it would have been ingratitude on his part. She wanted to know more about them. He swore that he had not touched Laura. The effect of his restraint was exactly the opposite of what he expected. What! exclaimed the infuriated Marchesa, you go to see her and do not touch her? What then do you do at her place? That is when that infernal jealousy arose which led her to make a hundred attempts on both of their lives, and consumed her with rage until the moment she died.

Other circumstances completed the work of kindling this furious passion, and restored this woman to her true character. I have already remarked that, with his rigorous integrity, Edward was lacking in delicacy. He gave the Marchesa the same present that Laura had sent back to him. She received it; not out of cupidity, but because they were on a footing that allowed for such gifts to each other; an exchange in which, in truth, the Marchesa was hardly the loser. Unfortunately she came to learn the first destination of this present, and how it had come back to him. I need not say that instantly the whole thing was broken to pieces and thrown out the window. Judge thereby what a jealous mistress and a woman of quality must have felt in such a situation.

However, the more Laura felt her shame, the less she tried to cast it off; she kept it out of despair; and the disdain she had for herself redounded upon her corruptors. She was not proud: what right would she have had? But a deep sentiment of ignominy which one would try in vain to repulse; the awful sadness of infamy which is felt and cannot be fled; the indignation of a heart that still has a sense of honor, yet feels forever dishonored—all this poured remorse and regret on pleasures abhorrent to love. A respect alien to those vile souls caused them to abandon their debauched tone; an involuntary malaise poisoned their transports; and, touched by their victim's fate, they returned home weeping for her and ashamed of themselves.

Grief consumed her. Edward, who little by little befriended her, saw that she was only too afflicted, and that he needed to cheer her and not disparage her. He went to see her; that was already a good deal in the way of consolation. His conversation did more, it encouraged her. His lofty and grand words restored to her downtrodden soul the vigor it had lost. What was not their effect issuing from a beloved mouth, and entering a wellborn heart that fate delivered to shame, but nature had made for honesty! In this heart they found a foothold and into it they fruitfully bore the lessons of virtue.

Through these beneficent attentions he finally made her think better of herself. If the only everlasting stigma is that of a corrupt heart, I feel in myself the means of blotting out my shame. I shall always be scorned, but I shall not deserve to be, I shall no longer scorn myself. Having escaped the horror of vice, at least that of contempt will seem to me less bitter. Ah! what will the whole world's disdain be to me when Edward thinks well of me? Let him see his handiwork and delight in it; he alone will make up for everything. Even if there is no benefit to honor in it, at least there will be to love. Yes, let us offer the heart it sets on fire a purer home. Delightful sentiment! I shall never again profane thy transports. I cannot be happy; I never shall be, that I know. Alas! I am unworthy of love's caresses; but I will never suffer others.

Her condition was too violent to last; but when she tried to get over it, she encountered difficulties she had not foreseen. She discovered that she who relinquishes the right to her person does not recover it at will, and that honor is a civil safeguard that leaves very vulnerable those who have lost it. She found no option for escaping oppression except to go plunge herself suddenly into a Convent and abandon her house almost to pillage; for she lived in an opulence common to her peers, especially in Italy, when their age and beauty make them sought after. She had said nothing to Bomston about her plan, finding it somewhat degrading to bring it up before carrying it out. Once she was in her sanctuary,[4] she sent him a note about it, begging him to protect her against powerful people who had an interest in her misconduct and would be offended at her retreat. He rushed to her house soon enough to save her personal effects. Though a foreigner in Rome, a great nobleman, highly regarded, wealthy, pleading forcefully the cause of honesty, soon mustered enough influence to maintain her in her Convent, and even to allow her the benefit of a pension which the Cardinal, to whom her parents had sold her, had left her.

He went to see her. She was beautiful; she was in love; she was penitent; she owed to him all she was to become. What claims to touch a heart like his! He came filled with all the sentiments that can inspire sensible hearts to do good; the only one missing was the very one that could have made her happy, and that was not in his power. Never had she had such great hopes; she was ecstatic; she already felt as though she had reached the station that one rarely can regain. She said: I am honest; a virtuous man takes an interest in me. Love, I no longer regret the tears, the sighs thou dost cost me; thou hast already repaid me for it all. Thou gavest me strength, and thou rewardest me; by making me take my duties to heart, thou becomest the foremost of them all. What happiness was reserved but to me alone! It is love that uplifts me and honors me; that wrests me from crime, from infamy; so long as there is virtue in my heart, love will be there still. O Edward! the day I again become contemptible, I will have ceased loving you.[5]

This retreat was much bruited about. Base souls, who judge others in terms of themselves, could not imagine that Edward had invested nothing more than the interest of honesty in this business. Laura was too lovable for the attentions a man paid her not always to be suspect. The Marchesa who had her spies was the first apprised of it all, and her fits of anger which she was unable to contain utterly gave her scheme away. Word of it reached the Marchese as far away as Vienna; and the following winter he came to Rome to get run through by a sword in order to restore his honor, which reaped no benefit from it.

Thus began these double liaisons, which in a country like Italy, exposed Edward to a thousand perils of every kind; now coming from an offended officer, now from a jealous and vindictive woman; now from those who had attached themselves to Laura and who were infuriated by her loss. Bizarre liaisons if ever there were, which, surrounding him needlessly with perils, tore him between two passionate mistresses without his being able to possess either one; refused by the courtesan he did not love, refusing the honest woman he worshipped; ever virtuous, it is true; but ever believing he was serving wisdom when he was listening to his passions alone.

It is not easy to say what sort of sympathy could unite two characters so opposite as those of Edward and the Marchesa; but, despite the difference in their principles, they were never able to detach themselves completely from each other. One can imagine the despair of this hotheaded woman when it dawned on her that she had given herself a rival, and what a rival! with her misguided generosity. Reproach, disdain, insults, threats, tender caresses, everything was tried in turn to detach Edward from this unworthy relationship, in which she could never believe that his heart played no part. He stood firm; he had promised he would. Laura had limited her expectation and her happiness to seeing him occasionally. Her nascent virtue needed support, it depended on him who had given birth to it; it was his task to sustain it. This is what he said to the Marchesa, to himself; and perhaps to himself he did not say all. Where is the man austere enough to flee the looks of a charming creature who demands of him no more than that he let himself be loved? where is he whose honest heart dost not swell a little at tears from two lovely eyes? where is the benefactor whose beneficial amour-propre is not pleased to enjoy the fruits of his attentions? He had made Laura too worthy of esteem to have no more than esteem for her.

The Marchesa, unable to prevail on him to stop seeing this unhappy girl, became furious; lacking the courage to break with him, she conceived a sort of horror for him. She shuddered when she saw his carriage enter, the sound of his footsteps coming up the staircase made her throb with fright. She was on the verge of fainting when he appeared. Her heart was heavy all the while he stayed with her; when he left she hurled curses at him; as soon as she lost sight of him, she would weep with rage; she talked about nothing but vengeance: her bloody spite inspired in her nothing but schemes worthy of her. Several times she had Edward attacked as he was leaving Laura's Convent. She set traps for her also to get her to come out and to abduct her. None of that was able to cure him. The next day he would return to see the woman who had tried to have him assassinated the day before, and having always his illusory scheme for restoring her to reason, he exposed his own, and fed his weakness with his virtue's zeal.

After a few months, the Marchese, ill recovered from his wound, died in Germany,[6] perhaps from grief at his wife's misconduct. This event, which should have brought Edward and the Marchesa closer together, served only to distance him even further. He found her so eager to put her recovered freedom to good use that he shuddered to take advantage of it. His very suspicion that the Marchese's wound might have contributed to his death affrighted his heart and stifled his desires. He said to himself: a husband's rights die with him for anyone else; but for his murderer they survive him and become inviolable. Even if humanity, virtue, the law, had nothing to say on this point, does reason alone not tell us that the pleasures attached to the reproduction of men ought not to be the reward for their blood; otherwise the means destined for giving us life would become sources of death and the human race would perish through the ministrations that should preserve it![7]

He spent several years thus torn between two mistresses; ever wavering from one to the other: often intending to renounce them both and able to give up neither, repelled by a hundred reasons, recalled by a thousand sentiments, and each day drawn more tightly into his shackles by his vain efforts to break them: yielding sometimes to his penchant and sometimes to his duty, going from London to Rome and from Rome to

London without being able to settle anywhere. Ever ardent, impulsive, passionate, never weak or culpable, and strong in his great and beautiful soul when he thought he was only strong in his mind. In a word, every day contemplating follies, and every day coming to his senses, ready to break his unworthy fetters. It was in his first moments of disaffection that he very nearly attached himself to Julie, and it seems certain that he would have done so had he not found the position occupied.

Meanwhile the Marchesa was constantly losing ground with her vices; Laura was gaining it with her virtues. Furthermore, the perseverance on both sides was equal; but the merit was not the same and the disgraced Marchesa, degraded by so many crimes, ultimately offered her hopeless love the supplements that Laura's had refused to tolerate. At each sojourn, Bomston found new perfections in the latter. She had learned English, she knew by heart everything he had advised her to read; she educated herself in all the fields of knowledge he seemed to love: she sought to mold her soul on his, and the remaining part of it that was hers did not unbecome it. She was still of an age when beauty grows with the years. The Marchesa was in one where it can but decline, and although she possessed that sentimental tone that pleases and moves, spoke graciously of humanity, fidelity, and virtues, all this became ridiculous given her conduct, and her reputation belied all those fine words. Edward knew her too well to hope for anything more from her. He detached himself from her imperceptibly without being able to do so entirely, he came ever closer to indifference without ever being able to achieve it. His heart constantly summoned him back to the Marchesa's; his feet carried him there without his intending it. A sensible man never forgets, however he may try, the intimacy of their former relationship.[8] By dint of machinations, ruses, horrors, she finally succeeded in making him despise her, but he despised her without ever ceasing to pity her; without ever forgetting what she had done for him or what he had felt for her.

Thus ruled by his habits even more than by his penchants, Edward could not break the attachments that attracted him to Rome. The bliss of a happy home made him desire to establish one like it before he grew old. Sometimes he accused himself of injustice, even of ingratitude toward the Marchesa, and imputed her character's vices only to her passion. Sometimes he forgot about Laura's earlier station, and his heart unintentionally crossed the barrier that separated him from her. Ever seeking to rationalize his penchant, he used his last journey as a pretext for testing his friend, forgetting that he was exposing himself to a test in which he would have succumbed without him.

The outcome of this enterprise and the denouement of the scenes related to it are recounted in the twelfth Letter of part V and in the third of part VI, in such a way as to be fully comprehensible after the preceding summary. Edward, loved by two mistresses while possessing neither, at first seems in a laughable situation. But his virtue gave him an inner delight sweeter than that of beauty, and one that does not like beauty exhaust itself. Happier with the pleasures he denied himself than is the voluptuary with those he indulges, he loved longer, remained free, and enjoyed life more than those who use it up. Blind men that we are, we all spend it chasing our illusions! Ah! shall we never learn that of all of men's follies, only the just man's makes him happy?

CHAPTER THIRTEEN

Pygmalion

Lyric Scene

The Theater represents a sculptor's studio. On the sides are seen blocks of marble, groups, rough-hewn statues. At the rear is another statue hidden under a canopy of light and brilliant fabric, ornamented with fringes and garlands.

Pygmalion, seated and leaning on his elbow, dreams with the attitude of a restless and sad man; then suddenly rising, he takes from a table the tools of his art, at intervals he goes to give some blows with the chisel on some of his rough statues, steps back, and looks with a discontented and discouraged air.

PYGMALION

There is neither soul nor life there; it is only stone. I shall never make anything of all that.

Oh, my genius, where are you? My talent, what has become of you? All my fire is extinguished, my imagination is frozen, the marble departs cold from my hands.

Pygmalion, no longer make Gods: you are only a common artist. . . . Vile instruments that are no longer those of my glory, go, do not dishonor my hands.

> *He throws his tools with disdain, then walks*
> *for a while dreaming, his arms crossed.*

What has become of me? what strange revolution has occurred in me? . . .

Tyre, opulent and superb city, the monuments of the arts with which you shine no longer attract me, I have lost the taste I had for admiring

SOURCE: Jean-Jacques Rousseau, *Letter to D'Alembert and Writings for the Theater. Collected Writings of Rousseau* X, trans. and ed. Allan Bloom, Charles Butterworth, and Christopher Kelly (Hanover, N.H.: University Press of New England, 2004).

them. The commerce of Artists and Philosophers becomes insipid for me. Conversation with Painters and Poets has no attraction for me. Praise and glory no longer elevate my soul. The praise of those who will receive it from posterity no longer touches me. Even friendship has lost its charms for me.

And you, young objects, masterpieces of nature that my art dared to imitate, and following whose steps pleasures ceaselessly attracted me, you my charming models who set me aflame with the fires of love and genius at the same time, since I have surpassed you, you are all indifferent to me.

He sits down and contemplates everything around him.

Kept in the studio by an inconceivable charm, I do not know how to do anything here, and I cannot go away. I wander from group to group, from figure to figure. My feeble, uncertain chisel no longer submits to its guide: these clumsy works, left in their timid outline, no longer feel the hand that once would have animated them . . .

He gets up impetuously.

It's over, it's over; I have lost my genius. . . . Still so young, and I outlive my talent.

But then what is this internal ardor that devours me? What do I have in me that seems to set me on fire? What! In the languidness of an extinguished genius, does one feel these emotions, does one feel these bursts of impetuous passions, this insurmountable restlessness, the secret agitation that torments me and whose cause I cannot unravel?

I feared that admiration for my own work caused the distraction that I brought to my labors. I have hidden it under the veil . . . my profane hands have dared to cover this monument of their glory. Since I no longer see it, I am sadder and no more attentive.

How dear it will be to me, how precious it will be to me, this immortal work! When my extinguished mind will no longer produce anything great, beautiful, worthy of me, I shall show my Galatea, and I shall say: This is my work! Oh my Galatea! When I have lost everything, you will be left to me, and I shall be consoled.

He approaches the canopy, then withdraws, goes, comes, and stops sometimes to look at it while sighing.

But why hide it? What do I gain by doing so? Reduced to idleness, why deprive myself of the pleasure of contemplating the most beautiful of my works? . . . Perhaps there remains some flaw in it that I have not noticed; perhaps I shall still be able to add some ornament to its adornment; no imaginable charm should be missing to such a charming object. . . . Perhaps this object will revive my languishing imagination. I must see her again, examine her anew. What am I saying? Ah! I have not yet examined her: up to now I have only admired her.

He goes to lift the veil, and lets it fall again as if frightened.

I know not what emotion I suffer when touching this veil; a fright seizes me; I believe that I touch the sanctuary of some Divinity. . . . Pygmalion! it is a stone; it is your work. What does it matter? Gods are served in our temples who are of no other material and who have been made by no other hand.

Trembling, he lifts the veil, and prostrates himself. The statue of Galatea is seen posed on a pedestal that is very small, but raised by a marble tier formed by some semicircular steps.

Oh Galatea! receive my homage. Yes, I was mistaken: I wished to make you a Nymph, and I made you a Goddess: Even Venus is less beautiful than you.

Vanity, human weakness! I cannot grow weary of admiring my work; I intoxicate myself with amour-propre; I adore myself in what I have made. . . . No, never has anything so beautiful appeared in nature; I have surpassed the work of the Gods . . .

What! so many beauties come out of my hands? My hands have touched them then? My mouth could then have . . . Pygmalion! I see a flaw. This garment covers the nakedness too much; it must be opened up some more; the charms it harbors should be better announced.

He takes his hammer and chisel, then slowly advancing, he climbs, while hesitating, the tier of the statue that he seems not to dare to touch. Finally, having already raised the chisel, he stops himself.

What trembling! what agitation! I hold the chisel with an unsteady hand. . . . I cannot . . . I dare not . . . I will spoil everything.

He encourages himself, and at last, presenting his chisel, he gives it a single blow, and seized with fright, he lets it fall, while uttering a great cry.

Gods! I feel the palpitating flesh repelling the chisel! . . .

He climbs down, trembling and confused.

Vain terror, foolish blindness! . . . No, I shall not touch it at all; the

Gods terrify me. Doubtless she has already been consecrated to their rank.

He considers it anew.

What do you want to change? Look; what new charms do you want to give it? . . . Ah! Its flaw is caused by perfection. . . . Divine Galatea! Less perfect, you would be lacking nothing.

Tenderly.

But you lack a soul: your form cannot do without one.

With even more tenderness.

How beautiful the soul made to animate such a body must be!

He stops for a long time, then, returning, sits down, he says with a slow and changed voice.

What desires have I dared to form? What senseless wishes! What do I feel? . . . Oh heaven! The veil of the illusion falls, and I do not dare to look in my heart: I would have too much with which to be indignant.

Long pause in a deep depression.

. . . This, then, is the noble passion that leads me astray! It is then for this inanimate object that I dare not leave here . . . a piece of marble! a rock! an unformed and hard mass, worked on with this iron! . . . Senseless man, return to yourself; bemoan yourself, see your error . . . see your madness . . .
. . . But no . . .

Impetuously.

No, I have not lost my senses; no, I do not extravagate; no, I do not reproach myself for anything. It is not at all this dead marble with which I am infatuated, it is with a living being who resembles it; it is with the form that it offers to my eyes. Wherever that adorable form may be, whatever body may bear it, and whatever hand may have made it, she will have all the wishes of my heart. Yes, my only madness is to discern beauty, my sole crime is to be sensitive to it. There is nothing in that for which I should blush.

In a less lively manner, but still with passion.

What shafts of fire seem to come from that object to set my senses ablaze, and return to their source with my soul! Alas! it stays immobile and cold, while my heart, set ablaze by its charms, would like to leave my body to warm its body. In my delirium I believe that I can soar out of myself; I believe that I can give it my life, and animate it with my soul. Ah! that Pygmalion might die in order to live in Galatea! . . . Oh Heaven, what am I saying! If I were she, I would not see her, I would not be the one who loves her! No, that my Galatea live, and that I not be she. Ah! that I might always be another, in order to wish always to be she, to see her, to love her, to be loved by her. . .

Rapture.

Torments, wishes, desires, rage, impotence, terrible love, fatal love . . . oh! all hell is in my agitated heart. . . . Powerful Gods! Beneficent Gods! Gods of the people who knew the passions of men! Ah! you have performed so many prodigies for less important causes. See this object, see my heart; be just and deserve your altars!

With a more pathetic enthusiasm.

And you, sublime essence who hides yourself from the senses, and makes yourself felt in hearts! soul of the universe, principle of all existence; you who through love gives harmony to the elements, life to matter, feeling to bodies, and form to all beings, sacred fire! celestial Venus, by whom everything preserves itself and ceaselessly reproduces itself! Ah! where is your equilibrium? where is your expansive force? where is the law of nature in the feeling that I am experiencing? where is your life-giving heat in the inanity of my vain desires? All your fires are concentrated in my heart and the cold of death remains on this marble; I perish from the excess of life that it lacks. Alas! I do not expect a miracle; it exists, it ought to cease; order is troubled, nature is outraged; restore their empire to its laws, reestablish its beneficent course and equally pour forth your divine influence. Yes, for the plenitudes of things two beings are lacking. Divide between them this devouring ardor that consumes one without animating the other. It is you who formed by my hand these charms and features that await only sentiment and life. . . . Give it half of mine, give it all, if necessary, it will be enough for me to live in her. Oh you who deign to smile at the homage of mortals! what feels nothing does not honor you. Extend your glory with your works. Goddess of beauty, spare nature this affront, that such a perfect model be the image of that which is not.

He returns to himself by degrees with a
movement of assurance and joy.

I am recovering my senses. What an unexpected calm! what unhoped-for courage reanimates me! A mortal fever sets my blood on fire: a balm of confidence and hope flow through my veins: I believe I feel myself being reborn.

Thus the sentiment of our dependence sometimes serves as our consolation. However unhappy mortals may be, when they have invoked the Gods, they are more tranquil . . .

But this unjust confidence fools those who make senseless wishes. . . . Alas! In the state I am in, one invokes everything and nothing hears one. The hope that abuses us is more senseless than the desire.

Ashamed of so much distraction, I no longer even dare to contemplate its cause. When I wish to raise my eyes to this fatal object, I feel a new agitation, a palpitation suffocates me, a secret fright stops me . . .

Bitter irony.

. . . Ah! look wretch! become intrepid, dare to gaze at a statue.

He sees her come to life, and turns away with fright and his heart broken with sadness.

What have I seen? Gods! What did I believe I saw? The coloring of flesh . . . a fire in the eyes . . . even movements . . . It was not enough to wish for the prodigy; for the peak of misery, at last, I have seen it . . .

Excess of depression.

Unfortunate one! then it has happened . . . your delirium has reached its final term; your reason abandons you as well as your genius! . . . Don't regret it, oh, Pygmalion! Its loss will cover your disgrace.

Lively indignation.

It is too funny for the lover of a stone to become a man of visions.

He turns around and sees the statue moving and descending by herself the steps by which he climbed onto the pedestal. He throws himself on his knees and raises his hands and eyes to Heaven.

Immortal Gods! Venus! Galatea! Oh trick of a frenzied love!

GALATEA, *touches herself and says.*
   I.

PYGMALION, *enraptured.*
   I!

GALATEA, *touching herself again.*
   It is I.

PYGMALION.
   Ravishing illusion that is transmitted even to my ears, ah, never leave
my senses.

GALATEA, *takes several steps and touches a piece of marble.*
   This is I no more.

> *Pygmalion, in an agitation, in raptures that he can hardly contain,
> follows all her movements, listens to her, observes her with a
> greedy attention that hardly allows him to breathe.*

> *Galatea approaches him and looks at him.*

> *He gets up precipitously, reaches out his arm, and looks at her with
> ecstasy. She lays a hand on him; he shudders, takes this hand,
> carries it to his heart, then covers it with ardent kisses.*

GALATEA, *with a sigh.*
   Ah, still I.

PYGMALION.
   Yes, dear and charming object: yes, worthy masterpiece of my hands,
of my heart, and of the Gods . . . it is you, it is you alone: I have given
you all my being; I shall no longer live except through you.

CHAPTER FOURTEEN

On Love

❧❦❧

[*These two passages come from the end of book IV of* Emile. *In this book Rousseau's fictional student is introduced to the moral world by being exposed to compassion, religion, beauty, and love. They give Rousseau's clearest statement about what love is.*]

Those who want to guide the young wisely, in order to safeguard them from the snares of the senses, make love horrifying to them. They would willingly make it a crime to think of it at their age, as if love were made for old men. All these deceptive lessons, to which the heart gives the lie, do not persuade. The young man, guided by a surer instinct, laughs in secret at the sad maxims with which he pretends to agree, and waits only for the moment to make them vain. All of that is against nature. By following a contrary road, I shall arrive more surely at the same goal. I shall not be afraid to indulge in him the sweet sentiment for which he is avid. I shall depict it for him as the supreme happiness of life, because in effect it is. As I depict it for him, I want him to surrender to it. By making him feel what a charm the union of hearts adds to the attraction of the senses, I shall disgust him with libertinism, and I shall make him chaste by making him fall in love.

*   *   *

Nothing of all that. My expedient alone takes care of everything. Your heart, I say to the young man, needs a companion. Let us go seek the one who suits you. We shall not easily find her, perhaps; true merit is always rare. But let us not hurry, nor let ourselves be discouraged. Doubtless there is one, and we shall find her in the end, or at least the one who comes closest to her. With a project so flattering for him, I introduce him into the world. What more do I need to say about this? Do you not see that I have done everything?

By depicting for him the mistress I destine for him, imagine whether I shall know how to make him listen to me; whether I shall know how to make agreeable and dear to him the qualities he must love; whether I shall know how to determine all of his sentiments with respect to what he must seek or flee? I would have to be the clumsiest of men if I do not make him passionate in advance without knowing about whom. It does not matter that the object I shall paint for him is imaginary. It is enough that it disgusts him with those that might tempt him; it is enough that he everywhere finds comparisons that make him prefer his chimera to the real objects that will strike him. And what is true love itself, if not chimera, lie, illusion? One loves far more the image one makes for oneself than the object to which one applies it. If one saw what one loves exactly as it is, there would no longer be love on earth. When one stops loving, the person one loved stays the same as before, but one no longer sees her as the same. The veil of illusion falls, and love vanishes. Now, by supplying the imaginary object, I am the master of comparisons, and I easily prevent illusion regarding real objects.

I do not, for all that, want one to mislead a young man by depicting for him a model of perfection that could not exist. But I shall so choose the defects of his mistress that they will suit him, they will please him, and they will serve to correct his. Neither do I want one to lie to him by affirming falsely that the object one depicts for him exists. But if he is pleased by the image, he will soon wish for an original. The journey from wish to supposition is an easy one; it is a matter of a few adroit descriptions that, by means of more tangible traits, will give to this imaginary object a greater air of truth. I would want to go so far as to name her. I shall say, laughing: let us call your future mistress *Sophie.* *Sophie* is a name that augurs well. If the one you will choose does not bear it, she will at least be worthy of bearing it; we can honor her with it in advance. After all these details, if without affirming or denying it one escapes by evasions, his suspicions will change into certainty. He will believe that one is making a mystery of the wife being destined for him, and that he will see her when it is time. If he once reaches this point, and one has chosen well the traits that one must show him, all the rest is easy. One can expose him in society almost without risk. Only protect him from his senses; his heart is safe.

CHAPTER FIFTEEN

On Love

[*In this part of the* Letter to d'Alembert *Rousseau observes that romantic love is the predominant subject of contemporary drama, which no longer has serious political concerns. This is the situation he had thought he could remedy when he had the idea of writing* The Death of Lucretia. *Here he spells out the effects of this focus on love.*]

Love is women's realm. They are the ones who necessarily give the law in it; because, according to nature's order, resistance belongs to them, and men cannot vanquish this resistance except at the expense of their freedom. A natural effect of these sorts of pieces is, then, to extend the empire of the *Female Sex,* to make women and young girls into the public's preceptors, and to give them the same power over the spectators that they have over their lovers. Do you think, Sir, that there are no inconveniences in this order, and that men will be better governed by increasing women's ascendancy with so much care?

In the world there might be some women worthy of being listened to by a decent man;[1] but in general is it from them that he should take advice, and would there be no means of honoring their sex, short of debasing ours? Nature's most charming object, the most capable of moving a sensitive heart and leading it to the good, is, I admit it, a lovable and virtuous woman. But where is this celestial object hiding itself, and is it not very cruel to contemplate it with so much pleasure at the theater, in order to find such different ones in society? Nevertheless the seductive tableau has its effect. The enchantment caused by these prodigies of wisdom turns to the profit of women without honor. If a young man has seen the world only on the Stage, the first means that offers itself to him to proceed to virtue is to look for a mistress who will lead him there; hoping very well to find a Constance or at least a Cenie.*[2]

*I do not cite Cenie at all carelessly here, even though this charming Piece is the work of a woman; for, seeking the truth in good faith, I do not know how to disguise

It is this way that, based on faith in an imaginary model, based on a modest and touching air, based on a counterfeit gentleness, *nescius area fallacis*,[3] the foolish youngster rushes to ruin himself, while thinking he is becoming a wise man.

This provides me the occasion to propose a sort of problem. In general the ancients had a very great respect for women;* but they showed this respect by abstaining from exposing them to the public's judgment, and believed they honored their modesty, by keeping quiet about their other virtues. They had a maxim according to which the country in which morals were purest, was the one in which the women were least spoken about and that the most decent woman was the one who was least spoken about. It is, based on this principle, that a Spartan, hearing a foreigner give magnificent praises of a Lady of his acquaintance, angrily interrupted him: "Won't you stop," he said to him, "slandering a good woman?" From that also came the fact that in their Comedy, the roles of lovers and marriageable girls never depicted anyone except slaves or streetwalkers. They had such an idea of the Female Sex's modesty that they would have believed they were lacking in the respect that they owed to it, by putting a decent girl on the stage, even in representation.** In a word, the image of open vice shocked them less than that of offended modesty.

Among us, on the contrary, the most esteemed woman is the one who causes the most commotion; who is most spoken about; who is most seen in high society; at whose home one dines most often; who most imperiously sets the tone; who judges, settles, decides, pronounces, assigns to talents, merit, virtues, their degrees and their places, and for whose favor the humble learned men beg most basely. On the Stage, it is even worse. At bottom, in high society they do not know anything, although they judge about everything: But in the theater, learned with men's learning, philosophers (thanks to the authors) they crush our Sex

---

what acts against my sentiment; and it is not to a woman, but to women that I refuse men's talents. I honor all the more willingly those of the author of *Cenie* in particular, as, having cause to complain about her speeches, I am rendering her a pure and disinterested homage, as are all the praises that have come from my pen.

*They gave them many honorable names that we no longer have, or that are low and old-fashioned among us. It is known what use Virgil made of that *Matres* on an occasion when the Trojan Mothers were hardly prudent.[4] In its place we have only the word *Ladies*, which does not suit all of them, which even is gradually growing old, and which has been completely proscribed from the fashionable tone. I observe that the ancients willingly drew their titles of honor from the rights of nature, and that we draw ours only from the rights of rank.

**If they made use of them differently in tragedies, that is because, following the political system of their theater, they were not sorry for it to be believed that people of high rank have no need of modesty, and are always exceptions to the rules of morality.

with its own talents and the imbecilic Spectators go naively to learn from women what they have taken care to dictate to them. All that, in truth, is to make fun of them; it is to accuse them of having a puerile vanity, and I do not doubt that the wisest are indignant about it. Leaf through the majority of modern plays, it is always a woman who knows everything, who teaches everything to men; it is always the Lady of the court who makes the little Jean de Saintré[5] say his catechism. A child would not know how to eat his bread if it is not cut by his governess. That is the image of what happens in new plays. The Nanny is on the stage and the children are in the pit. Once again, I do not deny that this method might have its advantages, and that such preceptors might be able to give some weight and value to their lessons; but let us return to my question. Of the ancient practice and ours, I ask which is the more honorable to women, and renders better to their Sex the true regards that are due to it?

The same cause that gives the ascendancy to women over men in our tragic and comic plays, also gives it to young people over the elderly; this is another reversal of natural relations that is not any less reprehensible. As the interest in them is always for the lovers, it follows that the characters who are advanced in age can never play anything in them except roles that are subordinate. Or, in order to form the crux of the intrigue, they serve as obstacle to the wishes of the young lovers, and then they are hateful; or they are lovers themselves, and then they are ridiculous. *Turpe senex miles.*[6] In tragedies they are made into tyrants, usurpers; in comedies, jealous men, usurers, pedants, unbearable fathers, whom the whole world is conspiring to deceive. Behold under what an honorable aspect old age is shown in the theater; behold what respect is inspired for it in young people! Let us thank the illustrious author of Zaïre and of Nanine for having shielded from this disdain the venerable Luzignan and the good old Philippe Humbert.[7] There are also several others; but is that enough to halt the torrent of public prejudice, and to erase the debasement in which the majority of authors are pleased to show the age of wisdom, of experience, and of authority? Who can doubt that the habit of always seeing the elderly as odious characters at the Theater, does not help to have them rejected in Society, and that by getting used to confusing those whom one sees in the world with driveling idiots and Gerontes of the Comedy, one does not despise them both equally? Observe in a gathering at Paris, the smug and vain air, the firm and trenchant tone of an impudent youth, while the Old Men, fearful and modest, either do not dare to open their mouths, or are barely listened to. Does one see anything similar in the provinces, and in the places where Shows are not at all established; and throughout the earth, outside of the large cities, do not a bald head and white hair always leave an impression of respect? I shall be told that at Paris the elderly contribute to making themselves despicable, by renouncing the bearing that suits them, in order indecently to put on the adornment and manners of youth, and that, playing at being gallant after its example, it is only normal that youth be preferred to them in its own trade. But it is exactly the opposite: because they have no other way of making themselves put up with, they are constrained to have recourse to that one, and they prefer to be put up with in favor of their ridiculousness, than not to be put up with at all. It is certainly not the case that by playing the fellows who dance attendance they become such in fact, and that a gallant sexagenarian is an extremely charming personage. But his very indecency turns to his profit; this is one triumph more for a woman, who, dragging a Nestor in her train, believes she is showing that the frost of age does not at all safeguard against the fires that she inspires. That is why women encourage these Deans of Cithera the best they can, and have the malice of treating as charming men old fools, whom they would find less lovable if they were less extravagant. But let us return to my subject.

These effects are not the only ones that are produced by the interest of the Stage founded solely upon love. Many others, more serious and more important, are attributed to it whose reality I do not examine here, but that have been often and strongly alleged by ecclesiastical Writers. It has been responded to them that the dangers that the tableau of a contagious passion can produce are forestalled by the manner of presenting it. The love that is exposed in the theater is rendered legitimate there. Its goal is decent; often it is sacrificed to duty and to virtue; and as soon as it is guilty, it is punished. Very good; but is it not pleasant that they claim to regulate the movements of the heart based on the precepts of reason this way *after* the fact, and that one has to wait for the outcome in order to know what impression one ought to receive from the situations that lead to them? The evil that one reproaches the theater for is not precisely that of inspiring criminal passions, but of disposing the soul to feelings that are too tender, that one afterward satisfies at the expense of virtue. The sweet emotions that one experiences there do not in themselves have a settled object, but they cause the need for one to be born; they do not exactly cause one to love, but they prepare one to feel it; they do not choose the person that one should love, but they force us to make this choice. Hence they are innocent or criminal only by the use that we make of them in accordance with our character, and this character is independent of the example. Even if it were true that only legitimate passions are depicted in the theater, does it follow that its impressions are any weaker, that its effects are less dangerous? As if the vivid images of an innocent tenderness were less sweet, less seductive, less capable of exciting a sensitive heart than those of a criminal love, to which the horror of vice at least serves as an antidote? But if for a few moments the idea of innocence embellishes the feeling that it accompanies, soon circumstances are erased from the memory, while the impression of such a sweet passion remains graven in the depths of the heart. When the Patrician Manilius was expelled from the Senate of Rome for having given a kiss to his wife in the presence of his daughter, considering that action only in itself, what was reprehensible in it? Nothing, without a doubt; it even proclaimed a praiseworthy feeling. But the chaste ardors of the mother could inspire impure ones in the daughter. That was therefore to make of a very decent action an example of corruption. That is the effect of the permitted loves of the theater.

They claim that they cure us of love by the depiction of its weaknesses. I do not know how authors go about doing that, but I see that the spectators are always on the weak lover's side, and that often they are sorry that he is not even weaker. I ask whether that is a great way of keeping from resembling him?

Do you remember, Sir, a play that I believe I remember having attended with you, several years ago, and that gave us a pleasure that we were hardly expecting, either because in fact the author had put more theatrical beauties in it than we had thought, or because the actress lent her characteristic charm to the role which she set off. I want to talk about Racine's Berenice. In what disposition of mind does the spectator see this play begin? In a feeling of disdain for the weakness of an Emperor and a Roman who hesitates, like the lowest of men, between his mistress and his duty; who, ceaselessly fluctuating in a dishonorable uncertainty, debases with effeminate complaints that almost divine character that history gives him; who causes one to look for the benefactor of the world and the delights of the human race in a vile bedroom[8] suitor. What does the same spectator think about him after the performance? He ends by pitying that sensitive man whom he despised; by taking an interest in that very passion that he made into a crime for him; by muttering in secret about the sacrifice that he is forced to make of it to the fatherland's laws. That is what each of us experienced at the performance. The role of Titus, very well rendered, might have brought about some effect had it been more worthy of him. But everyone felt that the principal interest was for Bérénice, and that it was the fate of her love that determined the type of the catastrophe; not that her continuous complaints gave a great emotion during the course of the play; but in the fifth act when, ceasing to complain, gloomy, dry-eyed and voice faint, she made speak a cold suffering approaching despair, the actress's art added to what was pathetic in the role, and the spectators, keenly touched, began to weep when Berenice wept no more. What did that signify, other than that one was terrified that she might be sent away; that one felt in advance the suffering with which her heart would be penetrated; and that each person would have wanted Titus to let himself be overcome, even at the risk of esteeming him less for it? Is that not a tragedy that has fulfilled its objective well, and that has well taught the spectators to surmount the weaknesses of love?

The outcome contradicts these secret wishes, but what difference does that make? The denouement does not at all erase the play's effect. The Queen leaves without the Pit's leave; the Emperor sends her away *invitus invitam*, one can add *invito spectatore.*[9] Titus might well remain a Roman; he is alone on his side; all the spectators have married Bérénice.

Even if one could dispute this effect with me; even if one maintains that the example of strength and virtue that one sees in Titus, conqueror of himself, is the basis for the interest of the Play, and makes it so that while pitying Berenice one is very glad to pity her; in that one would do nothing but return to my principles; because, as I have already said, the sacrifices made to duty and virtue always have a secret charm, even for corrupt hearts; and the proof that this sentiment is not at all the work of the play is that they have it before it begins. But that does not prevent certain satisfied passions from seeming to them preferable to virtue itself, and that, if they are content to see Titus virtuous and magnanimous, they might not be even more so to see him happy and weak, or at least that they might willingly consent to be so in his place. To make this truth tangible, let us imagine a denouement completely contrary to the author's. That after having better consulted his heart, Titus, wanting neither to break the laws of Rome, nor to sell happiness to ambition, comes, with opposite maxims to abdicate the Empire at the feet of Bérénice; that penetrated by such a great sacrifice, she feels that her duty would be to refuse her lover's hand, and that nevertheless she accepts it; that both of them intoxicated by the charms of love, peace, innocence, and renouncing empty greatness, make, with that sweet joy that the true movements of nature inspire, the decision to go to live happily and unknown in a corner of the earth; that such a touching scene be animated by the tender and pathetic feelings that the subject provides and that Racine would have known how to set off so well; that upon leaving the Romans Titus addresses a speech to them, of the sort called for by the circumstances and the subject—is it not clear, for example, that unless the author is totally lacking in skill, such a speech ought to make the entire audience melt into tears? Ending this way, the play will be, if you wish, less good, less instructive, less in conformity with history—but will it cause less pleasure, and will the spectators leave it less satisfied? The first four acts would remain just about as they are, and nevertheless a completely opposite lesson would be drawn from them. So true is it that the tableaux of love always make more of an impression than the maxims of wisdom, and that the effect of a tragedy is entirely independent of that of the denouement.*

Does one want to know whether it is certain that by showing the fatal consequences of immoderate passions, tragedy teaches how to protect oneself against them? Let experience be consulted. These fatal consequences are represented very strongly in Zaïre; it costs the two lovers their life and Orosmane much more than life: because he kills himself only in order to deliver himself from the cruelest sentiment that can enter into a human heart; remorse at having stabbed his mistress. There, then, are certainly very energetic lessons. I would be curious to find someone, man or woman, who would dare to boast about having left a performance of Zaïre well protected against love. As for me, I believe I hear every Spectator say in his heart at the end of the tragedy: "Ah! Give me a Zaïre; I will certainly act so as not to kill her." If women have not been able to keep themselves from running in a crowd to that enchanting play, and from making the men run there, I shall not say that it is in order to encourage themselves by the Heroine's example to imitate a sacrifice that succeeded so ill for her; but it is because, of all the tragedies that are in the theater, no other shows the power of love and the empire of beauty with more charms, and because as additional profit in it one also learns not to judge one's mistress based on appearances. Let Orosmane immolate Zaïre to his jealousy; a sensitive woman sees the rapture of passion in that without fright: for to perish by one's lover's hand is less of a misfortune than to be loved in a mediocre way by him.

Let them depict love to us as they wish: it seduces, or it is not love. If it is badly depicted, the play is bad; if it is well depicted, it eclipses everything that accompanies it. Its strife, its ills, its sufferings, make it even more touching than if it had no resistance to overcome. Far from its sad effects discouraging, it only becomes more interesting by means of its very misfortunes. One says to oneself in spite of oneself, that such

---

* In the seventh volume of *Pamela*[10] there is a very judicious examination of Racine's *Andromache*, from which one sees that this Play does not proceed to its self-proclaimed goal any better than all the others do.

a delightful sentiment consoles for everything. Such a sweet image imperceptibly softens the heart; from passion, one takes what leads to pleasure; from it, one leaves aside what torments. No one believes himself to be obliged to be a Hero, and this is how, admiring decent love, one abandons oneself to criminal love.

What completes making its images dangerous, is precisely what is done to make them pleasant; it is that one never sees it rule on the stage except between decent souls, it is that the two lovers are always models of perfection. And how can one not take an interest in such a seductive passion, between two hearts whose character is already so interesting by itself? I doubt that in all our dramatic plays one finds a single one of them in which mutual love does not have the spectator's favor. If some unfortunate burns with an unreciprocated love, he is made into the butt of the pit. One believes that one is performing marvels by making a lover estimable or hateful, in accordance with whether he is well or ill received in his loves, by making the feelings of his Mistress always approved by the public, and by giving to tenderness all the interest of virtue. Instead of which it would be necessary to teach young people to distrust love's illusions, to flee the error of a blind inclination that always believes it is based upon esteem, and sometimes to fear to deliver a virtuous heart over to an object unworthy of its cares. I know hardly any except *the Misanthrope* in which the Hero of the play has made a bad choice;* to make the misanthrope in love was nothing; the stroke of genius is to have made him in love with a coquette. All the rest of the theater is a treasury of perfect women. One would say that they have all taken refuge there. Is that the faithful image of society? Is that the way that one renders a passion that ruins so many wellborn people suspect to us? They very nearly make us believe that a decent man is obliged to be in love, and that a female lover who is loved would not know how not to be virtuous. Behold us extremely well instructed!

Once again, I am not at all undertaking to judge whether it is good or bad to base the principal interest of the theater on love: But I do say that, if its depictions are dangerous sometimes, they are so always, whatever might be done to disguise them. I say that it is speaking in bad faith or without knowing it, to want to rectify its impressions by other alien impressions that do not accompany them all the way to the heart, or from which the heart has soon separated them; impressions that even disguise the dangers, and give this deceiving feeling a new attraction by which it ruins those who abandon themselves to it.

* Let us add *The Merchant of London*,[11] an admirable play and whose moral goes more directly to the goal than any French Play that I know.

CHAPTER SIXTEEN

Letters to Sara[1]

Jam nec spes animi credula mutui.[2]
—Horace

It will be understood without difficulty how a sort of dare could have caused these four letters to be written. Someone asked whether it was possible for a half-century-old lover not to make people laugh. It seemed to me that one could be caught by surprise at any age, that a Greybeard could even write as many as four love letters, and still be interesting to decent people, but that he could not proceed to six without dishonoring himself. I do not need to state my reasons here: one can feel them upon reading these letters; after reading them, one will judge about them.[3]

First Letter

You[4] read in my heart, young Sara; you have seen through me, I know it, I feel it. A hundred times a day your curious eye comes to spy out the effect of your charms. From your satisfied manner, from your cruel kindnesses, from your scornful flirting, I see that you are secretly enjoying my misery; you are congratulating yourself with a mocking smile for the despair into which you are plunging a wretch, for whom love is no longer anything but a disgrace. You are mistaken, Sara; I am to be pitied, but I am not at all to be scoffed at: I am not at all worthy of scorn, but of pity, because I do not deceive myself either about my appearance or about my age, because, while loving, I feel myself to be unworthy of pleasing, and because the fatal illusion that is leading me astray keeps me from seeing you as you are, without keeping me from seeing myself as I am. You can deceive me about everything aside from myself: you

SOURCE: Jean-Jacques Rousseau, *Autobiographical, Scientific, Religious, Moral, and Literary Writings. Collected Writings of Rousseau* XII, trans. and ed. Christopher Kelly (Hanover, N.H.: University Press of New England, 2007).

can persuade me of anything in the world, except that you can share my insane ardors. To see myself as you see me is the worst of my tortures; for me your deceiving caresses are only a further humiliation, and I love with the horrible certainty of not being capable of being loved.

Be content then. Ah well, yes, I adore you; yes, I burn for you with the cruelest of passions. But try, if you dare, to chain me to your chariot, as a suitor with grey hair, as a greybeard lover who wants to dance attendance, and, in his extravagant delirium, imagines himself to have rights over a young object. You will not have that glory at all, oh Sara, do not flatter yourself on that score: you will not see me at your feet wishing to amuse you with the jargon of gallantry, or to soften you with languid words. You can wrest tears from me, but they are less of love than of fury. Laugh if you will at my weakness: at least you will not be laughing at my credulity.

I am speaking to you about my passion with fervor, because humiliation is always cruel, and disdain is hard to bear: but my passion, completely mad as it is, is not at all fervent; it is lively and sweet at the same time, as you are. Deprived of all hope, I am dead to happiness and live only from your life. Your pleasures are my only pleasures; I cannot have any enjoyments other than yours, nor form any wishes other than your wishes. I would love even my Rival if you loved him; if you did not love him, I would want him to be able to deserve your love; to have my heart in order to love you more worthily, and make you happy. This is the only desire permitted to anyone who dares to love without being lovable. Love and be loved, oh Sara. Live satisfied, and I shall die satisfied.

Second Letter

Since I have written to you,[5] I want to write to you again. My first fault attracts another one; but I shall know how to stop, be sure of it; and it is the manner in which you will have treated me during my delirium that will determine my sentiments with regard to you when I have recovered from it. Pretend though you do that you have not read my Letter: you are lying, I know it, you have read it. Yes, you are lying without saying anything to me, by the equable air with which you believe you are deceiving me about it: if you are the same as before, this is because you have always been false, and the simplicity that you are putting on with me, proves to me that you never had any. You are dissimulating about my folly only to increase it; you are not satisfied that I am writing to you unless you also see me at your feet: you want to make me as ridiculous as I can be; you want to make a spectacle of me for yourself, perhaps for others, and you do not believe yourself to be triumphant enough, unless I am dishonored.

I see all that, wily girl, in that feigned modesty by which you are hoping to deceive me, in that feigned equability by which you seem to want to tempt me to forget my fault, by appearing to know nothing about it yourself. Once again, you have read my Letter; I know it, I have seen it. I saw you, when I was entering your room, hurriedly put down the Book in which I had put it; I saw you blush and show signs of agitation for a moment. Seductive and cruel agitation that perhaps is yet another of your traps, and that has done me more harm than all your glances. What did I become upon seeing that aspect that still perturbs me? A hundred times in a moment, ready to throw myself at the feet of the proud one, what struggles, what efforts to hold myself back! I left, nevertheless, I left palpitating with joy at escaping from the unworthy base action that I was going to commit. This sole moment avenges me for your[6] insults. Be less proud, oh Sara, of an inclination that I can conquer, because once in my life I have already triumphed over you.

Unlucky one![7] I impute to your vanity some fictions of my amour-propre. If only I had the happiness of being able to believe that you are concerned about me, if only in order to tyrannize over myself! But to deign to tyrannize over a greying lover would still be doing him too much honor. No, you have no art other than your indifference; your disdain makes up all of your coquetry, you devastate me without thinking about me. I am unfortunate to the point of not being able to concern you even with my ridiculousness, and you despise my folly to the point of not deigning even to make fun of it. You have read my Letter, and you have forgotten it; you did not speak to me at all about my ills, because you were no longer thinking about them. What! am I nothing for you then? Far from exciting your pity, my raging, my torments do not even excite your attention? Ah! where is that sweetness that your eyes promise? Where is that so tender sentiment that appears to enliven them? . . . Barbarian! . . . insensitive to my condition, you must be insensitive to every decent feeling. Your face promises a soul; it lies, you have nothing but ferocity. . . . Ah Sara! From your good heart I would have expected some consolation in my misery.

Third Letter

Finally, nothing more is lacking to my shame, and I am as humiliated as you wanted. It is to this then that my vexation, my struggles, my resolutions, my constancy led? I would be less debased if I had resisted less. Who, me! I have acted on my love like a young man? I have passed two hours at a child's knees? I have shed torrents of tears upon her hands? I have put up with her consoling me, with her pitying me, with her wiping my eyes dimmed by age? I have received lessons of reason, of courage, from her? I have profited very well from my long experience and my sad reflections! How many times have I blushed at having been at twenty years what I am becoming again at fifty! Ah, I have, then, lived only in order to dishonor myself! If only a true repentance was bringing me back to more decent sentiments: but no; in spite of myself I take pleasure in those you inspire in me, in the delirium in which you plunge me, in the abasement into which you have reduced me. When I imagine myself at my age on my knees before you, my entire heart rises up, and becomes angry; but it forgets itself and loses itself in the raptures I felt there. Ah! I did not see myself then; I saw nothing but you, adored girl: your charms, your feelings, your speeches filled, formed my entire being: I was young with your youth, wise with your reason, virtuous with your virtue. Could I disdain the one that you honored with your esteem? Could I hate the one that you deigned to call your friend? Alas! that father's tenderness that you asked me for in such a touching tone, that name of daughter that you wanted to receive from me soon made me return to myself: your remarks so tender, your caresses so pure enchanted me and tore me apart, tears of love and rage flowed from my eyes. I felt that I was happy only from my misery, and that if I had been more worthy of pleasing I would not have been treated so well.

No matter. I have been able to make tenderness enter your heart. Pity closes it to love, I know it, but for me it has all its charms. What! I have seen your beautiful eyes become moist for me? I have felt one of your tears fall upon my cheek? Oh that tear, what a consuming blaze it caused! And I am not the happiest of men? Ah, how much I am beyond my most prideful expectation!

Yes, let those two hours return endlessly, let them fill the rest of my life with their return or their memory. Ah, what has my life had to compare with what I felt in that posture? I was humiliated, I was insane, I was ridiculous; but I was happy, and in that short space I tasted more pleasures than I have had in the whole course of my years. Yes, Sara, yes, charming Sara, I have lost all repentance, all shame; I no longer remember myself, I feel only the fire that is devouring me; in your chains I can brave the jeers of the entire world. What does it matter to me how I might appear to others? I have the heart of a young man for you, and that is enough for me. Winter might well have covered Etna with its ice; its bosom is no less set aflame.

Fourth Letter

What! it was you[8] of whom I stood in fear, it was you whom I blushed at loving? Oh Sara, adorable girl, soul more beautiful than your face! Henceforth if I esteem myself for anything, it is for having a heart made to feel all your worth. Yes, doubtless, I blushed from the love that I had for you, but that is because it was too fawning, too languid, too weak, too little worthy of its object. For six months my eyes and my heart have been devouring your charms, for six months you alone have been occupying me and I have not lived for anything but you: but it is only since yesterday that I learned to love you. While you were speaking to me and speeches worthy of Heaven were leaving your mouth, I believed I was seeing your features, your air, your bearing, your face change; I know not what supernatural fire was gleaming in your eyes; rays of light seemed to surround you. Ah Sara, if you are really not a mortal, if you are the Angel sent from Heaven in order to bring round a heart that is going astray, tell me so; perhaps there is still time. Do not let your image be profaned any longer by desires formed in spite of myself. Alas! if I am deceiving myself in my wishes, in my raptures, in my reckless homage, cure me of an error that offends you; teach me how you must be adored.

You[9] have subjugated me, Sara, in all ways and if you make me love my folly, you make me feel it cruelly. When I compare your behavior to mine, I find a wise man in a young girl, and in myself I feel only an elderly child. Your sweetness, so full of dignity, reason, seemliness, has told me everything that a more severe reception would not have told me; it made me blush more over myself than your reproaches would have done; and the slightly more serious accent that you put into your speeches yesterday easily made me know that I should not have exposed you to making them to me twice. I understand you, Sara, and I hope also to prove to you that if I am not worthy of pleasing you by my love, I am by the feelings that accompany it. My going astray will be as brief as it has been great; you have shown it to me, that is enough. I shall know how to get out of it, rest assured of it: however insane I might be, if I had seen its entire extent, I would never have made the first step. When I deserved censures you only gave me advice, and you were most willing to see me only as weak when I was criminal. What you have not said to me, I know how to say to myself; I know how to give my behavior toward you the name that you have not given it and if I may have committed a base act without knowing it, I shall make you see that I do not at all bear a base heart. Doubtless it is less my age than yours that makes me guilty. My contempt for myself kept me from seeing all the indignity of my proceeding. Thirty years of difference showed me only my shame and hid your dangers from me. Alas! what dangers? I was not vain enough to presume any: I did not imagine that I was capable of laying a trap for your innocence and if you had been less virtuous, I was a suborner without knowing anything about it.

Oh Sara! Your[10] virtue is proof against more dangerous trials, and your charms have better to choose from. But my duty does not depend on either your virtue or your charms; its voice speaks to me and I shall follow it. If only an eternal oblivion could hide my errors from you! If only I could forget them myself! But no, I feel it, I have them for life, and the dart buries itself deeper from my efforts to tear it out. It is my fate to burn until my last breath with a fire that nothing can extinguish, and from which each day removes a degree of hope and adds one of unreasonableness. That is what does not depend on me, but here, Sara, is what does depend on me. I give you[11] my word as a man who has never broken it, that never again in my life shall I speak to you about that ridiculous and unfortunate passion that I perhaps could have kept from being born, but that I can no longer stifle. When I say that I shall not speak to you about it, I understand that nothing in me will speak to you about what I ought to keep silent. I impose the same silence upon my eyes as upon my mouth: but, have mercy, impose it upon yours not to come to wrest this sad secret from me. I am proof against everything, aside from your glances: you know too well how easy it is for you to make me forswear myself. Could such a triumph, so sure for you and so dishonoring for me, flatter your beautiful soul? No, divine Sara, do not profane the Temple in which you are adored, and leave at least some virtue in this heart from which you have taken everything.

I am neither able nor wish to take back the unfortunate secret that escaped from me; it is too late, it must remain with you, and it is of so little concern for you that it would soon be forgotten if the admission were not ceaselessly renewed. Ah! I would be too much to be pitied in my misery if I could never tell myself that you pitied it, and that you ought to pity it all the more as you will never have to console me for it. You will always see me as I ought to be, but know me always as what I am: you will no longer have to censure my speeches, but permit my Letters; that is all that I ask of you. I shall draw near you only as a Divinity before which one imposes silence on one's passions. Your virtues will suspend the effect of your charms; your presence will purify my heart; I shall not at all fear being a seducer by telling you nothing that it does not suit you to hear; I shall cease to believe myself ridiculous when you will never see me as such; and I would like no longer to be guilty when I shall be able to be so only far from you.

My Letters? No. I ought not even desire to write to you, and you ought not ever to put up with it. I would esteem you less if you were capable of it. Sara, I give you[12] this weapon, in order to use it against me. You can be the depositary of my fatal secret; you cannot be its confidante. It is enough for me that you know it, it would be too much for me to hear it repeated. I shall keep silent: what more would I have to say to you? Banish me, despise me henceforth, if you ever see your lover again in the friend you have chosen for yourself. Without being able to flee you, I bid you farewell for life. This sacrifice was the final one that I had left to make to you. It was the only one that was worthy of your virtues and of my heart.

[Fifth Letter][13]

No, there is no peace at all on the earth, because my heart does not enjoy it. It is not your fault, dear Sara, it is mine; or rather it is fate's that put so far from me the sole good that could make me happy. This good was the possession neither of your heart nor of your person. My imagination leaves you always too far from my hope to ever expose you to my desires. My passion, my fatal passion, never blinds me to that point; it led me astray without seducing me, and I let myself be dragged by its force alone without seeing any goal that could attract me. The height of my wishes was that you might see my folly and that it might not excite your disdain. You became acquainted with it, you pitied it, you consoled me: I was satisfied. I shall be so if that condition, so sweet, could last forever: my happiness would last the same. If you could love nothing and let yourself be adored in silence, I would pass my days in that delightful occupation, without desiring anything, without perceiving anything beyond it. But I enjoy my passion without being able to give you any. But my heart is full, yours is empty; it cannot be so for very long and I am not the one who can fill it. You will love, Sara, if you do not love already; that is the horrible torment that is reserved for me, and that the certainty of experiencing some day already causes me to feel in advance. I have known too well how to do justice to myself in order not to submit to my fate, but I feel with fright that yours will depend on someone else. No, my despair is not from not being loved at all, but that another must be loved. It is for you, angelic girl, that I am afflicted. Let him have my heart and I shall forgive him; but who will know how to love you as I do?

V

FAMILY

CHAPTER SEVENTEEN

The Naturalness of the Family

235-298

❧❦❧

[*This passage and note come from part I of Rousseau's* Discourse on the Origin and Foundations of Inequality Among Men (Second Discourse). *Having described "physical man," Rousseau undertakes to describe him from the "Metaphysical and Moral side." This leads him to the topic of the origin of languages and the natural status of family relations.*]

Let me be allowed to consider for a moment the perplexities about the origin of Languages. I could be satisfied with citing or repeating here the researches that the Abbé de Condillac has made on this matter, all of which fully confirm my sentiment, and which, perhaps, gave me its first idea. But, as the manner in which this Philosopher resolves the difficulties that he himself raises on the origin of instituted signs shows that he has assumed what I am calling into question, namely a sort of society already established among the inventors of language, in referring to his reflections I believe I ought to join my own to them in order to set forth the same difficulties in the light that suits my subject. The first that presents itself is to imagine how languages could have become necessary; for, as Men did not have any connection with each other, nor any need to have any, one conceives neither the necessity of this invention nor its possibility if it were not indispensable. I might well say, as many others do, that Languages were born in the domestic intercourse of Fathers, Mothers, and Children: but aside from the fact that this would not resolve the objections, this would be to commit the mistake of those who in reasoning about the State of Nature carry over into it ideas taken from Society and always see the family gathered into one and the same habitation, and its members keeping among themselves as intimate and as permanent a union as among us, where so many common interests unite them; whereas in that primitive state, having neither Houses nor Huts, nor property of any sort, each found somewhere to stay at random, and often for a single night; the males and females united fortuitously depending on encounter, occasion, and desire, without speech being an extremely necessary interpreter of the things they had to say to each other. They left each other with the same ease. (X.*) At first the mother nursed her Children for her own (X.* need; then, habit having made them dear to her, afterward she nourished them for theirs; as soon as they had the strength to seek their own food, they did not delay in leaving even the Mother; And because there was almost no other way to find each other again than not to lose sight of each other, they were soon at the point of not even recognizing each other. Note also that the Child, having all its needs to explain, and consequently more things to say to the Mother than the Mother has to the Child, it must make the greatest expenditures of invention, and that the language it uses must be in great part its own work; which multiplies Languages by as many times as there are individuals to speak them, which is also contributed to by the wandering and vagabond life that does not leave any idiom time to take on any consistency; for to say that the Mother dictates to the Child the words that he must use in order to ask her for one thing or another: that shows very well how one teaches already formed Languages, but that does not instruct us about how they are formed.

Note

(X.*) I find in Locke's *Civil Government* an objection that appears too specious for me to be allowed to conceal it. "For the end of society between Male and Female," says this philosopher, "being not barely procreation, but the continuation of the species, this society ought to last, even after procreation, at least as long as is necessary to the nourishment and preservation of the progeny, that is to say till they are able to provide for their own needs themselves. This rule, which the infinite wisdom of the creator hath set to the works of his hands, we find creatures inferior to man steadily and precisely obey. In those animals which feed on grass, the Society between male and female lasts no longer than each act of copulation: because the teats of the Dam being sufficient to nourish the Young, till they be able to feed on Grass, the male is satisfied with begetting but does not concern himself after that with the female or young, to whose sustenance he can contribute nothing. But in beasts of prey, Society lasts longer: because the Dam not being able well to provide for her own subsistence and to feed her young at the same time by her own prey alone, a more laborious, as well as more dangerous way of living, than by feeding on grass, the assistance of the male is entirely necessary to the maintenance of their common family, if one can use this term; which cannot subsist till they are able to seek some prey for themselves, but by the care of the Male and the Female. The same is to be observed in all birds except some Domestick ones, which are to be found in places where the continual abundance of food excuses the male from the care and feeding of the young brood. It is seen that while the young need food in the nest, the cock and hen provide it till the Young are able to fly, and provide for their own subsistence.

"And herein I think lies the chief, if not the only reason why the male and female in Mankind are obliged to a longer Society than is kept by other creatures. The reason is that the woman is capable of conceiving, and is commonly pregnant and gives birth to a new child long before the former is in a condition to do without its parents' help, and able to provide for his own needs. Hence a Father, who is obliged to take care for those he hath begot and to take this care for a long time, is also under an obligation to continue in conjugal Society with the same woman with whom he has had them, and to remain in this Society much longer than the other creatures, whose young being able to subsist of themselves, before the time of a new procreation arrives, the bond of male and female dissolves of itself, and both of them find themselves at complete liberty, until that season, whose custom it is to solicit the animals to join one another, obliges them to choose new mates. And here one cannot admire enough the wisdom of the creator, who having given to man qualities suited to laying up for the future as well as for the present, hath willed and arranged it so that the Society of man should be much more lasting, than that of male and female amongst other creatures; that so the industry of the man and woman might be more encouraged, and their interests better united, with the aim of making provision and laying up goods for their children, nothing being more detrimental to Children than an uncertain and vague conjuncture or an easy and frequent dissolution of the conjugal Society."[1]

The same love of truth that has made me set forth this objection sincerely, urges me on to accompany it with several remarks, if not to resolve it, at least to clarify it.

1. To begin with I shall observe that moral proofs do not have great force in matters of Physics and that they serve rather to justify existing facts than to verify the real existence of these facts. Now such is the sort of proof that Mr. Locke uses in the passage I have just cited; for, although it might be advantageous to the human species that the union of man and woman be permanent, it does not follow that it was established that way by Nature; otherwise it would be necessary to say

that Nature also instituted Civil Society, the Arts, Commerce, and everything that one claims to be useful to men.

2. I do not know where Mr. Locke found that among animals of
prey the Society of Male and Female lasts longer than among those who
live on grass, and that the one helps the other to nourish the young: For
one does not see that the Dog, the Cat, the Bear, or the Wolf recognize
their female any better than the Horse, the Ram, the Bull, the Stag or
all other Quadrupeds recognize theirs. On the contrary, it seems that if
the help of the male were necessary to the female to preserve her young,
this would be so above all in the species that live only on grass, because
the Mother needs an extremely long time to graze, and during all that
interval she is forced to neglect her brood, whereas the prey of a female
Bear or Wolf is devoured in a moment and because she has more time to
nurse her young without suffering hunger. This reasoning is confirmed
by an observation on the relative number of teats and young that distin-
guishes the carnivorous from the frugivorous species, and about which
I spoke in Note (*6).[2] If this observation is correct and general, as the
woman has only two teats and rarely produces more than one child at a
time, this is a strong additional reason to doubt that the human species
is naturally Carnivorous, so that it seems that in order to draw Locke's
conclusion, it would be necessary to turn his argument completely up-
side down. There is no more solidity in the same distinction applied
to birds. For who will be able to persuade himself that the union of
the Male and the Female is more durable among vultures and Ravens
than among Turtledoves? We have two species of domestic birds, the
Duck and the Pigeon, which provide us with examples directly contrary
to this author's System. The Pigeon, which lives only from grain, stays
united to its female, and they nourish their young in common. The
Duck, whose voraciousness is known, recognizes neither its female nor
its young, and does not aid in their subsistence in any way. And among
Chickens, a species that is scarcely less carnivorous, one does not see that
the Rooster troubles himself at all about the brood. If in other species
the Male shares with the Female the care of nourishing the young; it is
because Birds, which cannot fly at first and which the Mother cannot
nurse, are much less in a condition to do without the Father's assistance
than the Quadrupeds for whom the Mother's teat suffices, at least for
some time.

3. There is much uncertainty over the principal fact that serves as the
basis of Mr. Locke's entire argument. For in order to know whether, as
he claims, in the pure state of Nature the woman is ordinarily pregnant
again and produces a new child long before the preceding one can pro-

vide for his needs by himself, experiments would be needed that Locke certainly did not perform and that are beyond anyone to perform. The continual cohabitation of the Husband and Wife provides such an immediate opportunity to be exposed to a new pregnancy that it is very difficult to believe that the fortuitous encounter or the sole impulsion of temperament produced such frequent effects in the pure State of Nature as it does in conjugal Society; a delay that might perhaps contribute to making children more robust, and that moreover might be compensated for by the faculty of conceiving, prolonged into a greater age among women who would have abused it less in their youth. With regard to Children, there are many reasons to believe that their strength and their organs develop later among us than they did in the primitive state about which I am speaking. The original weakness that they draw from the Parents' constitution, the efforts that are taken to swaddle them and constrain all their members, the softness in which they are brought up, perhaps the use of a different milk than their Mother's—everything opposes and retards the first progressions of Nature in them. The application they are obliged to give to a thousand things upon which their attention is continuously fixed while no exercise is given to their bodily strength can also cause a considerable diversion to their growth; so that, if instead of overburdening and fatiguing their minds in a thousand ways to begin with, their Bodies were allowed to be exercised by the continuous movements that Nature seems to require of them, it is to be believed that they would be in a condition to walk, to act, and to provide for their needs much earlier.

4. Finally, Mr. Locke proves at most that there could very well be in the man a motive to remain attached to the woman when she has a Child; but he in no way proves that he must have been attached to her before the birth and during the nine months of pregnancy. If a given woman does not interest the man during these nine months, if she even becomes unknown to him, why will he help her after the birth? Why will he aid her to bring up a Child that he does not even know belongs to him, and whose birth he has neither chosen nor foreseen? Mr. Locke evidently assumes what is in question: For it is not a matter of knowing why the man will remain attached to the woman after the birth, but why he will become attached to her after the conception. Once appetite is satisfied the man no longer needs a given woman, nor the woman a given man. He does not have the slightest concern or perhaps the slightest idea of the consequences of his action. One goes off in one direction, the other in a different one, and there is no appearance that at the end of nine months they would have the memory of having known each other:

For this sort of memory by which one individual gives the preference to one individual for the act of procreation requires, as I prove in the text,[3] more progress or corruption in human understanding than one can assume in it in the state of animality that is at issue here. Another woman can, then, satisfy the man's new desires as conveniently as the one he has already known, and another man satisfy the woman in the same way, it being assumed that she is urged on by the same appetite during the state of pregnancy, which one can reasonably doubt. If in the state of Nature the woman no longer is affected by the passion of love after the conception of the child, the obstacle to her Society with the man becomes even greater from it, as then she no longer needs either the man who impregnated her nor any other. There is not, then, for the man, any reason to seek out the same woman, nor, for the woman, any reason to seek out the same man. Locke's argument, then, falls apart, and all of this Philosopher's Dialectic does not protect him from that error that Hobbes and others have committed. They had to explain a fact of the State of Nature; that is to say, a state in which men lived isolated, and in which a given man did not have any motive to stay near any given man, nor perhaps for men to stay near each other, which is even worse; and they did not consider carrying themselves back beyond the Centuries of Society; that is to say, beyond these times in which men always have a reason to stay near each other, and in which a given man often has a reason to remain near a given man or a given woman.

CHAPTER EIGHTEEN

Mothers and Infants

[*This passage is from Book I of* Emile. *It should be kept in mind that Rousseau begins this book by saying that it is addressed to a tender and foresighted mother. It is preceded by an attack on swaddling children, as opposed to giving them relative freedom of motion. It is followed by an attack on overprotectiveness.*]

Not satisfied with having stopped nursing their children, women stop wanting to have them. The consequence is natural. As soon as the condition of motherhood becomes onerous, the means to free themselves from it altogether are soon found. They want to do a useless work in order always to start it over again, and they turn to the prejudice of the species the attraction given in order to multiply it. This practice, added to the other causes of depopulation, proclaims to us the impending fate of Europe. It will not be long before the sciences, the arts, philosophy, and the morals it engenders, make a desert of it. It will be peopled by ferocious beasts; its inhabitants will not have changed much.[1]

I have sometimes seen the little maneuvers of young women who pretend to want to nurse their children. One knows how to get oneself urged to renounce this whim: one adroitly makes husbands, doctors, and especially mothers, intervene. A husband who would dare to consent to his wife nursing his child would be a ruined man. He would be made an assassin who wants to get rid of her. Prudent husbands, one has to immolate paternal love for the sake of peace. Lucky for you that women more continent than yours are found in the countryside! Even more lucky if the time that the latter gain is not destined for others than you!

Women's duty is not in doubt. But it is disputed whether, given the contempt they have for it, it is all the same whether children are nursed with their milk, or another's. I take this question, on which the doctors are judges, to be decided according to the wishes of women. As for me,

I too would certainly think it better for the child to suck the milk of a healthy wet nurse than of a spoiled mother, if he had some new ill to fear from the same blood from which he is formed.

But must this question be considered only on the physical side, and does the child need a mother's cares any less than her breast? Other women, even beasts, could give him the milk they refuse him. Maternal solicitude cannot be replaced. She who nurses another's child instead of her own is a bad mother; how could she be a good nurse? She could become one, but slowly. Habit will have to change nature; and the child, who is badly cared for, will have the time to perish a hundredfold, before his nurse has acquired the tenderness of a mother toward him.

From this very advantage results an inconvenience that alone must take from every sensitive woman the courage to have her child nursed by another. It is that of sharing the right of motherhood—or, rather, of alienating it. It is to see one's child love another woman as much, and more, than her; to feel that the tenderness he keeps for his own mother is a favor, and the one he has for his adoptive mother a duty. For where I have found a mother's cares, do I not owe a son's attachment?

The way in which this inconvenience is remedied is to inspire in children contempt for their nurse, by treating them as actual servants. When their service is completed, the child is taken back, or the nurse dismissed. By dint of being badly received, she is rebuffed from coming to see her nursling. At the end of a few years, he no longer sees her, he no longer knows her. The mother is mistaken who believes that she takes her place, and makes up for her negligence by her cruelty. Instead of making a tender son of a denatured nursling, she trains him in ingratitude; she teaches him to despise one day her who gave him life, just as he despises her who fed him with her milk.

How much I would insist on this point if it were less discouraging to repeat useful subjects in vain over and over again! This is related to more things than one thinks. Do you want to restore each to his first duties? Begin with mothers. You will be astonished by the changes you will produce. Everything comes successively from this first depravity. The whole moral order deteriorates: naturalness is extinguished in all hearts. The interior of homes takes on a less lively air; the touching spectacle of a budding family no longer attaches husbands, no longer imposes respect on strangers; one has less respect for the mother whose children one does not see. One no longer resides with one's family; habit no longer reinforces the bonds of blood. There are no longer fathers nor mothers, nor children, nor brothers nor sisters. All hardly know one another; how could they love one another? Each thinks of nothing but himself. When home is nothing but a sad solitude, one certainly has to go cheer oneself up elsewhere.

But let mothers deign to nurse their children: morals will reform themselves, the sentiments of nature will awaken in all hearts, the State will be repeopled. This first point, this point alone will unify every-thing. The attraction of domestic life is the best antidote for bad morals. The bother of children, believed to be importunate, becomes pleasant. It makes father and mother more necessary, dearer, to one another. It tightens the conjugal bond between them. When the family is lively and animated, domestic cares are the dearest occupation of the wife, and the sweetest amusement of the husband. Hence from the correction of this sole abuse, a general reform will soon result. Soon nature will have taken back all of its rights. Once women become mothers again, soon men will again become fathers and husbands.

Superfluous speech! Even boredom with the pleasures of society never brings one back to those. Women have stopped being mothers. They will no longer be mothers; they no longer want to be. If they wanted to, they could hardly be mothers. Now that the contrary practice is estab-lished, each would have to combat the opposition of all those who come near her, allied against an example that some did not give, and that others do not want to follow.

Yet sometimes there are still young persons to be found with a good disposition who, daring to brave on this point the empire of fashion and the clamors of their sex, fulfill with a virtuous intrepidity this so sweet duty that nature imposes on them. May their numbers increase by the attraction of the goods destined for those who yield to it! Based on consequences that result from the most simple reasoning, and on obser-vations that I have never seen contradicted, I dare promise these worthy mothers a solid and constant attachment on the part of their husbands, a truly filial tenderness on the part of their children, the esteem and the respect of the public, fortunate deliveries without accidents and without consequences, a vigorous and firm health, and finally, the pleasure of one day seeing themselves imitated by their daughters, and cited as an example to those of others.

No mother, no child. Between them the duties are reciprocal, and if they are fulfilled badly on one side, they will be neglected on the other. The child must love his mother before he knows that he must. If the voice of blood is not fortified by habit and by cares, it is extinguished in the first years, and the heart dies, so to speak, before being born. Here we are, with the very first step, outside of nature.

CHAPTER NINETEEN

Domestic Life (from Julie)

[*After years of separation Saint Preux returns to see his beloved Julie who is now married to Wolmar. He writes a letter to his friend, Milord Edward, describing the domestic arrangements in the Wolmars' household.*]

To Milord Edward

What pleasures learnt too late have I enjoyed these past three weeks! How sweet to while one's days in the bosom of a tranquil friendship, safe from the storm of impetuous passions! Milord, what a lovely and moving spectacle is a simple and well-regulated house where order, peace, and innocence reign; where is assembled without pretention, without ostentation, everything that corresponds to man's veritable destination! The countryside, the seclusion, the repose, the season, the vast expanse of water spread out before me, the mountains' rugged look, everything here reminds me of my delightful island of Tinian.[1] It seems to me I am witnessing the realization of the fervid wishes I entertained so many times there. Here I lead a life to my liking, here I find a society after my heart. All that is missing in this place to bring all my happiness together is two people, and it is my hope to see them here soon.

In the meanwhile, until you and Madame d'Orbe come to crown such sweet and pure pleasures as I am learning to enjoy in this place, I wish to give you an idea of them through the description of a domestic economy that reflects the felicity of the masters of the house and causes it to be shared with those who live here. I hope, with respect to the plan you have in mind, that my reflections will some day have their use, and this hope helps also to inspire them.

I shall not describe to you the house at Clarens. You are familiar with it. You know what charm it has, what significant memories it affords

SOURCE: Jean-Jacques Rousseau, *Julie; or, The New Heloise. Collected Writings of Rousseau* VI, trans. and ed. Philip Stewart and Jean Vaché (Hanover, N.H.: University Press of New England, 1997).

me, how dear it must be to me, both for what it reveals to me, and for what it reminds me of. Madame de Wolmar rightly prefers to reside here rather than at Étange, a magnificent and grand chateau; but old, gloomy, uncomfortable, and its surroundings offer nothing comparable to what one sees around Clarens.

Since the masters of this house have established their home here, they have put to their use everything that served only as ornament; it is no longer a house made to be seen, but to be lived in. They have walled up long rows of rooms to change doors that were awkwardly situated,[2] they have divided rooms that were too large so as to have lodgings better laid out. They have replaced old-fashioned and sumptuous pieces of furniture with simple and convenient ones. Everything here is agreeable and cheerful; everything bespeaks plenty and elegance, nothing reeks of wealth and luxury.[3]

There is not a single room where one is not recognizably in the country, and where one fails to find all the conveniences of the city. The same changes can be noticed out of doors. The farmyard has been enlarged by reducing the size of the coach house. In place of an old, dilapidated billiard room they have put a fine wine press, and a dairy where once lived noisy Peacocks which have been got rid of. The vegetable garden was too small for the kitchen; the flower bed has been turned into a second one, but so elegant and so well designed that this bed thus disguised is more pleasing to the eye than before. The mournful Yews that covered the walls have been replaced with good espaliers of fruit trees. Instead of the useless horse chestnut, young black mulberry trees are beginning to shade the courtyard, and they have planted two rows of walnut trees down to the road instead of the old linden trees that flanked the avenue. Everywhere they have replaced attractive things with useful things, and attractiveness has almost always come out the better. As far as I am concerned at least, the noises of the farmyard, the cocks' crowing, the cattle's mooing, the harnessing of the carts, the meals in the fields, the return home of the workers, and all the instruments of rural economy give this house a more pastoral, more lively, more spirited, more festive appearance, a certain something that radiates joy and well-being, that it did not possess in its dreary dignity.

Their lands are not leased out but farmed under their own supervision, and this farming accounts for much of their occupations, their possessions, and their pleasures. The Étange Barony has only meadows, fields, and woods; but the production of Clarens is in vineyards, which are extensive, and as the difference of cultivation here has a more considerable effect than is the case with wheat, this constitutes yet another

economic reason for having preferred to reside here. Nonetheless they
go almost every year for the harvesting at their estate, and Monsieur
de Wolmar goes there alone rather frequently. They follow the maxim
of extracting from the land all it can yield, not to obtain a larger gain
from it, but to feed more men. Monsieur de Wolmar contends that land
produces in proportion to the number of hands that till it; better tilled it
yields more; this excess production furnishes the means of tilling it better
still; the more men and beasts you put on it, the more surplus it supplies
over and above their subsistence. It is not known, he says, where this
continual and reciprocal increase in product and laborers might end. On
the contrary, neglected fields lose their fertility: the fewer men a region
produces, the fewer commodities it produces. It is the paucity of inhabitants that prevents it from feeding the few it has, and the inhabitants of
any area that loses population must sooner or later die of hunger.[4]

Possessing then much land and farming it all very industriously, they
require, besides the farmyard domestics, a large number of day-workers;
which provides them the pleasure of providing subsistence for many
people without inconvenience to themselves. When choosing these
day-workers, they always prefer local ones and neighbors to foreigners
or strangers. If they lose something by not always choosing the most
robust, they are well repaid by the affection this preference inspires in
those who are chosen, by the advantage of always having them around,
and being able to count on them at all times, although they pay them
only part of the year.

With all these workers they always fix two prices. The first is manda-
tory and rightful, the current local price, which they agree to pay them
for their work. The other, a bit higher, is a bonus, which they are paid
only insofar as they are found satisfactory, and it almost always turns
out that what they do to prove satisfactory is worth more than the extra
pay they are given. For Monsieur de Wolmar is principled and stern,
and never allows the procedures of favor and benevolence to degenerate
into custom and abuse. These workers have supervisors who prod and
observe them. These supervisors are farm hands who themselves work
and have an interest in the others' work because of the small share they
are allotted beyond their own wages, on all that is brought in thanks to
them. Moreover, Monsieur de Wolmar checks on them himself nearly
every day, often several times a day, and his wife likes to join in these
rounds. Finally, during the peak labors, Julie each week gives a gratification of twenty batz*[5] to the one worker of all, day-workers or servants

* Local small coin.

all taken together, who in the master's judgment has been the most diligent during that week. All these incentives for emulation which appear expensive, applied with prudence and justice, imperceptibly make everyone industrious, diligent, and ultimately pay back more than they cost; but as its benefit becomes apparent only with consistency and time, few know how and care to make use of it.

However an even more effective means, the only one that appears not to be inspired by economic views and is more suited to Madame de Wolmar, is to win the affection of these good folk by extending hers to them.[6] She does not believe that money can suffice to pay for the pains taken on her behalf, and thinks she owes services to anyone who has rendered some to her. Workers, domestics, all those who have served her even for a single day all become her children; she shares in their pleasures, in their sorrows, in their lot; she inquires about their business, their interests are hers; she takes on a thousand cares in their behalf, she gives them advice, she patches up their disputes, and expresses the affability of her character not with honeyed, ineffectual words, but with genuine services and continual acts of kindness. They, in return, drop everything at her slightest sign; they fly when she speaks; a mere look from her inspires their zeal, in her presence they are content, in her absence they talk about her and inspire each other to serve her. Her charms and words do much, her gentleness, her virtues do more. Ah Milord! how powerful and worthy of worship is the empire of beneficent beauty!

As to the masters' personal service, they have eight domestics in the house, three women and five men, not counting the baron's valet or the Farmhands. It is rare to be badly served by a small number of Domestics; but one would think from the zeal of these, that each one, in addition to his own service, feels responsible for that of the seven others, and from their concord, that a single one does it all. You never see them idle and unoccupied diddling in an antechamber or romping in the courtyard, but always engaged in some useful task; they help out in the farmyard, in the Wine cellar, in the Kitchen; the gardener has no help other than them, and what is particularly agreeable is that it can be seen they do all these things gaily and with pleasure.

They choose young to get them the way they want them. The maxim here is not the one I saw prevailing in Paris and London, of hiring fully trained Domestics, in other words fully confirmed Rascals, ever changing jobs, who in every house where they touch down adopt the shortcomings of both servants and masters, and make it their business to serve everyone, without ever attaching themselves to anyone. Neither honesty nor loyalty nor zeal can prevail in the midst of such folk, and this pile of riffraff brings ruin to the master and corrupts the children in all affluent houses. Here the selection of Domestics is an important matter. They are not merely regarded as mercenaries of whom only diligent service is required; but as members of the family, which a wrong choice could unsettle. The first thing that is required of them is to be honest, the second is to love their master, the third is to serve him as he sees fit; but provided a master is reasonable and a domestic intelligent, the third always follows from the other two. They are therefore drawn not from the city but from the country. Their first position is here, and it will surely be the last for all those who prove to be of some worth. They are picked from some large family overburdened with children, whose fathers and mothers themselves come to offer them. They are chosen young, of good constitution, in good health and of pleasant physiognomy. Monsieur de Wolmar questions them, examines them, then presents them to his wife. If they please both, they are admitted, first on probation, then to the number of the servants, that is to say, the children of the house, and a few days are spent teaching them with much patience and care what they are expected to do. The service is so simple, so regular, so uniform, the masters are so little inclined to whims and bad humor, and their domestics take to them so promptly, that it is soon learned. Their situation is easy; they enjoy a well-being they did not have at home; but they are not allowed to go soft with idleness, the mother of vice. They are not allowed to turn into Gentlemen and become haughty in servitude. They continue to work as they did in the paternal household; they have, in a manner of speaking, merely changed father and mother, and acquired more affluent ones. In this manner, they do not come to disdain their former rustic life. If ever they were to leave here, there is not one who would not rather resume his peasant condition than to bear being a servant elsewhere. In all, I have never seen a household where each performed his service better, and thought of it less as service.

So it is that by training and drilling one's own Domestics one has no need to entertain this objection, as common as it is senseless: I will have trained them for others. Train them as you should, it could be answered, and they will never serve others. If you think only of yourself when you train them, then they are quite right to think only of themselves when they leave you; but attend a bit more to them and they will remain attached to you. Intention alone creates obligations, and a person who takes advantage of something I want only for myself owes me no gratitude.

So as doubly to prevent the same difficulty, Monsieur and Madame de Wolmar employ yet another means that seems to me very well calculated. When setting up their household they counted up the number of domestics they could maintain in a house fitted out at about the level of their fortune, and they found that the number came to fifteen or sixteen; to be served better they reduced it to half that; so that with less display their service is much more diligent. In order to be served better yet, they motivated the same servants to serve them for a long time. A domestic entering their service earns the standard wage; but this wage increases every year by a twentieth; thus after twenty years it would be more than doubled and the domestics' keep would then be roughly proportional to the master's means: but it does not take a great algebrist to see that the outlay for this increase is more apparent than real, that they will have few double wages to pay, and that were they obliged to pay them to all, the advantage of having been well served for twenty years would more than compensate for the additional expenditure. You can well appreciate, Milord, that this is a sure expedient for making the domestics ever more attentive and attaching them to oneself to the degree one becomes attached to them. There is not merely prudence, but also equity in such a setup. Is it fair for a newcomer, having no affection, and who is perhaps just a ne'er-do-well, to receive upon entry the same salary that is given an old servant, whose zeal and loyalty are proven by long service, and who moreover as he ages is approaching a time when he will be unable to earn his living? Besides, this latter reason does not apply here, and you can well believe that such humane masters do not neglect duties that many masters lacking in charity ostentatiously fulfill, and that they do not abandon those of their servants who lose their capacity to serve due to infirmities or advancing age.

At this very moment I have a fairly striking example of this consideration. Baron d'Étange, intending to reward the long service of his valet with an honorable retirement, had sufficient credit to obtain for him from Their Excellencies[7] an easy and lucrative employment. Julie has just received from this old domestic a letter fit to draw tears, in which he begs her to get him permission to decline this employment. "I am old," he tells her, "I have lost all my family; I have no relatives left but my masters; all I long for is to end my days peacefully in the house where I have spent them. . . . Madame, when I held you in my arms at your birth, I asked God also to hold your children one day; he has granted me this favor; do not refuse me the favor of seeing them grow and prosper like you. . . . I who am accustomed to living in a house of peace, where shall I find another one like it to rest my old age? . . .

Pray have the charity to write to Monsieur le Baron on my behalf. If he is displeased with me, let him dismiss me and give me no employment: but if I have faithfully served him for forty years, may he let me end my days in his service and yours; for me there could be no better reward." It is useless to ask whether Julie did write. I can see she would be just as dismayed to lose this old fellow as he would be to leave her. Am I wrong, Milord, to compare masters so cherished to fathers, and their domestics to their children? You see that that is what they consider themselves.

There has been no instance in this house of a domestic requesting his leave. It is even rare that they threaten someone with dismissal. This threat is all the more frightening because of how pleasant and easy service here is. The best fellows are always the most alarmed by it, and it is never necessary to resort to execution except with those who will be little missed. There is a further rule for this. When Monsieur de Wolmar has said: *You are fired*, one may implore the intercession of Madame, sometimes obtain it and a return to favor through her pleading; but a dismissal she gives is irrevocable, there is no more mercy to hope for. This convention is very well calculated to temper both the excessive confidence that might be placed in the wife's gentleness, and the extreme fear that the husband's inflexibility could cause. Yet these words are always extremely dreaded coming from an equitable and dispassionate master; for besides the fact that one is not certain to obtain mercy, and that it is never granted twice to the same person, these words alone entail loss of seniority, and a new term of service is begun upon re-entry, which deters old domestics from insolence and increases their circumspection, in proportion to what they have to lose by it.

The three women are, the chambermaid, the children's governess, and the cook. The latter is a most proper and clever peasant whom Madame de Wolmar has taught to cook; for in this still simple country* young ladies of all stations learn to perform themselves all the tasks that the women in their service will one day perform in their house, so they will know how to direct them as needed and not be pushed around by them. The chambermaid is no longer Babi; she has been sent back to Étange where she was born; she has been put in charge of the chateau and made overseer of the receipts, which in a way makes her comptroller of the Steward. Monsieur de Wolmar had been urging his wife for a long time to make this arrangement, without managing to persuade her to send away one of her mother's former domestics, even though

* Simple! Then it must have greatly changed.

she had more than one reason to complain of her. Finally after their latest discussion on the subject, she consented, and Babi has left. This woman is intelligent and loyal, but indiscreet and garrulous. I suspect she has more than once betrayed her mistress's secrets, that Monsieur de Wolmar is not unaware of this, and that in order to avert a similar indiscretion with respect to some stranger, this wise man has found a way to put her to use so as to take advantage of her good qualities without being exposed to the bad ones. Her replacement is that same Fanchon Regard of whom you heard me speak formerly with such pleasure. Despite Julie's prediction, her kindnesses, her father's, and yours, this young woman, so honest and decent, has not been happy in her marriage. Claude Anet, who had borne his poverty so well, was not able to endure an easier situation. Finding himself well off he neglected his trade, and having gotten himself deeply into debt he fled the country, leaving his wife with a child which she has since lost. Julie after taking her in taught her all the simple skills of a chambermaid, and I was never more pleasantly surprised than when I found her on duty the day I arrived. Monsieur de Wolmar makes much of her, and both have entrusted her with the duty of keeping an eye both on their children and on their governess. The latter is a simple and credulous, but attentive, patient, and docile villager; so nothing has been overlooked to prevent city vices from infiltrating a house whose masters neither have nor tolerate them.

Although all the domestics have just one common table, on the other hand there is little communication between the two sexes: this item is considered very important here. They do not share the opinion of those masters who are indifferent to everything beyond their own interests, who want only to be served well, without bothering additionally about what their servants are up to. They think, on the contrary, that those who wish only to be served well cannot be for long. Too intimate relations between the sexes never lead to anything but trouble. Most of the disorders in a household stem from gossip sessions among the chambermaids. If the head butler takes a liking to one of them, he does not fail to seduce her at his master's expense. Agreement amongst the men alone or amongst the women is not firm enough to create much of a problem. But it is always from a combination of men and women that secret monopolies become established which in the long run bring the most affluent families to ruin. Here they therefore keep watch on the proper behavior and modesty of the women, not only for reasons of good morals and honesty, but also through well-calculated self-interest; for no matter what they say, no one discharges his duty well if he does not take it to heart, and there never were any but honorable people who managed to take their duty to heart.

To forestall a dangerous intimacy between the two sexes, they are not constrained here by explicit laws which they would be tempted to break secretly; but without any apparent intention, customs are instituted that are more powerful even than authority. They are not forbidden to see each other, but it happens by design that they have neither the opportunity nor the will to do so. This is achieved by assigning to them entirely different occupations, habits, tastes, pleasures. Given the admirable order that reigns here, they sense that in a well-run house men and women should have little communication with each other. Even someone who might accuse his master's orders on this subject of arbitrariness, submits without reluctance to a way of living that is not formally prescribed to him, but that he himself judges the best and most natural. Julie asserts it is that indeed; she maintains that neither love nor conjugal union imply continual contact between the sexes. According to her, wife and husband are certainly destined to live together, but not in the same manner; they must act in concert without performing the same acts. The life that would charm the one would, she says, be unbearable to the other; the inclinations nature imparts to them are as various as the functions she assigns them; their amusements differ no less than do their duties; in a word, both work toward mutual happiness by different means, and this division of labors and duties is their union's strongest tie.

For my part, I admit that my own observations are rather favorable to this maxim. Indeed, is it not a uniform practice of all peoples on earth, aside from the French and their imitators, that men live amongst themselves, and women likewise? If they see each other, it is rather by appointment and almost furtively like the Spouses of Lacedaemon,[8] than by indiscreet and perpetual mingling likely to confound and disfigure in them nature's wisest distinctions. Even savages are not found indistinctly mixed, men with women. In the evening the family gathers together; every man spends the night with his wife; separation begins again at daybreak, and the two sexes have nothing further in common except meals at most. Such is the order that its universality shows to be the most natural, and even in the countries where it is perverted one can still see its vestiges. In France where men have subjected themselves to living in the manner of women and remaining forever enclosed in a room with them, the involuntary restlessness they retain shows that it is not for this they were destined. Whereas the women remain tranquilly seated or reclining on their loungechair, you see the men rise, walk to and fro, sit back down with a continual restlessness, a mechanical instinct constantly struggling against the constraint in which they place themselves, and urging them willy-nilly toward that active and laborious life nature assigned them. This is the only people on earth where men remain standing at the theater, as if they went to the pit[9] to relieve themselves from having sat all day long in the salon. And so they feel so strongly the tedium of this effeminate and domesticated indolence that in order to provide themselves at least some sort of activity they yield at home their place to strangers, and go try to temper this aversion in the company of other men's wives.

Madame de Wolmar's maxim is very well supported by the example of her own household. Everyone belonging, as it were, wholly to his own sex, the women here live quite separate from the men. In order to prevent suspect relationships between them, her big secret is to keep the ones and the others constantly occupied; for their tasks are so different that only idleness can bring them together. In the morning everyone goes about his duties, and no leisure is left to anyone for troubling someone else's. In the afternoon the men's department is the garden, the farmyard, or other rural chores; the women are busy in the nursery until it is time for them to walk the children, often even with their mistress, and which they find pleasant since it is the only moment when they take the air. The men, sufficiently exercised by the day's labor, have no desire to go walking and rest indoors.

Every Sunday after the evening sermon the women gather together again in the nursery with some lady relative or friend they invite by turns with Madame's permission. There as they await a small feast she treats them to, they chat, sing, play shuttlecock, jackstraws, or some other game of skill of a kind the children like to watch, until the time they can enjoy doing it themselves. The collation arrives, consisting of some dairy foods, waffles, pastries, merveilles* or other dishes to the children's and women's liking. Wine is always excluded, and the men, who seldom enter this little Gynaeceum** at any time, never partake of this collation, which Julie rarely fails to attend. So far I am the only man to have been so privileged. Last Sunday by greatly insisting I received permission to accompany her. She took considerable pains to see that I appreciated this favor. She told me out loud that she would grant it to me this one time, and that she had refused it to Monsieur de Wolmar himself. Imagine whether petty feminine vanity was flattered, and whether a lackey would have been well received had he wished to be admitted to the exclusion of the master?[10]

* A local sort of cake.
** The women's apartment.

I had a delicious snack. Are there any dishes in the world comparable to the milk products hereabouts? Think what they must be like
coming from a dairy over which Julie presides, and eaten by her side.
Fanchon served me *grus* and *céracée*,*[11] waffles, gingerbread. All of it
instantly disappeared. Julie laughed at my appetite. I see, she said giving me another plateful of cream, that your stomach does itself credit
everywhere, and that you do as well by women's fare as you did with
the Valaisans;[12] and with no more impunity, I retorted; one sometimes
becomes as drunk with the one as the other, and reason can go astray
just as well in a chalet as in a cellar.[13] She lowered her eyes without
replying, blushed, and started caressing her children. This was sufficient
to elicit my remorse. Milord, that was my first indiscretion, and I hope
it will be the last.

There reigned in this gathering a certain air of age-old simplicity that
touched my heart; I saw on all the faces the same gaiety and more can-
dor, perhaps, than if there had been men present. Founded on confidence
and attachment, the familiarity that reigned between the servants and
the mistress only strengthened respect and authority, and the services
rendered and received seemed to be only tokens of reciprocal friendship.
The very choice of dishes helped to make them interesting. Milk products and sugar are one of the sex's natural tastes and as it were the sym-
bol of the innocence and sweetness that constitute its most endearing
ornament. Men, on the contrary, usually seek strong flavors and spirits,
foods more suited to the active and laborious life that nature requires
of them; and when it happens that these diverse tastes are perverted and
confounded, it is an almost infallible mark of a disorderly mingling of
the sexes. Indeed I have observed that in France, where women live all
the time in the company of men, they have completely lost the taste for
dairy products, the men largely that for wine, and in England where
the two sexes are less confounded, their specific tastes have survived
better. In general, I think one could often find some index of people's
character in the choice of foods they prefer. The Italians who live largely
on greenery are effeminate and flaccid. You Englishmen, great meat eat-
ers, have something harsh that smacks of barbarity in your inflexible
virtues.[14] The Swiss, naturally cold, peaceful, and simple, but violent
and extreme in anger, like both kinds of food, and drink both milk and
wine. The Frenchman, flexible and changeable, consumes all foods and
adapts to all characters. Julie herself could serve as my example: for although she is sensual and likes to eat, she likes neither meat, nor stews,

*Excellent milk derivatives made on mount Salève. I doubt they are known under
this name in the Jura, especially at the other end of the lake.

nor salt, and has never tasted wine straight. Excellent vegetables, eggs, cream, fruit; those are her daily fare, and were it not for fish of which she also is very fond, she would be a true Pythagorean.[15]

It serves no purpose to restrain the women if the men are not restrained as well, and this part of the rule, no less important than the other, is yet more difficult; for attack is generally more vigorous than defense: such is the intention of the preserver of nature. In a Republic citizens are restrained by morals, principles, virtue: but how can domestics, mercenaries, be contained other than by constraint and coercion? The master's whole art consists in hiding this coercion under the veil of pleasure or interest, so that they think they desire all they are obliged to do. Sunday's idleness, and the right, of which one can hardly deprive them, of going wherever they wish when their functions do not keep them at home, often destroy in a single day the examples and lessons of the other six. The frequentation of the cabaret, the conversation and maxims of their comrades, the company of loose women, soon ruin them for their masters and for themselves, and render them through a thousand flaws incapable of serving, and unworthy of freedom.

This problem is remedied by retaining them at home by means of the same motives that led them to go out. What were they going elsewhere to do? To drink and gamble at the cabaret. They drink and gamble at home. The whole difference is that the wine costs them nothing, they do not get drunk, and there are winners in the game without anyone ever losing. Here is how this is achieved.

Behind the house is a shaded avenue, where they have set up a game field. There the liveried servants and the farmyard workers gather in summer on Sunday after the sermon to gamble several rounds, not for money, it is not allowed, nor for wine, it is provided; but for a stake put up by the masters' generosity. This stake is always some small item or some furnishing for their own use. The number of rounds is proportional to the stake's value, so that when this stake gets to be pretty valuable as with silver buckles, a collar clasp, silk stockings, a fine hat, or something similar, they usually take several sessions to compete for it. They are not limited to a single kind of game, these are varied, so that the ablest in one does not walk away with all the stakes, and to make them all more skillful and strong through a variety of exercises. Sometimes the object is to capture on the run a goal placed at the other end of the avenue; sometimes to throw the same stone the farthest; sometimes to carry the same burden the longest. Sometimes the prize is decided by shooting at a target. To most of these games is added some ceremony that prolongs them and makes them entertaining. The master and mistress often honor them with their presence; sometimes the children are brought along, even strangers come attracted by curiosity, and some would ask nothing better than to compete; but none is ever admitted without the masters' approval and the consent of the players, who would have nothing to gain by granting it easily. Little by little this custom has turned into a sort of spectacle where the actors motivated by the public attention prefer the glory of applause to the attraction of the prize. By growing more vigorous and agile, they take more pride in themselves, and becoming accustomed to deriving their value from themselves rather than from what they possess, although they are mere servants, honor becomes dearer to them than money.

It would take too long to list for you all the advantages gained here thanks to a stratagem that is so puerile in appearance and always scoffed at by vulgar minds, whereas it is the nature of true genius to produce great effects by small means.[16] Monsieur de Wolmar told me it cost him scarcely fifty écus[17] a year for these little institutions which his wife was the first to think up. But, he said, how many times over do you think I get that sum back in my household and business thanks to the vigilance and attention devoted to their service by loyal servants who derive all their pleasures from their masters; thanks to the interest they take in the service of a house they regard as their own; thanks to the advantage of profiting in their labors from the vigor they acquire in their games; thanks to the advantage of keeping them always healthy by protecting them from the customary excesses of their peers, and the illnesses that are the usual consequence of such excesses; thanks to the advantage of preventing in them the thievery that disorder infallibly brings with it, and keeping them always honest folk; finally thanks to the pleasure of having at home and at little expense recreations pleasant even for ourselves? And if by chance there were some one among our servants, man or woman, who cannot adapt to our rules and prefers the freedom of running off wherever he likes under various pretexts, we never refuse him permission to do so; but we regard this taste for license as a very suspect indication, and we lose no time getting rid of those who possess it. Thus these same entertainments that keep us some good people; also serve as a test for selecting them. Milord, I admit that I have never seen anywhere but here masters training at the same time, in the same men, good domestics for their personal service, good peasants to till their lands, good soldiers to defend the fatherland, and fine people for all the stations to which fortune may call them.

In winter the pleasures change in kind as do the labors. On Sunday, all the house servants and even the neighbors, men and women alike, gather after the service in a lower Room where they find a fire, wine, fruit, cakes, and a fiddle to dance by. Madame de Wolmar never fails to come by at least for a few minutes, in order to maintain order and modesty through her presence, and it is not rare for her to dance as well, even with her own servants. When I learned of this rule at first it seemed to me less in keeping with the strictness of protestant morals.[18] I told Julie so; and here is more or less what she answered me.

Pure morality is so burdened with strict duties that if in addition it is overburdened with unimportant formalities, it is nearly always at the expense of what is essential. They say that is the case for most Monks, who, subjected to a thousand useless rules, do not know what honor and virtue are. This flaw is less prevalent among us, but we are not entirely exempt from it. Our Churchmen, as superior in wisdom to all kinds of Priests as our Religion is superior to all the others in holiness, yet hold a few maxims that seem to be grounded more in prejudice than in reason. Such is the one that censures dancing and assemblies, as if there were more evil in dancing than in singing, as if each of these entertainments were not equally an inspiration of nature, and it were a crime to frolic together in innocent and honest recreation. As far as I am concerned, I think on the contrary that every time there is a participation of the two sexes any public diversion becomes innocent by the very fact it is public, whereas the most praiseworthy occupation is suspect when two people are alone together.*[19] Man and woman are destined for each other, it is nature's goal that they be united in marriage. Every false Religion combats nature; ours alone, which follows and corrects her, heralds an institution that is divine and suited to man. Thus it should not with respect to marriage add to the complications of the civil order difficulties not prescribed by the Gospel, and contrary to the spirit of Christianity. But tell me where young marriageable persons will have the opportunity to develop a taste for each other, and meet with more decency and circumspection than in a gathering where the eyes of the public, constantly focused on them, oblige them to watch themselves extremely carefully? In what way is God offended by a pleasant and beneficial activity, suited to the vivacity of young people, which consists in presenting themselves to each other with grace and propriety, and on which the spectator imposes a solemnity that no one would dare to disrupt? Can one imagine a more honest means of deceiving no one at least insofar as looks are concerned, and showing oneself with the

---

*In my *Letter to Monsieur d'Alembert on Spectacles* I transcribed from this one the following passage, and a few others; but because at the time I was just preparing this edition, I thought I ought to wait until its publication to cite what I had taken from it.

attractions and shortcomings one may possess to people whose interest it is to know us well before taking on the obligation of loving us? Does not the duty of cherishing each other supersede that of pleasing each other, and is it not worth the trouble for two virtuous, Christian persons who are planning to unite, thus to prepare their hearts for the mutual love that God prescribes to them?

What happens in those places where a perpetual constraint prevails, where the most innocent merriment is punished as a crime, where young people of both sexes never dare assemble in public, and where a Pastor's indiscreet strictness has nothing to preach in God's name but servile constriction, and gloom and boredom? They evade an insufferable tyranny that nature and reason disavow. For permissible pleasures that playful and frolicking young people are deprived of, they substitute more dangerous ones. Cleverly contrived private encounters take the place of public gatherings. By dint of hiding as if one were guilty, one is tempted to become so. Innocent joy likes to break forth in broad daylight, but vice is the friend of shadows, and never were innocence and secrecy bedfellows for long. My dear friend, she said to me, pressing my hand as if to convey her repentance to me and infuse into my heart the purity of hers;[20] who ought to feel better than we the importance of this maxim? What sufferings and pains, what remorse and tears we would have spared ourselves over so many years, if we two, loving virtue as we always have, had been able to foresee further in advance the dangers it runs when two people are alone together!

Once more, continued Madame de Wolmar in a more subdued tone, it is not in crowded gatherings where everyone watches and listens to us, but in private conversations where secrecy and liberty prevail, that morals can incur risks. It is on this principle, that when my domestics of both sexes assemble, I am very pleased if they all attend. I even approve their inviting those of the neighborhood youth whose association cannot harm them, and I learn with great pleasure that in order to praise the morals of one of our young neighbors, they say: he is welcome at Monsieur de Wolmar's. In this we have yet another objective. The men who serve us are all bachelors, and among the women the children's governess is yet unmarried; it is not right for the reserve in which both men and women live here to deprive them of an honest establishment. We try in these small gatherings to provide them this opportunity under our watch in order to help them choose better, and by working thus toward the formation of happy couples we increase the happiness of our own.

Perhaps in addition I should justify myself for dancing with these good folk; but I would rather plead no contest on this point, and I frankly admit that my principal motive in this is the pleasure it gives me. You know that I have always shared my Cousin's passion for the dance; but after losing my mother I gave up balls and all public gatherings for life; I kept my word, even at my wedding, and will keep it, and do not believe I am going against it by dancing sometimes at home with my guests and domestics. It is an activity useful to my health during the sedentary life we are forced to live here in the wintertime. It entertains me innocently; for when I have had a good dance my heart finds no fault with me. It also entertains Monsieur de Wolmar, my coquetry in this goes no farther than pleasing him. It is for me that he comes to the place where we dance; his servants are all the happier to be honored by their master's watching; they also express joy at seeing me among them. Finally I find that this moderate familiarity forms between us a bond of tenderness and attachment that brings back a little natural humanity[21] by mitigating the lowliness of servitude and the rigor of authority.

There, Milord, you have what Julie told me on the subject of the dance, and I marvelled how such affability could exist alongside such subordination, and how she and her husband could descend and put themselves so often on the same level with their domestics, without the latter being tempted to take them literally and put themselves on the same level in their turn. I do not believe there are Sovereigns in Asia served in their Palaces with more respect than these good masters are in their house. I know nothing less imperious than their orders and nothing so promptly executed: they entreat and the servants fly; they forgive and the servants feel their mistakes. I have never understood better how little the force of the things we say depends upon the words we use.

This led me to another reflection on the vain solemnity of masters. Namely, that it is not so much their familiarities as their flaws that engender contempt for them in their own house, and that the insolence of domestics indicates a vice-ridden master rather than a weak one: for nothing makes them bolder than acquaintance with his vices, and all those they discover in him are as they see it so many excuses for disobeying a man they can no longer bring themselves to respect.

The servants imitate the masters, and since they imitate them clumsily they expose in their conduct the flaws which the gloss of education hides better in others. In Paris I used to ascertain the morals of the women I knew by the air and tone of their chambermaids, and this rule never failed me. Besides the fact that the chambermaid once in her mistress's confidence makes her pay dearly for her discretion, she acts as the other thinks and discloses all her maxims by practicing them crudely. In all things the masters' example is stronger than their authority, and it is not natural for their domestics to seek to be more honest than they are. There is no use in yelling, cursing, abusing, firing, replacing them all; all that does not result in good service. When he who gives not a whit about his servants' contempt and hatred nonetheless believes he is well served, that is because he is satisfied with what he sees and their seeming punctiliousness, without taking into account the thousand secret wrongs constantly perpetrated on him, the source of which he never perceives. But where is the man so devoid of honor that he can bear the disdain of his whole retinue? Where is the woman so depraved that slander no longer fazes her? How many Ladies, in Paris and in London, think they are much honored, who would melt in tears if they heard what is said about them in their antechamber? Fortunately for their peace of mind they take comfort in taking these Arguses[22] for imbeciles, flattering themselves that their servants do not perceive what they do not bother to hide from them. And so in their reluctant obedience they in turn hide nothing of their contempt for their mistresses. Masters and servants mutually sense that it is useless to try making the others respect them.

Domestics' judgment seems to me the surest and most difficult test of their masters' virtue, and I remember, Milord, having thought well of yours in the Valais before I knew you, simply from the fact that though you spoke rather roughly to your servants, they were not for that less attached to you, and that they manifested among themselves as much respect for you in your absence as if you had been within hearing. It has been said that no one is a hero to his valet;[23] that may be, but the just man has his valet's respect; which sufficiently shows that heroism has but a vain appearance, and that there is nothing solid but virtue. In this house especially one recognizes the extent of its empire in the domestics' approval. An approval all the surer in that it does not consist in vain praises, but in the natural expression of what they feel. Never hearing anything here to make them believe that other masters are not just like their own, they do not praise them for virtues they hold common to all; but in their simplicity they praise God for having placed the rich on earth for the happiness of those who serve them, and for the relief of the poor.

Servitude is so unnatural to man that it cannot possibly exist without a measure of discontent. Yet one respects the master and says nothing about it. Should some grumbling against the mistress be vented, it is better than praise. No one complains that she lacks benevolence for himself, but that she showers just as much on others; no one can suffer her comparing his zeal to that of his comrades, and each would like to be first in favor as he believes he is in attachment. This is their sole complaint and their greatest injustice.

Subordination of inferiors is complemented by harmony between equals, and this aspect of domestic administration is not the least difficult. In the rivalries of jealousy and self-interest that forever divide the servants in a household, even in one as small as this one, they hardly ever remain united but at the master's expense. If they concert, it is to connive in stealing; if they are faithful each tries to look good at the expense of the others; they must be enemies or accomplices, and it is hard to see how one can avoid both their larceny and their quarrels. Most heads of households are familiar only with alternation between these two difficulties. Some, choosing their own interest over honesty, encourage this inclination of Servants to make secret reports and think they are achieving a masterpiece of prudence by turning them into each others' spies and overseers. Others more indolent would rather be robbed and let everybody live in peace; they make it almost a point of honor always to give a cool reception to information that a pure zeal sometimes extracts from a faithful Servant. All are equally mistaken. The former, by provoking within their household continual disruptions, inconsistent with discipline and order, merely gather a band of rascals and snitchers who betray their comrades in training for perhaps some day betraying their masters. The latter, by refusing to learn what goes on in their household, countenance leagues against themselves, encourage the bad ones, discourage the good ones, and maintain at great cost nothing but arrogant and lazy knaves who, concerting at the master's expense, consider their services as favors, and their thefts as rights.*

It is a great mistake in domestic as in civil economy to attempt to combat one vice with another or create between them a sort of equilibrium, as if what saps the foundations of order could ever serve to establish it! With this bad system one only ends up compounding all the difficulties. The vices tolerated in a house are not the only ones that prosper therein; let one sprout, a thousand others will follow. Soon they undo the servants who have them, ruin the master who suffers them, corrupt or scandalize the children keen on observing them. What unworthy father would dare place some advantage in the balance with this latter evil? What honorable man would wish to be the head of a

---

* I have studied fairly closely the system of large households, and I have clearly seen that it is impossible for a master who has twenty domestics ever to find out whether there is an honorable man among them, and not to take for such the nastiest knave in the bunch. That alone would kill any desire I might have of being one of the rich. One of life's sweetest pleasures, the pleasure of confidence and respect, is lost to these unhappy people. They pay very dearly for all their gold.

household, if it were impossible for him to conciliate peace and loyalty in his house, and if he had to purchase his domestics' zeal at the price of their mutual goodwill?

Anyone who had seen this house alone would not even imagine that such a difficulty could exist, so greatly does the union of its members appear to arise from their attachment to the heads. It is here one finds the palpable example that there is no way to love the master sincerely without loving all those who are dependent upon him: a truth which serves as foundation to Christian charity. Is it not entirely to be expected that the children of the same father should treat each other as brothers? That is what they tell us every day at Church without bringing us to feel it; it is what all the inhabitants of this house feel without being told.

This propensity toward concord begins with the choice of Subjects. When he hires them Monsieur de Wolmar does not examine solely whether they suit his wife and himself, but whether they suit one another, and a conspicuous antipathy between two excellent domestics would suffice to get one of them dismissed at once: for, says Julie, so small a household, one within which they constantly remain, and are continually in each other's presence, has to suit them all equally well, and would be like hell for them if it were not a house of peace. They must regard it as the paternal household where all are one single family. A single person who alienated the others could make them loath it, and this displeasing object being continually before their eyes, they would not be well off here either in terms of themselves or of us.

After matching them up as well as possible, they unite them so to speak despite themselves by means of the services they are more or less forced to render to each other, and they make it so that each one has a palpable interest in being loved by all his comrades. No one is as welcome seeking mercy for himself as for another; thus he who desires to obtain it tries to prevail upon another to speak for him, and this is all the easier in that whether one grants or refuses a favor thus requested, it is always counted as a merit to the one who served as intercessor. On the contrary, those who are good only for themselves are rebuffed. Why, they are told, should I grant what is being asked for you when you have never asked anything for another? Is it fair for you to be luckier than your comrades, because they are more willing to help than you? They go further; they invite them to help each other silently, unostentatiously, without making a show of it. Which is all the less difficult to obtain in that they know very well that the master, witness to this discretion, thinks the more of them for it; thus self interest gains thereby and amour-propre is not hurt. They are so persuaded of this general disposition, and such confidence reigns amongst them, that when someone has some mercy to ask, he brings it up at their table by way of conversation; often without doing anything more than that he finds that it has been asked and received, and not knowing whom to thank, he is indebted to all.

It is by this means and others like it that they inspire among them an attachment born of the one each has for his master, and subordinate to it. Thus, far from conspiring to his detriment, they are all united only to serve him better. Whatever interest they may have in loving each other, they have an even greater one in pleasing him; zeal for his service takes precedence over their mutual goodwill, and considering themselves injured by losses that would impede his ability to reward a good servant, all of them are equally unable to suffer in silence the wrong that anyone of them might try to do to him. To me there is something sublime about this part of the system established in this house, and I cannot admire enough how Monsieur and Madame de Wolmar managed to transform the vile role of accuser into a function of zeal, integrity, courage, as noble, or at least as praiseworthy as it was among the Romans.

They began by destroying or deterring, clearly, simply, and with perceptible examples, that criminal and servile morality, that mutual tolerance at the master's expense, that a bad servant does not fail to preach to the good ones under the guise of a charitable maxim. They made them well understand that the precept of covering the faults of one's neighbor applies only to those that do no one harm, that an injustice witnessed and silenced, and that hurts a third person, is an injustice one commits oneself, and that since it is only the sentiment of our own failings that impels us to forgive those of others, no one likes to suffer knaves who is not a knave himself. Based on these principles, true in general man to man, and much more rigorous yet in the closer relationship between servant and master, they hold here as indisputable that whoever sees a wrong perpetrated against his masters without reporting it is even more guilty than the one who committed it; for the latter is deceived in his act by the profit he anticipates from it, but the former composedly and without advantage has no other motive for his silence than a profound indifference to justice, to the good of the house he serves, and a secret desire to imitate the example he conceals. So that when the fault is great, he who committed it can still sometimes hope for forgiveness, but the witness who kept it silent is unfailingly dismissed as a man prone to evildoing.

On the other hand they suffer no accusation that can be suspected of injustice and calumny; that is to say that none is heard in the absence of the accused. If someone comes singly to report something against his comrade, or to complain of him personally, they ask him whether he is adequately informed, whether he has first talked it over with the person he has just complained about? If he says no, they further ask how he can judge an action of which he does not know the motives well enough? This action, they tell him, may have to do with some other one you know nothing about; there is perhaps some circumstance that tends to justify or excuse it, that you do not know. How dare you condemn this conduct before you know the reasons of the person who acted? A word of explanation would perhaps have justified it in your eyes? Why take the risk of condemning it unjustly and exposing me to sharing in your injustice? If he insists that he has first talked it over with the accused; why then, they reply, are you appearing without him, as if you were afraid he might belie what you have to say? What right have you to neglect for me the precaution you thought you needed to take for yourself? Is it proper to want me to assess on your word an act you did not wish to assess based on what you witnessed, and would you not be responsible for the biased assessment I might make of it, if I limited myself to your deposition alone? Then they propose to send for the person he is accusing; if he agrees to it, the matter is soon resolved; if he is opposed, he is sent away after a stern reprimand, but they keep the secret, and they watch both of them so closely that it is not long before they know which of the two was in the wrong.

This rule is so well known and established that a domestic of this house is never heard to speak ill of one of his absent comrades, for they know it is a way to pass for a coward or a liar. When one of them accuses another, it is openly, candidly, and not only in his presence, but in the presence of all their comrades, so that among the witnesses of what he says he will find guarantors of his good faith. When it is a matter of personal quarrels, these are almost always settled by mediators without intruding on Monsieur or Madame; but when the master's sacred interest is at stake, there is no way the matter can remain secret; the guilty party must either turn himself in or he must have an accuser. These petty pleadings are very rare and take place only at table during the rounds Julie makes every day at her servants' dinner or supper and which Monsieur de Wolmar in jest calls her grand sessions.[24] Then after calmly listening to the complaint and the reply, if the matter concerns her service, she thanks the accuser for his zeal. I know, she tells him, that you love your comrade, you have always spoken well of him, and I applaud the fact that for you the love of duty and justice outweighs individual affections: such is the way of a faithful servant and honorable man. Then, if the accused is not in the wrong, she always adds some praise to his vindication. But if he is really guilty, she spares him some of the shame in the presence of the others. She assumes he has something to say in his defense, which he does not wish to proclaim in front of everyone; she assigns him a time to hear him in private, and that is when she or her husband speaks to them[25] as the case requires. What is singular about this is that the harsher of the two is not the more dreaded, and that they fear Monsieur de Wolmar's stern reprimands less than Julie's stirring reproaches. The former, giving voice to justice and truth, humiliates and confounds the guilty parties; the latter makes them feel a mortal regret for it, by expressing her own at having to deprive them of her good will. Often she wrings from them tears of grief and shame, and it is not rare for her to melt at witnessing their repentance, in the hope she will not be obliged to keep her word.

Anyone who formed an opinion about all these precautions on the basis of what goes on in his own or his neighbors' house would perhaps judge them pointless or bothersome. But you, Milord, who have such exalted ideas about the duties and pleasures of the paterfamilias, and who know the natural empire that genius and virtue have over the human heart, you see the importance of these details, and you sense what makes them successful. Riches do not make a man rich, says the *Romance of the Rose*.[26] A man's goods are not in his coffers, but in the usage he makes of them; for he takes possession of the things he owns only through their employment, and abuses are always more inexhaustible than riches; and so it is that his pleasure is proportional not to his expenditure, but to his ability to regulate it. A fool can throw ingots into the sea and say they have given him pleasure: but what comparison is there between this extravagant pleasure and that which a wise man could have procured for a lesser sum? Only the order and discipline that multiply and perpetuate the usage of goods can transform pleasure into happiness. For if it is from the relation of things to us that genuine ownership arises;[27] if it is rather the use of riches than their acquisition which gives them to us, what duties are more important to the paterfamilias than the domestic economy and the good administration of his home, where the most perfect relations go directly to him, and the well-being of every member then adds to the head's?

Are the richest the happiest? What then does affluence do for felicity? But every well-regulated house is the image of the master's soul. Gilt panelling, luxury, and magnificence testify only to the vanity of him who displays them, whereas any time you see order reign without gloom, peace without slavery, plenty without profusion, then say confidently: it is a happy being who commands here.

For my part, I think that the most assured sign of true contentment of spirit is the withdrawn and domestic life, and that those who constantly go about seeking their happiness in others' homes do not have it in their own. A paterfamilias who takes pleasure in his house is rewarded for the continual cares he assumes there by the continual enjoyment of nature's sweetest sentiments. Alone among mortals, he is master of his own felicity, because he is happy like God himself, without desiring anything more than what he already has: like that immense Being he does not worry about expanding his possessions but of making them truly his own through the most perfect relations and the shrewdest direction: if he does not become richer through new acquisitions, he becomes richer by better possessing what he has. He had been enjoying only the income from his lands, he further enjoys those very lands by supervising their cultivation and visiting them continually. His Staff were strangers to him; he makes them his own, his children, he takes possession of them. He held rights only over their acts, he acquires new ones to their will. He was master only for a price, he becomes master through the sacred empire of respect and charitable deeds. Were fortune to strip him of his wealth, it could not take from him the hearts he has won to himself, it will not take children from their father; the whole difference is that he fed them yesterday, and tomorrow they will feed him. This is how one learns truly to enjoy one's possessions, one's family, and oneself; this is how the details of a household become delightful for the honorable man who is able to appreciate their value; this is how, far from regarding his duties as a burden, he makes them his happiness, and derives from his affecting and noble functions the glory and pleasure of being a man.

Now if these precious advantages are scorned or little known, and if even the few who seek them so rarely obtain them, all this is owing to the same cause. There are simple and sublime duties that few people are called to love and fulfill. Such are those of the paterfamilias; the air and bustle of the world inspire nothing but distaste for them, and they are still poorly fulfilled if one inclines to them only for reasons of avarice and self-interest. A man who thinks himself a good paterfamilias may be nothing more than a vigilant bursar; his property may prosper and his household go very badly. It takes loftier notions to enlighten, direct this important administration and give it a happy outcome. The first precaution by which the ordering of a house must begin is to suffer therein only honest folk who do not bring in the secret desire to upset that order. But are servitude and honesty compatible enough so one could hope to find domestics who are honest folk? No, Milord, to have them one must not look for them, but make them, and only a man of honor knows the art of fashioning other men of honor. In vain does a hypocrite attempt to adopt the voice of virtue, he can inspire the taste for it in no one, and if he knew how to make it desirable he would desire it himself. What use are frigid lessons contradicted by a continual example, if not to give the impression that he who delivers them is making sport of others' credulity? What great absurdity speak those who exhort us to do as they say and not as they do! He who knows not what he is saying never says it well; for the language of the heart that moves and persuades is lacking. I have sometimes heard those awkwardly stilted conversations, which masters deliver in front of domestics as if in front of children to teach them lessons indirectly. Far from thinking they were for an instant duped by them, I have always seen them smile secretly at the ineptitude of the master who was taking them for idiots, by heavily intoning in front of them maxims they well knew not to be his.

All these vain subtleties are unknown in this house, and the great art of masters to make their domestics as they wish them is to show themselves to them as they are. Their conduct is always candid and open, because they do not fear lest their acts belie their words. As they do not have for themselves a moral different from the one they wish to impart to others, they have no need to be circumspect in what they say; a word that foolishly escapes them does not overturn the principles they have endeavored to establish. They do not indiscreetly reveal all their business, but they freely state all their maxims. At table, out strolling, in private or in front of everyone, they always maintain the same language; they state candidly what they think on every matter, and without their having anyone in mind, everyone finds some instruction in it. Since the domestics never see their master do anything that is not right, just, fair, they by no means regard justice as the poor man's tribute, as the wretched man's yoke, as one of the miseries of their condition. The care they take not to make workers travel needlessly, and waste whole days coming to request payment for their working days, accustoms them to appreciate the value of time. Seeing the masters' concern to save others' time, each concludes that his own is precious to them and counts idleness as a greater crime. The confidence of their servants in their integrity lends their practices a force that gives them stature and avoids abuses. No one fears that in each week's gratification the mistress will always find that it is the youngest or strongest who has been the most diligent. An old domestic is not afraid they will cavil at some trifle so as to save on the supplementary wages he is given. They have no hope of taking advantage of a disagreement between their masters to promote their own interests and obtain from one what the other has refused. Those who are marriageable are not afraid their establishment will be impeded so as to keep them longer, and their good service will thus work against them. Were some outside Servant to come and tell the servants in this house that a master and his domestics have reached a real state of war, that in doing him all the harm they can they are merely exercising a right of reprisal, that masters being usurpers, liars, and scoundrels, there is nothing wrong in treating them the way they treat the Prince or the People or individuals, and cleverly return the harm they do with open violence; the man who spoke thus would be understood by no one; they don't even worry here about how to counter or prevent such talk; only those who provoke it are obliged to refute it.

There is never either sullenness nor reluctance in the obedience, because there is neither arrogance nor whim in the command, because they demand nothing but what is reasonable and useful, and they have enough respect for the dignity of man albeit in servitude to put him only to tasks that do not abase him. Moreover, here nothing is base save vice, and all that is useful and just is honest and seemly.

They suffer no intrigue without, nor is anyone tempted to have one. They know very well that their most secure fortune is dependent on the master's, and that they will never want for anything so long as the house prospers. By serving it they therefore attend to their own estate, and increase it while making their service pleasant; that is their greatest interest. But this word is hardly in its proper place in this instance, for I have never seen a system in which interest was more wisely channelled and where however it had less influence than here. Everything is done out of attachment: one would say that these venal souls are purified upon entering this abode of wisdom and union. One would say that a part of the master's wisdom and the mistress's sentiments had been transmitted to each of their servants; so judicious, beneficent, honest, and superior to their condition do they appear. To be well thought of, to be well considered, to have their masters' good will, is their greatest ambition, and they count the kind words said to them, as elsewhere the presents they are given.

There, Milord, are my principal observations on the part of this house's economy that concerns domestics and paid laborers. As for the masters' manner of living and the governance of the children, each of these items well deserves a letter of its own.[28] You know the purpose with which I began these remarks;[29] but in truth, it all makes for such a delightful tableau that one can enjoy looking at it without any other interest than the pleasure it gives.

CHAPTER TWENTY

"A Household on Rue Saint-Denis" [1]

The woman makes more noise, the man does more harm.

In Paris I saw a woman who was very much the most wicked Prude of the whole rue St. Denis and whose husband passed for the neighborhood Saint; when they had some quarrel together, which happened rather frequently, the wife spewed out torrents of insults against her husband with frightful shouts and this uproar lasted for two to three hours and more, but admire if you please the easygoingness of the gawker who was no more disturbed than a rock and listened to this beautiful litany from beginning to end with an angelic patience; it is true that when his better half found it appropriate to conclude he coolly took up a stick, rained blows on her, left her lying for dead, and calmly went to drink with his friends, overwhelmed with insults and weariness.

Just because an example is drawn from the dregs of the people, it is no less conclusive: men show themselves everywhere, the lower the level they are in, the less nature is disguised.

SOURCE: Jean-Jacques Rousseau, *Autobiographical, Scientific, Religious, Moral, and Literary Writings. Collected Writings of Rousseau* XII, trans. and ed. Christopher Kelly (Hanover, N.H.: University Press of New England, 2007).

CHAPTER TWENTY-ONE

Emile and Sophie; or, The Solitaries

[This incomplete story is the sequel to Emile, *at the end of which Emile is married to Sophie and announces to his tutor that she is pregnant.]*

First Letter

I was free, I was happy, oh my master! You had made me a heart suited to savoring happiness, and you had given me Sophie. To the delights of love, to the outpourings of friendship, a growing family added the charms of paternal tenderness: everything proclaimed a pleasant life to me, everything promised me a sweet old age and a peaceful death in my children's arms. Alas! What has become of that happy time of enjoyment and hope, in which the future embellished the present; in which my heart, drunk with its joy, imbibed a century of felicity each day? Everything vanished like a dream; still young I lost everything—wife, children, friends, in sum, everything—even commerce with my fellows. My heart has been torn apart by all its attachments; it no longer holds onto anything except the least of all, the tepid love of a life without pleasures but exempt from remorse. If I outlive my losses for long, my fate is to age and die alone, without ever seeing a man's face again, and providence alone will close my eyes.

In this condition, what can still engage me to take care of this sad life that I have so little reason to love? Memories, and the consolation of being in order in this world, by subjecting myself to the eternal decrees without complaint. In everything that was dear to me I am dead: Without impatience and without fear I am waiting for what is left of me to rejoin what I have lost.

But you, my dear master, are you alive? Are you still mortal? Are you still on this earth of exile along with your Emile, or are you already living in the fatherland of just souls along with Sophie? Alas! Wherever you are, you are dead for me, my eyes will not see you again; but my heart will be occupied with you ceaselessly. Never have I known the value of your efforts better than after harsh necessity made me feel its blows so cruelly and deprived me of everything except myself. I am alone, I have lost everything, but I have myself left, and despair has not annihilated me. These papers will not reach you, I cannot hope for it. Doubtless they will perish without having been seen by any man, but it does not matter; they have been written, I gather them together, I bind them, I continue them, and it is to you that I address them: it is for you that I want to trace those precious memories that both nourish and distress my heart; it is to you that I wish to give an account of myself, of my feelings, of my conduct, of this heart that you gave me. I shall say everything, the good, the bad, my pains, my pleasures, my faults; but I believe that I have nothing to say that could dishonor your work.

My happiness bloomed early; it began from my birth, it was to end before my death. All the days of my childhood were fortunate days, passed in freedom, in joy as well as innocence: I never learned to distinguish my instructions from my pleasures. All men tenderly recall the games of their childhood, but I am perhaps the only one who does not mix with these sweet memories those of the tears he was made to shed. Alas! If I had died as a child I would have already enjoyed life, and would never have known its regrets!

I became a young man and did not cease being happy. In the age of passions I formed my reason by means of my senses; what serves to fool other people was the path to truth for me. I learned to judge soundly about the things that surrounded me and the interest that I should take in them; I judged about them based on true and simple principles; authority, opinion did not adulterate my judgments at all. In order to discover the relationships among things, I studied the relations of each of them to me. From two known terms I learned to find the third. In order to know the universe by means of everything that could concern me, it was enough for me to know myself; once my place was assigned, everything was found.

In this way I learned that the primary wisdom is to want what is, and to regulate one's heart according to one's destiny. That is all that depends on us, you told me; all the rest is from necessity. The one who struggles most against his fate is the least wise and always the most unhappy; what he can change in his situation relieves him less than he is tormented by the internal disturbance that he gives himself by doing so. He rarely succeeds, and gains nothing by succeeding. But what sentient being can live forever without passions, without attachments? That is not a man, it is a beast or it is a God. Thus, not being able to secure myself against all the affections that tie us to things, at least you taught me to select them, to open my soul only to the most noble, to attach it only to the worthiest objects that are my fellows, to extend, so to speak, the human I over all of humanity, and in this manner to preserve myself from the vile passions that concentrate it.

When my senses, awakened by age, asked me for a companion, you purified their fire by means of sentiments; it is by means of the imagination that animates them that I learned to subjugate them: I loved Sophie even before I knew her; that love preserved my heart from the traps of vice, it brought the taste for beautiful and decent things into it, it engraved the holy laws of virtue in it in indelible strokes. When at last I saw this worthy object of my worship, when I felt the empire of these charms, everything sweet, ravishing that can enter a soul penetrated mine with an exquisite feeling that nothing can express. Cherished days of my first loves, delightful days, why can't you begin again ceaselessly and fill all my being from now on! I would want no other eternity.

Empty regrets! Useless wishes! Everything has disappeared, everything has disappeared never to return . . . After so many ardent sighs, I obtained the prize for them, all my wishes were fulfilled. Husband, and still lover, in tranquil possession I found a happiness of another sort, but not less true than in the delirium of desires. My master, you believe you knew that bewitching girl. Oh, how much you deceive yourself: you knew my mistress, my wife; but you did not know Sophie. Her charms of every sort were inexhaustible, every moment seemed to renew them, and the last day of her life showed me some that I had not known.

Already a father of two children, I divided my time between an adored wife and the dear fruits of her tenderness; you helped me to prepare an education similar to my own for my son, and, under the eyes of her mother, my daughter would have learned to resemble her. All my business was limited to taking care of Sophie's patrimony; I had forgotten my fortune in order to enjoy my felicity. Deceitful felicity! Three times have I felt your inconstancy. Your duration is only a point, and when one is at the height one must soon decline. Was it through you, cruel father, that this decline was to begin? By what fatality could you leave that peaceful life that we were leading together, how did my attentiveness repel you from me? You took pleasure in your work; I saw it, I felt it, I was certain of it. You appeared happy because of my happiness; Sophie's tender caresses seemed to delight your paternal heart; you loved us, you were pleased to be with us, and you left us! Without your retreat I would still be happy; my son would perhaps be alive, or other hands would not have closed his eyes. His mother, virtuous and cherished, would herself be alive in her husband's arms. Fatal retreat, which abandoned me irrevocably to the horrors of my fate! No, under your eyes crime and its punishments would never have drawn near my family; by abandoning it you have done me more ills than you did me good in my whole life.

Soon Heaven ceased to bless a house in which you no longer lived. Ills, afflictions followed each other without respite. Within a few months we lost Sophie's father, mother, and finally her daughter, her charming daughter whom she had desired so much, whom she idolized, whom she wanted to follow. With this final blow her shaken constancy completely abandoned her. Up to that time, content and peaceful in her solitude, she had not known the bitter things of life, she had not at all armed that sensitive and easily moved soul against the blows of fate. She felt these losses as one feels one's first misfortunes: and so they were only the beginnings of ours. Nothing could dry her tears; her daughter's death made her feel her mother's more keenly: groaning, she ceaselessly called one or the other; she caused all the places where once she used to receive their innocent caresses to resound with their names and her regrets: all the objects that recalled them to her sharpened her pains; I resolved to take her away from these sad places. In the capital I had what is called business and what had never been such for me until then: I proposed that she follow there a friend whom she had made in the neighborhood and who was obliged to go there with her husband. She consented to do so in order not to be separated from me, not perceiving my motive. Her affliction was too dear to her to seek to calm it. To share her regrets, to weep with her was the only consolation anyone could give her.

Drawing near the capital, I felt myself struck by a grievous impression that I had never experienced before. The saddest presentiments rose up in my breast: everything I had seen, everything you had told me about large cities made me tremble about the stay in this one. I was frightened about exposing such a pure union to so many dangers that could adulterate it. Gazing at the sad Sophie, I shuddered at considering that I myself was dragging so many virtues and charms into that pit of prejudices and vices to which innocence and happiness proceed from every direction in order to be ruined.

Nevertheless, certain of her and of myself, I despised this advice of prudence that I took for an empty presentiment; while allowing myself to be tormented by it, I treated it as a chimera. Alas! I did not imagine that I would see it justified so soon and so cruelly. It hardly occurred to me that I was not going to seek peril in the capital, but rather that it was following me there.

How to speak to you about those two years that we passed in that fatal city, and about the cruel effect that this poisoned stay made on my soul and my fate? You knew only too well those sad catastrophes whose memory, erased in happier days, today comes to redouble my regrets, by taking me back to their source. What a change was produced in me by my indulgence of too pleasing ties, which habit was beginning to turn into friendship! How did example and imitation, against which you armed my heart so well, imperceptibly bring it to those frivolous tastes that I had known how to disdain when I was younger? How different it is to see things when distracted by other objects or merely occupied with those that strike us! This was no longer the time when my heated-up imagination sought nothing but Sophie, and repelled everything that was not her. I was no longer seeking her, I possessed her, and her charm then embellished the objects as much as it had disfigured them in my earliest youth. But soon these same objects weakened my tastes by dividing them. Blunted upon all these frivolous amusements, little by little my heart was imperceptibly losing its first resilience and becoming incapable of warmth and force; I wandered uneasily from one pleasure to another; I sought out everything and I was bored with everything; I was pleased only where I was not, and I dazed myself in order to amuse myself. I felt a revolution about which I did not want to be convinced; I left myself no time to turn back upon myself for fear of no longer finding myself there again. All my attachments had been loosened, all my affections had become lukewarm: I had put a jargon of sentiment and of morality in place of the reality. I was a man who was gallant without tenderness, a stoic without virtues, a wise man occupied with follies; of your Emile, I no longer had anything but the name and some speeches. By detaching themselves from me little by little, my frankness, my freedom, my pleasures, my duties, you, my son, Sophie herself, everything that previously animated, elevated my mind and formed the fullness of my existence, seemed to detach me from them, and left in my collapsed soul only an aching sentiment of emptiness and annihilation. Finally, I no longer loved or believed I no longer loved. That terrible fire, which appeared almost extinct, smoldered under the ashes, in order to burst out soon with more fury than ever.

A change a hundred times more inconceivable! How could she who constituted the glory and the happiness of my life constitute its shame and despair? How would I describe such a deplorable lapse? No, this awful detail will never leave my pen nor my mouth; it is too offensive to the memory of the worthiest of women, too overwhelming, too horrible for my memory, too discouraging for virtue; I would die from it a hundred times before it was finished. Morality of the world! Traps of vice and example, betrayals of a false friendship, human inconstancy and weakness: who among us is proof against you? Ah! If Sophie sullied her virtue, what woman will dare to count on hers? But how uniquely tempered must have been a soul that can return from so far to everything that it was before?

It is about your regenerated children that I have to speak. All their deviations have been known to you: I shall speak only about what pertains to their return to themselves and serves to link events.

Consoled, or rather distracted, by her friend and by the societies to which she led her, Sophie no longer had that settled taste for private life and for retreat: she had forgotten her losses and almost what she had left. Growing up, her son was going to become less dependent on her, and already the mother was learning to do without him. I myself was no longer her Emile, I was only her husband, and in big cities the husband of a decent woman is a man with whom one maintains all sorts of good manners in public, but whom one does not see at all in private. For a long time we frequented the same cliques. Imperceptibly they changed. Each of the two thought he was putting himself at ease far from the person who had the right of inspection over him. We were no longer one, we were two: the tone of high society had divided us, and our hearts no longer drew near each other. It was only our neighbors from the country and friends of the city who sometimes brought us together. The wife, after having often flirted with me—which I did not always find it easy to resist—was discouraged, and, attaching herself completely to Sophie, became inseparable from her. The husband lived extremely united with his wife, and consequently with mine. Their external conduct was regular and decent, but their maxims should have frightened me. Their good understanding came less from a genuine attachment than from a common indifference over the duties of their state. Hardly jealous of the rights they had over each other, they claimed to love each other much more by letting each other's tastes pass without constraint, and not taking offense at not being their object. "May my husband live happily in everything," said the wife. "May I have my wife as a friend, I am satisfied," said the husband. "Our feelings," they continued, "do not depend on us, but our behavior does. Each puts all that he can of his own into the other one's happiness. Can one love what is dear to us any better than to want everything that it desires? One avoids the cruel necessity of avoiding each other."

If this system had been uncovered this way at a stroke, it would have horrified us. But one does not know how much the outpourings of friendship make one pass over things that would be revolting without it; one does not know how much a philosophy so well adapted to the vices of the human heart, a philosophy that offers in place of feelings that one is no longer master of having, in place of hidden duty that torments, and that profits no one, only care, courtesies, propriety, attentions, only frankness, freedom, sincerity, confidence; one does not know, I say, how appealing everything that preserves the union between persons when hearts are no longer united is for the best natural dispositions, and becomes seductive under the mask of wisdom: reason itself would have found it hard to defend itself, if conscience did not come to its aid. That was what preserved between Sophie and me the shame of showing each other an eagerness that we no longer had. The couple that had subjected us offended against each other without constraint and believed they loved each other: but an old respect for each other that we could not vanquish forced us to flee each other so that we could offend against each other. While appearing to be a burden to each other mutually, we were closer to reuniting than were those who never left each other at all. To stop avoiding each other when each offends against the other is the way to be certain of never reuniting.

But at the moment when the distance between us was the most marked, everything changed in the most bizarre manner. Suddenly Sophie became as sedentary and withdrawn as she had been dissipated until then. Her mood, which was not always even, became constantly sad and somber. Closed up in her room from morning to night without speaking, without weeping, without caring about anyone, she could not bear being interrupted. Even her friend became unbearable to her; she told her so and received her badly without discouraging her: she begged me more than once to rid her of her. I battled her over this caprice, which I blamed on a little jealousy; I even told her so one day while joking. "No, Sir, I am not at all jealous," she said to me with a cold and resolute air, "but I am horrified by that woman: I ask you for only one favor, that is that I may never see her again." Struck by these words, I wanted to know the reason for her hatred: she refused to answer. She had already closed her door to the husband; I was obliged to close it to the wife, and we no longer saw them.

Nevertheless her sadness continued and became disquieting. I began to be alarmed at it; but how could I know its cause about which she persisted in keeping silent? One could not impose on that proud soul by means of authority: we had ceased being each other's confidantes for so long that I was hardly surprised that she disdained to open her heart to me; one had to deserve this confidence, and, either because her touching melancholy had heated up mine again, or because it was less cured than it had believed it was, I felt that it cost me little to give her the care with which I hoped finally to overcome her silence.

I did not leave her any longer, but, even though I had returned to her and had marked this return with the most tender attentiveness, I saw with pain that I was not making any progress. I wanted to reestablish a Husband's rights, too long neglected; I experienced the most invincible resistance. These were no longer those exciting refusals, made to give a new value to what one is granting. Nor were they those tender, modest, but absolute refusals that intoxicated me with love and that one nevertheless had to respect. These were the serious refusals of a decided will that was indignant that one could doubt it. She forcefully reminded me of the engagements taken formerly in your presence.[1] "Whatever may be the case for me," she said, "you ought to esteem yourself and forever respect Emile's word. My wrongs do not at all authorize you to violate your promises. You can punish me, but you cannot constrain me, and be sure that I shall never put up with it." What to respond, what to do, if not to seek to bend her, to touch her, to overcome her obstinacy as a result of perseverance? These vain efforts irritated my love and my amour-propre at the same time. The difficulties inflamed my heart, and I made it a point of honor for myself to surmount them. Perhaps never after ten years of marriage, after such a long cooling off, has the passion of a Husband been rekindled in so burning and keen a way; never during my first loves had I shed so many tears at her feet: everything was useless, she remained unshakable.

I was as surprised as I was afflicted, knowing well that this hardness of heart was not in her character. I did not become at all discouraged, and if I did not overcome her stubbornness, finally I believed I saw less curtness in it. Some signs of regret and pity tempered the sharpness of her refusals, sometimes I judged that they cost her; her dull eyes let fall upon me some glances no less sad but less fierce, and that seemed to be moved toward tenderness. I thought that the shame of such an excessive caprice kept her from going back on it, that she kept it up for lack of being able to excuse it, and that perhaps she was only waiting for a little constraint in order to appear to cede to force what she no longer dared to grant willingly. Struck by an idea that flattered my desires, I indulgently gave myself over to it: to save her from the embarrassment of giving herself after having resisted for so long was one more piece of consideration that I wanted to have for her.

One day, carried away by my raptures, I joined the most ardent caresses to the most tender supplications, I saw her moved; I wanted to

complete my victory. Oppressed and palpitating, she was ready to succumb when, suddenly changing tone, bearing, expression, she pushed
me back so suddenly, with such an unbelievable violence, and looking at
me with an eye that rage and despair made frightening, she said to me:
"Stop, Emile, and know that I am no longer anything to you. Another
has sullied your bed. I am pregnant; you will not touch me again in my
life"; and on the spot she threw herself impetuously into her dressing
room and closed the door.[2]

I stay there crushed. . . .

My master, this is not the story of the events of my life; they are
hardly worth the trouble of writing; this is the story of my passions, of
my feelings, of my ideas. I must expand upon the most terrible revolution that my heart has ever experienced.

The great wounds of the body and soul do not bleed the moment
they are made; they do not impress their keenest sufferings that soon.
Nature gathers itself together in order to sustain all their violence, and
often the mortal blow is struck a long time before the wound makes
itself felt. At this unexpected scene, at these words that my ears seemed
to push away, I remain immobile, annihilated; my eyes close, a mortal
cold flows through my veins; without having fainted I feel all my senses
arrested, all my functions suspended; my distressed soul is in a total disturbance, similar to the chaos of the theatrical scenery at the moment
it changes, at the moment that everything recedes and proceeds to take
on a new aspect.

I do not know how long I remained in that condition, on my knees as
I was, and almost not daring to move, out of fear of assuring myself that
what was happening was not at all a dream. I would have wanted this
daze to last forever. But having finally reawakened in spite of myself, the
first impression that I felt was a spasm of horror for everything that surrounded me. Suddenly I get up, I throw myself out of the room, I walk
down the stairway without seeing anything, without saying anything to
anyone. I leave, striding along, I go away with the rapidity of a stag that
believes that, with its speed, it is fleeing the arrow that it bears sunk in
its flesh.

I rush this way, without slowing my pace, all the way to a public garden. The sight of day and the Sky was a burden to me, I sought darkness
under the trees; finally, finding myself out of breath, I let myself fall
half-dead on a lawn. . . . "Where am I, what have I become? What have
I heard? What catastrophe? Madman! What chimera have you chased
after? Love, honor, faith, virtues, where are you? The sublime, the noble
Sophie is only a despicable woman!" This exclamation that my delirium

caused to burst forth was followed by such a rending of the heart that, wracked with sobs, I could neither breathe nor groan: without the rage and fit of anger that followed, this shock would doubtless have suffocated me. Oh, who could unravel, express this confusion of numerous feelings that shame, love, rage, regrets, tenderness, jealousy, frightful despair caused me to experience simultaneously? No, this situation, this tumult cannot be described. The blossoming of the extreme joy that seems to extend and rarify our entire being with a uniform emotion is easily conceived and imagined. But when excessive suffering gathers all the furies of hell into a wretch's bosom; when a thousand contradictory impulses tear him apart without his being able to distinguish a single one of them; when he feels himself broken into pieces by a hundred separate forces that drag him in opposite directions, he is no longer one, he exists wholly in each point of suffering, he seems to multiply himself in order to suffer. Such was my condition, such it was for several hours; how to paint its picture? In volumes I would not say what I was feeling at every moment. Happy men who, in a cramped soul and in a tepid heart, are unacquainted with any reversals other than those of fortune, nor passions other than vile self-interest: may you always be able to treat this horrible condition as chimerical and never experience the cruel torments that worthier attachments give, when they are broken, to hearts made for feeling them.

Our forces are limited and all violent outbursts are intermittent. During one of these moments of exhaustion, in which overwhelmed nature catches its breath in order to suffer, I suddenly happened to think about my youth, about you my master, about my lessons; I happened to think that I was a man and I immediately asked myself, "What harm have I received in my person? What crime have I committed? What have I lost of myself? If at this moment I fell from the clouds just as I am in order to begin to exist, would I be an unhappy being?"[3] This reflection, more rapid than a lightning bolt, cast into my soul a glimmer of light that I soon lost again but that was enough to make me recognize myself. I saw myself clearly in my place, and the utility of this moment of reason was to teach me that I was incapable of reasoning. The horrible agitation that reigned in my soul left no time for any object to make itself noticed there: I was in no condition to see anything, to compare anything, to deliberate, to resolve, to judge about anything. Thus to ponder what I had to do was to torment myself in vain, it was to sharpen my pains fruitlessly, and my sole care ought to be to gain time in order to steady my senses and settle my imagination. I believe that this is the only course of action that you could have taken yourself, if you had been there to guide me.[4]

Resolved to give vent to the violence of the transports that I could not vanquish, I abandon myself to them with a fury marked with an indefinable voluptuousness, as if I had put my suffering at its ease. I get up precipitately, I begin walking as before, without following any settled route: I run, I wander this way and that, I abandon my body to every agitation of my heart; I follow its impressions unconstrainedly; I make myself lose my breath, and, mixing my sharp sighs with my troubled breathing, I sometimes felt myself ready to suffocate.

The jolts of that hurried walk seemed to stupefy me and bring me relief. In violent passions, instinct dictates outcries, motions, gestures that give vent to the spirits and divert one from one's passion: as long as one is in motion one is only carried away; gloomy repose is more to be feared, it is close to despair. The same night I made an almost laughable test of this difference, if everything that shows human folly and misery ought ever to stir up laughter in anyone who might be subject to them.

After a thousand twists and turns made without my noticing them, I find myself in the middle of the City surrounded by Carriages at the hour for the shows, and in a street where there was one. I was about to be crushed in the confusion if someone, taking me by the arm, had not warned me of the danger: I throw myself into an open door; it was a café. I am accosted there by some acquaintances; they speak to me, they drag me I don't know where. Struck by a noise of instruments and a burst of lights I came back to myself, I open my eyes, I look: I find myself in the middle of the theater on the day of the premiere, crushed by the crowd, and unable to leave.

I shuddered but I made my decision. I did not say anything, I kept myself calm, however dearly this apparent calmness cost me. They made a lot of noise, they spoke a lot, they spoke to me; not understanding anything, what could I answer? But when by chance one of those who had brought me named my wife, at this fatal name I made a piercing cry that was heard by the entire gathering and caused some murmuring. I promptly recovered, and everything quieted down. Nevertheless, having attracted the attention of those around me with this cry, I sought the moment to escape, and, drawing near the door little by little, I finally left before they had finished.

Upon entering the street and mechanically withdrawing my hand, which I had held in my bosom during the entire performance, I saw my fingers covered with blood, and I believed I felt it running upon my chest. I uncover my chest, I look, I find it bleeding and torn just like the heart enclosed in it. One might think that a spectator who had paid this price for his calmness was not an extremely good judge of the Performance that he had just heard.

I hastened to flee, trembling at being met again. As the night favored my travels, I started roaming the streets again as if to compensate myself for the constraint I had just experienced; I walked for several hours without resting for a moment. Finally, scarcely able to hold myself up any longer and finding myself near my neighborhood, I return home, not without a frightful beating of the heart: I ask what my son was doing; they tell me that he was sleeping; I keep quiet and sigh. My people want to speak to me; I impose silence on them; I throw myself on a bed, ordering them to retire. After several hours of a rest worse than the agitation of the day before, I get up before daybreak and, crossing the apartments without any noise, I draw near Sophie's room. I go there, without being able to hold myself back; with the most detestable cowardice, I cover the threshold of her door with a hundred kisses and bathe it with a torrent of tears, then escaping with the fear and the precautions of a guilty man, I softly leave the dwelling resolved never to enter it again in my life.

Here ended my lively but brief madness, and I returned to my good sense. I even believe that I did what I should have done in giving way at first to the passion that I could not vanquish, in order to be able to govern it afterward after having allowed it some scope. The movement that I had just taken had disposed me to tenderness, the rage that had carried me away until then gave way to sadness, and I began to read well enough in the depths of my heart to see the most profound affliction engraved there in indelible strokes. Nevertheless I walked, I distanced myself from the dreadful place, less rapidly than the day before, but also without making any detour. I left the City and, taking the first highway, I set myself to following it with a slow and unconfident pace that showed weakness and despondency. In measure as the increasing daylight illuminated objects, I believed I saw another Sky, another earth, another universe: everything had changed for me. I was no longer the same as the day before—or, rather, I was no longer; it was my own death for which I had to cry. Oh, how many delightful memories came to lay siege to my heart, contracted with distress, and to force it to open itself to their sweet images in order to drown it in empty regrets! All my past enjoyments came to sharpen the feeling of my losses, and caused me more torments than they had given me voluptuous pleasures. Ah! Who knows the frightful contrast of suddenly leaping from the extreme of happiness to the extreme of misery, and to cross that immense interval without having a moment to prepare for it? Yesterday, even yesterday, at the feet of an adored wife, I was the happiest of beings; it was love that subjected me to its laws, that kept me dependent on her; her tyrannical power was the work of my tenderness, and I enjoyed even her rigors. Why was it not given to me to pass the course of centuries in that too lovable condition, to esteem her, to respect her, to cherish her, to groan at her tyranny, to wish to make her bend without ever succeeding in doing so, to ask, implore, beg, desire ceaselessly, and never to obtain anything. Those times, those charming times of expected return, of deceitful hope were even worth as much as those in which I possessed her. And now hated, betrayed, dishonored, without hope, without recourse I do not even have the consolation of daring to form wishes . . . I stopped myself, frightened with horror by the object that I had to substitute for the one that was occupying me with so many charms. To contemplate Sophie debased and despicable! What eyes could bear that profanation? My cruelest torment was not occupying myself with my misery; it was mixing with it the shame of the one who had caused it. This desolating picture was the only one that I could not bear.

The day before, my stupid and frenzied suffering had protected me from that horrible idea; I thought about nothing but suffering. But in measure as the feeling of my ills settled itself, so to speak, in the depths of my heart, forced to go back to their source, I kept going back over that fatal object in spite of myself. The emotions that had escaped me upon leaving showed only too well the unworthy inclination that was bringing me back to it. The hatred that I owed her cost me less than the disdain I had to add to it, and what tore me apart most cruelly was not so much to renounce her as to be forced to despise her.

My first reflections about her were bitter. "If the infidelity of an ordinary woman is a crime, what name must be given to hers? Vile souls do not debase themselves in committing base acts; they remain in their condition; there is no ignominy for them because there is no elevation. The adulteries of society women are only gallantries; but Sophie as an adulteress is the most odious of all monsters: The distance between what she is and what she was is immense; no, there is no debasement, no crime comparable to hers."

"But I," I resumed, "I who accuse her, and who has only too much right to do so, as I am the one against whom she is offending, as I am the one that the ingrate has killed, by what right did I dare to judge her so severely before having judged myself, before knowing what I should reproach myself for in her wrongs? You are accusing her of no longer being the same! Oh, Emile, and you, have you not changed? How different toward her have I seen you in this big city than you used to be!

Ah! Her inconstancy is the result of yours. She had sworn to be faithful to you; and you, hadn't you sworn to adore her always? You abandon her, and you want her to remain with you; you scorn her and you want to be always honored by her! It is your cooling off, your forgetfulness, your indifference that have torn you from her heart; one must not cease being lovable if one wants to be loved always. She violated her oaths only following your example; you had not to neglect her, and never would she have betrayed you.

"What subjects of complaint did she give you in the retirement in which you found her, and in which you should always have left her? What cooling off did you notice in her tenderness? Is she the one who begged you to take her out of that fortunate place? You know it: she left it with the most mortal regret. The tears that she shed there were sweeter to her than the frolicsome games of the City. There she passed her innocent life in causing the happiness of yours: but she loved you better than her own tranquillity; after having wanted to hold you back, she left everything in order to follow you. You are the one who dragged her from the bosom of peace and virtue into the abyss of vices and miseries into which you threw yourself. Alas! It depended only on you for her to be always reasonable, and for her to make you happy always.

"Oh Emile! You have lost her, you must hate yourself and feel sorry for her; but what right do you have to scorn her? Have you remained irreproachable yourself? Has high society not encroached at all on your morals? You did not share her infidelity, but didn't you excuse it by ceasing to honor her virtue? Didn't you incite it by living in places where everything that is decent is held in derision, where women would blush at being chaste, where the only reward for the virtues of their sex is raillery and incredulity? Was the faith that you did not violate exposed to the same risks? Did you receive, as she did, that fiery temperament that causes great weaknesses, as well as great virtues? Do you have that body too well formed by love, too exposed to perils by its charms and to temptations by its senses? Oh, how the fate of such a woman is to be pitied! What combats does she not have to make without respite, ceaselessly, against another, against herself? What invincible courage, what stubborn resistance, what heroic firmness are necessary for her! What dangerous victories does she have to win every day without any other witness of her triumphs than heaven and her own heart? And after so many fine years passed this way in suffering, ceaselessly combating, and vanquishing, a moment of weakness, a single moment of relaxation and forgetfulness sully that irreproachable life forever, and dishonor so many virtues. Unfortunate woman! Alas! A moment of going astray causes all your misfortunes and mine. Yes, her heart remained pure, everything assures me so; it is too well known to me to be able to deceive me. Ah, who knows in what skillful traps the perfidious ruses of a woman who is vicious and jealous of her virtues could have taken her innocent simplicity by surprise? Did I not see her regrets, her repentance in her eyes? Is it not her sadness that led me back to her feet, is it not her touching pain that gave me back all my tenderness? Ah, that is not the deceitful behavior of an unfaithful woman who is cheating on her husband and who revels in her treachery!"

Then afterward, happening to reflect more in detail over her behavior and her astonishing declaration, what didn't I feel in seeing that timid and modest woman vanquish shame by means of frankness, reject an esteem to which her heart gave the lie, disdain to preserve my trust and her reputation by hiding a fault that nothing forced her to admit by covering it with caresses that she rejected, and fear to usurp my tenderness as a father for a child that was not of my blood! What force did I not admire in that invincible loftiness of courage that, even at the price of honor and life could not debase itself to falsity, and brought the intrepid audacity of virtue even into crime! "Yes," I said to myself with secret applause, "even in the bosom of ignominy, that strong soul still preserves its resilience; it is guilty without being contemptible; it may have committed a crime, but not an act of cowardice."

This is how, little by little, my heart's inclination brought me back in her favor to gentler and more bearable judgments. Without justifying her I excused her; without pardoning her affronts, I approved her good conduct. I took pleasure in these feelings. I could not get rid of all my love, it would have been too cruel to preserve it without esteem. As soon as I believed I still owed it to her, I felt an unhoped-for relief. Man is too weak to be able to preserve extreme emotions for very long. In the very excess of despair providence arranges some consolations for us. In spite of the horror of my fate I felt a sort of joy in representing Sophie to myself as estimable and unhappy; I loved to give this foundation to the interest that I could not stop taking in her. In place of the dry-eyed pain that consumed me earlier, I felt the sweetness of being moved to the point of tears. "She is lost forever for me, I know it," I said to myself, "but at least I shall still dare to think of her, I shall dare to regret her, I shall sometimes still dare to moan and sigh without blushing."

Meanwhile I had pursued my route and, distracted by these ideas, I had walked the whole day without noticing it, until finally returning to myself and, no longer being sustained by the animosity of the day before, I felt a lassitude and an exhaustion that required nourishment and rest. Thanks to the exercises of my youth I was robust and strong. I feared neither hunger nor fatigue; but my sick mind had tormented my body, and you had protected me against violent passions much more than you had taught me to bear them. I had trouble reaching a village that was still a league away from me. As I had not taken any food for almost thirty-six hours, I dined, and even with appetite: I went to bed freed from the furors that had tormented me so much, satisfied at daring to think of Sophie, and almost joyful at imagining her to be less disfigured and more worthy of my regrets than I had hoped.

I slept peacefully until morning. Sadness and misfortune respect sleep and leave respite to the soul; only remorse leaves it none at all. Upon rising I felt my mind calm enough and in a condition to deliberate over what I had to do. But this was the most memorable as well as the cruelest period of my life. All of my attachments were ruptured or altered, all my duties had changed; I was no longer attached to anything in the same manner as before, I was becoming, so to speak, a new being. It was important to weigh the decision I had to make maturely. I made a provisional one in order to give me the leisure to reflect about it. I completed the path that was left to take to the closest town; I entered a master's home, and I set myself to work at my trade,[5] while waiting until the fermentation of my spirits had completely subsided, and I could see objects as they were.

I never felt the force of education better than in these cruel circumstances. Born with a weak soul, tender to all impressions, easy to disturb, timid at resolving, after the first moments given up to nature, I found myself master of myself and capable of considering my own situation with as much coolness as that of someone else. Subject to the law of necessity I ended my vain murmurs, I bent my will under the inevitable yoke, I regarded the past as foreign to me, I thought of myself as beginning to be born and, drawing the rules for my conduct from my present condition, while waiting to be well-enough informed about it, I set myself peacefully to work as if I had been the most content of men.

From childhood there is nothing that I learned so much from you as to be entirely where I am, never to do one thing and dream about another—which properly is to do nothing and to be entirely nowhere. Thus I was attentive to nothing but my labor during the day: in the evening I took up my reflections again and, relieving the mind and the body by each other without ever tiring either of the two, I made as good use of them as I could.

From the first night, following the thread of my ideas of the day before, I examined whether perhaps I was taking a woman's crime too much to heart, and whether what appeared to me as a catastrophe of my life was not too common an event to need to be taken so seriously. "It is certain," I said to myself, "that wherever morals are held in esteem the infidelities of women dishonor the husbands; but it is also certain that in all big cities, and anywhere where men, being more corrupt, believe themselves more enlightened, this opinion is held to be ridiculous and hardly sensible. 'Does a man's honor,' they say, 'depend on his wife? Must his misfortune cause his shame, and can he be dishonored by someone else's vices?' The other morality might well be more severe; this one appears more in conformity with reason.

"Moreover, whatever judgment people might pass on my behavior by my own principles, wasn't I above public opinion? What did it matter to me what people might think of me, provided that in my own heart I did not stop being good, just, decent? Was it a crime to be merciful? Was it an act of cowardice to pardon an offense? Based on what duties was I going to rule myself, then? Had I disdained men's prejudice for so long in order to sacrifice my happiness to it in the end?

"But even if this prejudice were well-founded, what influence can it have in a case so different from others? What relationship is there between an unfortunate woman in despair, from whom remorse alone tore the admission of her crime, and those faithless ones who cover theirs with lying and fraud, or who put effrontery in the place of frankness and boast about their dishonor? Every vicious woman, every woman who despises her duty even more than she offends against it is unworthy of consideration; to tolerate her infamy is to share it. But the one who is reproached more for a fault than a vice and who expiates it by her regrets is more worthy of pity than of hatred; one can feel sorry for her and pardon her without shame; the unhappiness for which she is reproached is a warrant for her for the future. Sophie, having remained estimable even in crime, will be respectable in her repentance; she will be all the more faithful because her heart made for virtue has felt what it costs to offend against it; she will have at the same time the firmness that preserves virtue and the modesty that makes it lovable; the humiliation of remorse will soften that prideful soul and make the empire that love gave her over me less tyrannical; she will be more careful and less proud for it;[6] she will have committed a fault only in order to cure herself of a defect."

When the passions cannot overcome us uncovered they put on the mask of wisdom in order to take us by surprise, and it is by imitating the language of reason that they make us renounce it. All these sophisms imposed on me only because they flattered my inclination. I would have wanted to be able to return to unfaithful Sophie, and I listened with indulgence to everything that seemed to authorize my cowardice. But try as I might, my reason, less tractable than my heart, could not adopt these follies. I could not dissimulate to myself that I was arguing in order to impose on myself, not in order to enlighten myself. I said to myself sadly but forcefully that the maxims of high society do not constitute a law for someone who wants to live for himself, and that, prejudice for prejudice, those of good morals have an additional one that favors them; that it is with reason that one imputes a wife's disorders to her husband, either for having chosen her badly, or for governing her badly; that I myself was an example of the justice of this imputation, and that if Emile had always been wise Sophie would never have been at fault; that one has the right to presume that the one who does not respect herself at least respects her husband, if he is worthy of it, and if he knows how to preserve his authority; that the wrong of not having prevented the dissoluteness of a wife is aggravated by the infamy of putting up with it, that the consequences of impunity are frightening, and that in such a case this impunity shows an indifference for decent morals in the offended man, and a baseness of soul unworthy of all honor.

Above all in my particular case I felt that what rendered Sophie still estimable was all the more hopeless for me: for one can support or reinforce a weak soul, and the one whom forgetfulness of duty causes to fail in it can be brought back to it by reason; but how to bring back the one who keeps, while sinning, all her courage, who knows how to have virtues in crime and does evil only as she is pleased by it? "Yes, Sophie is guilty because she wanted to be so. If that lofty soul could overcome shame, it could overcome every other passion; it would not have cost her any more to be faithful to me than to declare her heinous crime to me.

"In vain would I return to my Wife, she would no longer return to me. If the one who loved me so much, if the one who was so dear to me could offend against me, if my Sophie could break the first bonds of her heart, if the mother of my son could violate the still complete conjugal faith, if the fires of a love that nothing had offended against, if the noble pride[7] of a virtue that nothing had impaired, could not prevent her first fault, what would prevent relapses that no longer cost anything? The first step toward vice is the only painful one; one continues without even thinking about it. She no longer has either love, or virtue, or esteem to husband: she no longer has anything to lose by offending against me, not even regret at offending against me. She knows my heart, she has made me altogether as unhappy as I can be; it will no longer cost her anything to bring it to its term.

"No, I know her heart; never will Sophie love a man to whom she has given the right to despise her . . . She does not love me any more . . . hasn't the ingrate said it herself? She does not love me any more, the faithless woman! Ah! That is her greatest crime: I could have pardoned everything, aside from that."

"Alas!" I resumed bitterly, "I am still speaking about pardoning without considering that the offended one often pardons, but that the offender never does. Doubtless she wishes me all the evil that she has done me. Ah! How much she must hate me!

"Emile, how you mislead yourself when you judge about the future based on the past! Everything is changed. In vain would you still live with her; the happy days that she has given you will not come back again. You will no longer find your Sophie again, and Sophie will no longer find you again. Situations depend on the affections one brings to them: when hearts change, everything changes; even if everything remained the same, when one no longer has the same eyes one no longer sees anything as before.

"Her morals are not at all hopeless, I know it well: she can still be worthy of esteem, deserve all my tenderness; she can give me back her heart; but she cannot have not fallen, nor lose—and take away from me—the memory of her fault. Fidelity, virtue, love—all can come back, except for trust, and without trust there is no longer anything but disgust, sadness, boredom in marriage; the delightful charm of innocence has vanished. It is done, it is done, Sophie cannot be happy any longer either close or far, and I can be happy only from her happiness. That alone decides me; I prefer to suffer far from her than by her: I would rather regret her than torment her.

"Yes, all our bonds are broken, they are broken by her. By violating her engagements, she set me free from mine. She is no longer anything to me; hasn't she even said so? She is no longer my wife. Would I see her again as a stranger? No, I shall never see her again. I am free; at least I must be so: would that my heart were as free as my faith!

"But what! Will my affront remain unpunished? If the unfaithful woman loves someone else, what ill do I do her by releasing her from me? I am the one that I am punishing and not her: I am fulfilling her wishes at my expense. Is that the resentment of insulted honor? Where is justice, where is vengeance?

"Eh! Wretch, upon what do you wish to avenge yourself? Upon the person whom your greatest despair is to be unable to make her happy any longer. At least do not be the victim of your own vengeance. Do her, if it is possible, some ill that you do not feel. There are some crimes that must be abandoned to the remorse of the guilty; to punish them is almost to authorize them. Does a cruel husband deserve a faithful wife? Moreover by what right punish her, by what title? Are you her judge when you are not even her husband any more? When she violated her duties as a wife she did not preserve her rights as wife for herself. From the moment that she formed other ties, she broke yours and did not hide herself at all; she did not at all adorn herself in your eyes with a fidelity that she no longer had; she neither betrayed you, nor lied to you. In ceasing to be yours alone she declared that she was no longer anything to you: what authority can you have left over her? If you did have any left, you should abdicate it for your own advantage. Believe me, be good out of wisdom and clement out of vengeance. Distrust anger; be afraid that it might bring you back to her feet."

Thus tempted, either by the love that was calling me back or by the spite that wanted to seduce me, how many struggles did I have to make before being completely decided; and when I believed I was, a new reflection overturned everything. The idea of my son softened me toward his mother more than anything had done previously. I felt that this meeting point would always keep her from being a stranger to me, that children form a truly indissoluble bond between those who have given them life, and a natural and invincible reason against divorce. Such dear objects from which neither of the two can estrange themselves necessarily bring them closer to each other; it is a common interest that is so tender that it would take the place of society for them, if they did not have any other. But what became of this reason, which pleaded for the mother of my son, when applied to the mother of a child that was not mine? What! Nature itself will authorize crime; and my wife, by dividing her tenderness between her two sons, will be forced to divide her attachment between two fathers! This idea, more horrible than any that had entered into my mind set me ablaze with a new rage; all the furies came back to rend my heart as I thought about that horrible division. Yes, I would have preferred to see my son dead rather than to see one from another father belonging to Sophie. This imagination embittered me more, alienated me more from her than everything that had been tormenting me up to then. From that moment I decided irrevocably and, in order to leave no more foothold for doubt, I ceased to deliberate.

This well-formed resolution extinguished all my resentment. She was dead to me: I no longer saw her as guilty; I no longer saw her as anything but estimable and unhappy, and without thinking of her wrongs, I recalled with tenderness everything that made me regret her loss. As a consequence of that disposition I wanted to include in my proceedings all the good behavior that can console an abandoned wife; for, whatever I might have claimed to think of her in my anger, and whatever she might have said about it in her despair, I did not doubt that in the depths of her heart she was still attached to me, and that she felt my loss keenly. The first effect of our separation must be to take my son away from her. I shuddered at merely considering it, and after not knowing how to obtain vengeance, I could hardly bear the idea of that one. Tell myself as I might, while getting myself angry, that this child would soon be replaced by a different one, lean as I might on this cruel supplement with all the force of jealousy—all that did not hold up before the image of Sophie in despair at seeing herself torn from her child. Nevertheless I mastered myself; not without a wrench did I form that barbarous resolution, and regarding it as a necessary consequence of the first (in which I was certain of having reasoned well), I would certainly have executed it in spite of my repugnance if an unforeseen event had not constrained me to examine it better.

Another deliberation was left for me to make that I counted as hardly anything after the one that I had just extracted from myself. I had made my decision in relation to Sophie; I still had to make it in relation to myself, and to see what I wanted to become upon finding myself alone again. It had been a long time since I had been only an isolated being on the earth: as you had predicted to me, my heart held onto the attachments it had given itself. It had accustomed itself to being indissolubly united to my family; it was necessary to detach it from them, at least in part, and that was even more painful than to detach it completely. What a void is made in us, how much does one lose of one's existence when one has depended on so many things and one must no longer depend on anything but oneself—or what is worse, on what makes us ceaselessly feel our detachment from the rest. I had to seek whether I was still that man who knows how to fill his place in his species when no individual takes an interest in it any longer.

But where is that place for the one for whom all of his supports have been destroyed or changed? What to do, what to become? Where to direct my steps, for what to use a life that was no longer to constitute my happiness nor that of what was dear to me, and in which fate was depriving me even of the hope of contributing to anyone's happiness? For, if so many instruments prepared for my own had caused only my misery, could I hope to be more fortunate for anyone else than you had been for me? No, I still loved my duty but I no longer saw it. To recall its principles and rules, to apply them to) my new condition was not the business of a moment, and my tired mind needed a little respite in order to give itself over to new meditations.

I had made a great step toward peace. Freed from the uneasiness of hope, and certain of losing that of desire little by little this way, seeing that the past was no longer anything to me, I was trying to put myself completely in the condition of a man who is beginning to live. I said to myself that in fact we are never doing anything but beginning, and that there is no connection in our existence other than a succession of present moments, the first of which is always the one that is happening. We die and we are born every instant of our lives, and what interest can death leave us? If there is nothing for us other than what will be, we can be happy or unhappy only from the future, and to torment oneself about the past is to draw subjects of our misery from nothingness. "Emile, be a new man, you will no more have to complain about fate than about nature. Your misfortunes are null, the abyss of nothingness has swallowed them all; but what is real, what is existant for you is your life, your health, your youth, your reason, your talents, your enlightenment, your virtues, in sum, if you wish it, and consequently your happiness."

I resumed my labor, peacefully waiting for my ideas to arrange themselves in my head well enough to show me what I had to do, and, nevertheless, upon comparing my condition to the one that had preceded it I was calm; that is the advantage that all conduct in conformity with reason procures independently of events. If one is not happy in spite of fortune, when one knows how to maintain one's heart in order, one is at least calm in spite of fate. But how precarious this calm is in a sensitive soul! It is very easy to put oneself into order; what is difficult is to stay there. I nearly saw all my resolutions overturned at the moment that I believed them to be most solidified.

I had entered into the master's home without making myself noticed very much. In my clothing I had always preserved the simplicity that you had made me love; my manners were not any more elaborate, and the easy air of a man who feels himself in his place everywhere was less noticeable in a carpenter's home than in a Grandee's. Nevertheless it was obvious that my attire was not that of a worker; but, from my manner of setting myself to work they judged that I had been one, and that afterward, having advanced to some small position, I had lost it to return to my first station. A little parvenu who has fallen back does not inspire much consideration, and I was taken just about at my word concerning the equality into which I had put myself. Suddenly I saw the whole family's tone change toward me. Familiarity took on more reserve, at labor I was regarded with a sort of astonishment; everything that I did in the workshop (and I did everything better than the master) stirred up admiration; all my movements, all my gestures seemed to be closely watched. They tried to treat me as usual, but they could no longer do so without an effort, and one might have said that it was out of respect that they abstained from showing me any more respect. The ideas with which I was preoccupied kept me from noticing this change as soon as I would have done at any other time: but, quickly being brought back to what was being done around me by my habit in acting of always being wholly involved in the thing, it did not allow me to remain unaware for very long that for these good people I had become an object of curiosity that interested them very much.

Above all I noticed that the wife's eyes never left me. This sex has a sort of right over men without means that make them more interesting to it in some way. I did not make a stroke of the graver without her appearing frightened, and I saw her completely surprised that I had not wounded myself. "Madame," I said to her once, "I see that you do not trust my skill; are you afraid that I might not know my trade?" "Sir," she said to me, "I see that you know ours well; one would say that you have done nothing but that your whole life." At that word[8] I saw that I was known: I wanted to know how that had happened. After a great deal of secrecy, I learned that a young Lady had happened to get out of a carriage two days before at the master's door, that she had wanted to see me without permitting me to be notified, that she had stopped behind a door with a window in it from where she could perceive me at the back of the workshop, that she had gotten on her knees at that door with a small child beside her whom by intervals she squeezed in her arms with rapture, heaving long half-stifled sobs, shedding torrents of tears, and giving various signs of a suffering by which all the witnesses had been keenly moved; that several times they had seen her at the point of throwing herself into the workshop, that she had appeared to hold herself back only by violent efforts upon herself; that finally, after having gazed at me for a long time with more attentiveness and meditation, she had suddenly gotten up, and, pressing the child's face to her own, she had cried out in a low voice: *"No, he will never want to take your mother away from you; come, we have nothing to do here."* At these words she had left hurriedly; then after having gotten them to agree that they would say nothing about it to me, to get back in her carriage and leave in a flash was for her the work of an instant.

They added that the keen interest that they could not help having for that lovable Lady had kept them faithful to the promise they had made her and that she had demanded with such entreaties, that they were failing to keep it only with regret, that they saw easily from her attire, and even more from her features that this was a person of a high rank, and that they could not presume anything else from what she had done and her speech than that this woman was my wife, for it was impossible to take her for a kept woman.

Judge what passed in me during this narrative! How many things did all that imply! What anxieties must there have been, what researches must have been made in order to find my trail again this way? Does all that come from someone who does not love any longer? What a voyage! What motive could have caused her to undertake it! In what occupation had she caught me! Ah! This was not the first time: but then she was not on her knees, she did not melt into tears.[9] Oh times, happy times! What has happened to that angel from heaven? . . . But what is this woman doing here? . . . she brings her son . . . my son . . . and why? . . . Did she want to see me, speak to me? Why take flight? . . . to defy me? . . . Why in tears? What does she want from me, the faithless one? Does she come to insult me in my misery? Has she forgotten that she is no longer anything to me? I sought in some manner to get angry about this voyage in order to overcome the tender feelings that it was causing me, in order to resist the temptations to run after the unfortunate woman that were agitating me in spite of myself. Nevertheless, I stayed. I saw that this step did not prove anything except that I was still loved, and, as that very assumption had entered into my deliberation, it ought not to change anything in the decision it had caused me to make.

Then examining all the circumstances of this trip more calmly, weighing above all the last words that she had pronounced upon leaving, I believed that in them I disentangled the motive that had brought her and the one that had made her leave again suddenly without allowing herself to be seen. Sophie spoke simply, but everything she said brought shafts of light into my heart, and these few words were one of them. *"He will not take your mother from you,"* had she said? Thus it was the fear that he would be taken from her that had brought her, and it was the persuasion that this would not happen that had made her leave again. And from what did she draw that persuasion? What had she seen? Emile at peace, Emile at work. What proof could she draw from that sight, other than that in that condition Emile was not at all subjugated by his passions, and was forming nothing but reasonable resolutions? Thus, according to her, that of separating her from her son was not one, although according to me it was: which was wrong? Sophie's statement also settled this point; and, in fact, considering the child's interest alone, could that even be doubted? I had envisaged only the child taken away from the mother, and it was necessary to envisage the mother taken away from the child. Thus I was wrong. To take a mother away from her son is to take away from him more than one can return to him, especially at that age; it is to sacrifice the child in order to avenge oneself on the mother: it is an act of passion, never of reason, unless the mother is mad or denatured. But Sophie is the mother that should be desired for my son even if he had a different one. No longer being able to bring him up together, either she or I must bring him up, or he must be made into an orphan in order to satisfy my anger. But what shall I do with a child in the condition I am in? I have enough reason to see what I can or cannot do, not to do what I ought to. Shall I drag a child of that age into other countries, or shall I keep him under his mother's eyes, in order to defy a woman I ought to flee? Ah! For my own safety I shall never be far enough from her! Let us leave her the child, out of fear that he will bring the father back to her in the end. May he remain with her for my sole vengeance; may he recall to the unfaithful woman every day of his life the happiness of which he was the token and the husband whom she has taken away from herself.

It is certain that the resolution of taking my son away from his mother had been the effect of my anger. On this point alone passion had blinded me, and this was also the only point on which I changed my resolution. If my family had followed my intentions, Sophie would have brought up that child, and perhaps he would still be alive; but perhaps also from that point on Sophie would have been dead to me; consoled in that dear half of myself she might no longer have considered rejoining the other, and I would have lost the finest days of my life. How many sufferings were to make us expiate our faults before our reunion made us forget them!

We both knew each other so well that in order to guess the motive of her sudden retreat I needed only to feel that she had foreseen what would have happened if we had seen each other again. I was reasonable but weak, she knew it; and I knew even better how much inflexibility that sublime and proud soul preserved even in its faults. The idea of Sophie returned to favor was unbearable to her. She felt that her crime was one of those that cannot be forgotten; she preferred to be punished rather than pardoned: such a pardon was not made for her; to her taste even punishment debased her less. She believed that she could not erase her fault except by expiating it, nor do what justice obliged her to do except by undergoing all the evils she deserved. It is for that reason that, intrepid and barbarous in her frankness, she told her crime to you, to my whole family, at the same time remaining silent about what excused her, what perhaps justified her, hiding it, I say, with such obstinacy that she never told me a word about it, and that I never knew it until after her death.

Moreover, reassured about the fear of losing her son, she had nothing more to desire from me for herself. To move me to pity would be to debase me, and she was all the more jealous of my honor because she did not have any other left. Sophie could be criminal, but the husband that she had chosen for herself must be above an act of cowardice. These refinements of her amour-propre could not suit anyone but her, and perhaps I was the only one capable of penetrating them.

Even after having been separated from her, I also had this obligation to her for having brought me back from an unreasonable decision that vengeance had caused me to make. In the good opinion that she had of me she had been deceived on this point, but this error no longer was one as soon as I thought about it; upon considering only my son's interest I saw that it was necessary to leave him to his mother, and I made up my mind to do so. Moreover, confirmed in my sentiments, I resolved to distance his unhappy father from the risks that he had just been running. Could I be far enough away from her, as I must no longer draw near her? It was again she; it was her voyage that had just given me that wise lesson: in order to follow it, it was important for me not to remain in the position of receiving it twice

I had to flee; that was my great business, and the consequence of all my prior reasonings. But where to flee? It was upon that deliberation that I had remained, and I had not seen that there was nothing more indifferent than the choice of the place, so long as I went away. What good was it to hesitate over my retreat, as everywhere I would find what to live on or die, and that that was all that I had left to do? What stupidity of amour-propre always to show us all of nature concerned with the petty events of our life! Seeing me deliberate over my abode, wouldn't someone have said that it mattered a great deal to the human race that I went to live in one country rather than another, and that the weight of my body was going to rupture the equilibrium of the globe? If I estimated my existence only at what it was worth for my fellows, I would make myself less uneasy about going to seek duties to fulfill—as if they would not follow me wherever I might be, and as if as many of them as can be fulfilled by the one who loves them did not always turn up. I would say to myself that wherever I live, in whatever situation I might be, I shall always find my task as a man to perform, and no one would need others if each lived suitably for himself.

The wise man lives from day to day and finds all his daily duties around him. Let us not attempt anything beyond our strength and let us not carry our existence forward. My duties of today are my sole task, those of tomorrow have not yet come. What I ought to do at present is to distance myself from Sophie, and the path that I ought to choose is the one that takes me away from her most directly. Let us limit ourselves to that.

Having made this resolution, I put the order that depended on me into everything that I was leaving behind; I wrote to you, I wrote to my family, I wrote to Sophie herself. I put everything in order, I forgot nothing but the cares that could concern my person; none were necessary for me, and without valet, without money, without retinue, but without desires and without cares, I left alone and on foot: among the Peoples where I have lived, on the seas that I have traveled over, in the deserts I have crossed, wandering for so many years, I have regretted only one single thing, and that was the one whom I had to flee. If my heart had left me calm, my body would have lacked nothing.

Second Letter

"I have drunk the water of forgetfulness; the past is erased from my Memory and the universe is opening before me." That is what I said to myself upon leaving my Fatherland about which I had to blush, and to which I owed only disdain and hatred: because, happy and worthy of honor by myself, from it and its base inhabitants I had only the ills to which I was prey, and the opprobrium into which I had been plunged. In breaking the bonds that attached me to my country I extended it over the whole earth; and, in ceasing to be a Citizen, I became all the more a man.

In my long voyages I have noticed that it is only the remoteness of the end that makes the trip difficult. It never is difficult to go one day's journey from where one is, and why wish to do any more, if from day to day one can go to the end of the earth. But by comparing the extremities one takes fright at the gap; it seems that one must cross it with one leap, whereas by taking it by parts one merely takes some walks and one arrives. Travelers, always surrounding themselves with their practices, their habits, their prejudices, all their factitious needs, have, so to speak, an atmosphere that separates them from where they are, as so many other worlds different from their own. A Frenchman would want to carry all of France with him; as soon as he lacks something that he had, he counts the equivalents for nothing, and believes himself lost. Always comparing what he finds to what he has left, he believes he is ill when he is not in his own mode, and cannot sleep in the Indies if his bed is not made exactly as it is in Paris.

As for me, I followed the direction contrary to the object that I had to flee, as previously I had followed the opposite one from the shadow in the forest of Montmorency.[10] The speed that I did not put into my pace was compensated for by the firm resolution of not going backward at all. Two days of walking had already closed the barrier behind me by leaving me the time to reflect during my return, if I had been tempted to consider it. In taking myself away I drew breath, and I walked more at my ease in measure as I escaped the danger. Limited to the sole plan that I was executing, my only rule was to follow the same direction of the wind; sometimes I walked quickly, sometimes slowly, according to my convenience, my health, my mood, my strength. Provided, not with me, but in me, with more resources than I needed for living, I was troubled about neither my carriage nor my means of existence. I did not fear robbers at all; my purse and my passport were in my arms: my clothing formed my entire luggage; it was convenient and good for a workman. I renewed it without difficulty as it wore out. Because I was walking with neither the apparatus nor the uneasiness of a traveler, I did not excite anyone's attention; everywhere I passed for a man of the country. I was rarely stopped at borders, and when that did happen, it hardly mattered to me, I stayed there without impatience, I worked there exactly the same as anywhere else, I would have passed my life there without any difficulty if they had always retained me, and my lack of a hurry to go any farther finally opened all pathways to me. The preoccupied and worried air is always suspect, but a calm man inspires confidence; everyone left me free when they saw that they could dispose of me without getting me angry.

When I did not find any work in my trade, which was rare, I did other kinds. You had made me acquire the universal instrument.[11] Sometimes peasant, sometimes artisan, sometimes artist, sometimes even a man of talents, everywhere I had some knowledge that had currency, and I made myself master of their practice by means of my lack of hurry in showing off. One of the fruits of my education was to be taken at my word about what I gave myself out as, and nothing more; because I was simple in everything, and because in filling a post I did not angle for another one. Thus I was always in my place and I was always left there.

If I fell sick, a very rare accident in a man of my temperament who commits no excess, neither with foods, nor cares, nor labor, nor rest, I kept quiet, without tormenting myself about being cured, or frightening myself about dying. The sick animal fasts, remains in place, and is cured or dies; I did the same, and I found myself well for it. If I had made myself uneasy about my condition, if I had importuned people with my fears and my complaints, they would have been annoyed with me, I would have inspired less interest and attentiveness than my patience gave. Seeing that I did not disturb anyone, that I did not lament over myself, they were the first to do me a good turn that they would perhaps have refused me if I had implored them. A hundred times I have observed that the more one wants to demand from others, the more one disposes them to a refusal: they love to act freely, and if they ever do so much as to be good they want to have all the credit for it. To ask for a benefit is to acquire a sort of right to it; to grant it is almost a duty, and amour-propre would rather make a free gift than pay a debt.

In these pilgrimages, which would have been blamed in high society as the life of a vagabond because I did not make them with the pomp of an opulent traveler, if I sometimes asked myself: "What am I doing? Where am I going? What is my goal?" I answered myself, "What did I do in being born other than to begin a voyage that must end only at my death? I am performing my task, I am staying in my place, I am using up this short life with innocence and simplicity, I am still doing a great good by the evil that I am not doing among my fellows, I am providing for my needs by providing for theirs, I am serving them without ever harming them, I am giving them the example of being happy and good without cares and without trouble: I have repudiated my patrimony, and I am living; I do not do anything unjust, and I am living; I do not demand any charity at all, and I am living. Thus I am useful to others in proportion to my subsistence: for men do not give anything for nothing."

As I am not undertaking the history of my travels, I am passing over everything that is only descriptive. I arrive at Marseille: in order always to follow the same direction, I embark for Naples; it is a question of paying for my passage; you had provided for it by making me learn rigging: it is not any more difficult on the Mediterranean than on the Ocean, the entire difference was some changes of terms. I make myself into a sailor. The captain of the ship, a sort of puffed-up boss, was a renegade[12] who had been repatriated. He had been taken since by the Corsairs, and said that he had escaped from their hands without having been recognized. Some Neapolitan Merchants had entrusted another vessel to him and he was making his second trip since this reestablishment. He told his life to anyone who wanted to listen to it, and knew so well how to make himself important that while amusing he inspired confidence. His tastes were as bizarre as his adventures. He thought of nothing but diverting his crew: he had on board two pathetic pierriers[13] that he shot all day long; all night long he shot flares; never has a Boss of a ship been seen to be so gay.

As for me I amused myself by practicing seamanship, and when it was not my watch, I did not remain any less on the rigging or at the helm.[14] Attentiveness took the place of experience for me, and I did not delay in judging that we were veering very much to the west. The compass was nevertheless at the appropriate angle; but the course of the sun and the stars seemed to me to contradict its direction so strongly that according to me the needle had to be deviating prodigiously. I said so to the Captain; he beat around the bush while making fun of me, and as the sea was rising and the weather became hazy, it was not possible for me to verify my observations. We had a violent wind that cast us into the open sea; it lasted for two days: on the third we noticed land at our left. I asked the Boss what it was. He said to me: a possession of the Church. A sailor maintained that it was the coast of Sardinia; he was hooted at and paid for his welcome in that manner; for although he was an old sailor, he was new to this crew, just as I was.

It hardly mattered to me where we were; but because what that man had said reawakened my curiosity, I set myself to ferreting about the binnacle, in order to see whether some piece of iron put there inadvertently was not making the needle deviate. What was my surprise at finding a large magnet hidden in a corner![15] Upon removing it from its place I saw the needle moving to take back its direction. At the same moment someone shouted: "Sail!" The Boss looked with his Telescope, and said that it was a small French Ship; as its heading was toward us and we were not avoiding it, it was soon in plain sight, and everyone saw then that it was a Barbary sail. Three Neapolitan merchants that we had on board with all their property cried to high heaven. Then the enigma became clear to me. I drew near the Boss, and whispered in his ear: *"Boss, if we are taken, you are dead; count on that."* I had appeared so little moved, and I made him this speech in such a composed voice, that he hardly became alarmed and even pretended not to have heard it.

He gave some orders for defense, but not a weapon was found in condition, and we had burned so much powder that when we wished to charge the Pierriers there was barely enough left for two rounds. Defence would even have been quite useless to us; as soon as we were within range, instead of deigning to shoot at us, they shouted out to us to strike our colors, and we were boarded almost at the same instant. Until then the Boss, without seeming to do so, was observing me with some distrust: as soon as he saw the Corsairs onboard us, however, he

stopped paying attention to me and made his way toward them carelessly. At that moment I believed myself to be judge and executioner, in
order to avenge my companions in slavery, by purging the human race
of a traitor and the sea of one of its monsters. I ran to him and shout-
ing to him: *"I promised you, I am keeping my word,"* I made his head
fly off with a saber I had grabbed. Instantly, seeing the Leader of the
Barbary men coming impetuously toward me, I waited for him reso-
lutely, and presenting him the saber by the handle I said to him in the
lingua franca: *"Here Captain, I have just done justice; you can do it in
your turn."* He took the saber, he raised it over my head; I waited for the
blow silently: he smiled and, taking my hand, he forbade them to put
me in irons with the others. But he did not speak to me at all about the
armed enterprise that he had seen me perform; which confirmed to me
that he knew the reason for it well enough. This distinction, moreover,
lasted only until the port of Algiers, and upon landing we were sent to
the Prison, leashed together like hunting dogs.

   Until then, attentive to everything I saw, I was hardly occupied with
myself. But finally, when the first agitation had stopped, it allowed me to
reflect upon my change of condition, and the sentiment that still occupied me in its entire force made me say inside with a sort of satisfaction:
"Of what will this event deprive me? The power of doing something
stupid. I am more free than before." "Emile a slave!" I resumed, "Ah!
In what sense? What have I lost of my primitive freedom? Was I not
born a slave of necessity? What new yoke can men impose on me? Work?
Did I not work when I was free? Hunger? How many times have I willingly suffered it! Pain? All human force will not give me any more of it
than a grain of sand made me feel. Constraint? Will it be any rougher
than that of my first chains, and I did not want to leave them. Subjected
to human passions by my birth, whether their yoke is imposed on me
by someone else or by myself, is it not always necessary to bear it, and
who knows from what direction it will be more bearable to me? At least
I shall have all my reason to moderate them in someone else; how many
times has it not abandoned me in mine? Who will be able to make me
bear two chains? Did I not bear one before? There is no real servitude
other than that of nature. Men are only its instruments. Whether a master fells me or a rock crushes me, to my eyes it is the same event, and the
worst that can happen to me in slavery is not to move a tyrant to pity
any more than a stone. In the end if I had my freedom, what would I do
with it? In the condition I am in, what can I want? Ah! In order not to
fall into nothingness I need to be animated by someone else's will for
lack of my own."

From these reflections I drew the conclusion that my change of condition was more apparent than real; that, if freedom consisted in doing what one wills, no man would be free; that all are weak, dependent on things, on harsh necessity; that the one who best knows how to will everything that it orders is the most free, because he is never forced to do what he does not want.

Yes, my father, I can say it; the time of my servitude was that of my reign, and never did I have so much authority over myself as when I bore the chains of the people of Barbary. Subjected to their passions without sharing them, I learned to know my own better. For me their deviations were more lively instructions than your lessons had been, and under these rough masters I took a course in Philosophy even more useful than the one I had taken with you.

Nevertheless I did not experience all the rigors that I expected from servitude to them. I endured some bad treatment, but less, perhaps, than they would have endured among us, and I knew that these names of Moors and pirates carried with them prejudices from which I had not defended myself well enough. They are not inclined to pity but they are just, and, if neither gentleness nor clemency is to be expected from them, neither must one fear either caprice or wickedness. They want one to do what one can do, but they do not demand any more, and in their punishments they never punish impotence, but only ill-will. The Negroes would be only too happy in America if the European treated them with the same fairness: because, however, he sees in these wretches only instruments of labor, his behavior toward them depends solely on the utility that he draws from them; he measures his justice based on his profit.

Several times I changed owners: they called that selling me, as if one could ever sell a man. They sold the labor of my hands; but they certainly did not sell my will, my understanding, my being, everything by which I was myself and not someone else; and the proof of that is that the first time that I wanted the opposite of what my so-called master wanted, I was the one who was the victor. That event deserves to be recounted.

At first I was treated gently enough; they counted on my being redeemed, and for several months I lived in an inactivity that would have bored me if I could know boredom. But finally seeing that I was not scheming with the European Consuls and the Monks, that no one was speaking about my ransom and that I appeared not to be considering it myself, they wanted to put me to good use in some manner, and they made me work. This change neither surprised nor angered me. I feared hard labor little, but I preferred more amusing labor. I found the way to enter a workshop whose master did not take long to understand that I was his master in his trade. Because this labor became more lucrative for my owner than the one that he was making me do, he set me up for his advantage and made out well for doing so.

I had seen almost all of my former comrades of the prison dispersed. Those who could be ransomed had been. Those who could not be had had the same fate as I had, but not all had found the same softening. Among others, two knights of Malta[16] had been abandoned. Their families were poor: the Order does not ransom its captives, and the fathers, not being able to ransom everyone, just like the Consuls, gave a very natural, and not inequitable, preference to those whose gratitude could be more useful to them. These two knights, one young and the other old, were educated and did not lack merit, in their station. But this merit was lost in their present situation. They knew Strategy, tactics, Latin, fine literature. They had talents for shining, for commanding—which were not a great resource for slaves. In addition they bore their chains very impatiently, and philosophy, upon which they piqued themselves extremely, had not at all taught these proud gentlemen to serve commoners and bandits with a good grace; for they did not call their masters anything different. I pitied these two poor people; having renounced the station of men by their nobility, in Algiers they were no longer anything, they were even less than nothing. For among the corsairs, an enemy corsair made into a slave is very much beneath nothingness. I could not serve the old man except with my advice, which was superfluous to him: for more learned than I was, at least in that science that parades itself, he knew all morality to the bottom, and its precepts were very familiar to him. It was only its practice that he lacked, and one could not bear the yoke of necessity with a worse grace. The young one, even more impatient, but ardent, active, intrepid, lost himself in plans of revolt and conspiracies impossible to execute, and that, always uncovered, did nothing but aggravate his misery. I attempted to stir him up to make efforts following my example and to take advantage of his arms to make his condition more bearable, but he disdained my advice and told me proudly that he knew how to die. "Sir," I said to him, "it would be even better to know how to live." Nevertheless I succeeded in procuring him some relief that he received with a good grace and as a noble and sensitive soul, but that did not make him savor my views. He continued his plots to procure freedom for himself by means of a bold stroke, but his restless spirit wearied the patience of his master who was also mine. That man distrusted him and me; our relations had appeared suspect to him, and he believed that I was using the conversations, by means of which I was trying to turn him away from his scheming, in order to aid him in it. We were sold to a contractor of public works and condemned to work under the orders of a barbarous overseer, a slave as we were, but who, in order to show himself off to advantage to his master, overwhelmed us with more labors than human force was capable of bearing.

The first days were only games for me. Because they divided up the work to us equally and I was more robust and more spry than all of my comrades, I had accomplished my task before them; after which, I helped the weakest and relieved them of a portion of theirs. But, having noticed my diligence and the superiority of my strength, our overseer kept me from using them for others by doubling my task; and constantly increasing it by degrees, he ended by overloading me to such a point both with labor and blows that in spite of my vigor I was menaced with succumbing soon under the burden. All my companions, the strong as well as the weak, ill-nourished, and more ill-treated were wasting away under the excessive labor.

Because this condition was becoming completely unbearable I resolved to free myself from it at any risk: my young knight, to whom I communicated my resolution, keenly shared it. I knew him to be a man of courage, capable of constancy provided that he was under men's eyes; and as long as it was a question of brilliant actions and heroic virtues, I counted him for certain. My own resources nevertheless were entirely in myself and I did not need anyone's cooperation in order to execute my plan; nevertheless, it was true that it could have a much more advantageous effect executed in concert by my companions in misery and I resolved to propose it to them jointly with the Knight.

It was difficult to get him to agree to make this proposal simply and without preliminary intriguing. We took the mealtime when we were more gathered together and under less surveillance. First I addressed myself in my language to a dozen compatriots I had there, not wanting to speak to them in lingua franca out of fear of being heard by the people of the country. "Comrades," I said to them, "listen to me. What strength I have left cannot last for two more weeks of the labor with which they are overburdening me, and I am one of the more robust of the group; such a violent situation has to end quickly, either by total exhaustion or by a resolution that forestalls it. I am making the latter choice, and beginning tomorrow I am determined to refuse all labor at the risk of my life, and of all the treatment that this refusal must draw to me. My choice is an affair of calculation. If I remain as I am, I must infallibly perish in a very short time and, having no recourse, I am providing myself with one by this sacrifice of a few days. The decision I am making is capable of frightening our inspector and enlightening his master about his genuine interest. If that does not happen, although my fate would be accelerated, it could not be made any worse. This recourse would be tardy and null if my exhausted body were no longer capable of any labor: then, by sparing me, they would have nothing to gain; by finishing me off they would only save my food. Thus it is advisable for me to choose the moment at which my loss is still one for them. If anyone among you finds my reasons to be good, and wishes, following the example of this man of courage, to make the same decision as I do, our number will produce more of an effect and make our tyrants more manageable. But even if he and I are alone, we are not any less resolved to persist in our refusal, and we take you all as witnesses of the manner in which it will be maintained."

This simple speech, simply uttered, was heard without much emotion. Four or five of the group nevertheless told me to count on them and that they would act as I did. The others did not say a word and everything remained calm. The knight, dissatisfied with this tranquillity, spoke more vehemently to his people in his language; their number was great; he loudly gave them animated descriptions of the condition into which we had been reduced and of the cruelty of our executioners. He stirred up their indignation by means of the depiction of our debasement and their ardor by means of the hope for vengeance—finally, he inflamed their courage so much by means of admiration for the strength of soul that knows how to brave torments and that triumphs over power itself that they interrupted him with shouts and all swore to imitate us and to be unshakable even unto death.

The next day, upon our refusal to labor, we were, as we had expected, all very mistreated, uselessly however as to the two of us and as to my three or four companions of the day before, from whom our executioners did not wrest a single cry. But the Knight's work did not hold out so well. The constancy of his fiery compatriots was exhausted in several minutes, and soon by blows with a bludgeon, they were all brought back to labor as gentle as lambs. Outraged at this cowardice the Knight, while he was being tortured himself, loaded them with reproaches and insults to which they did not listen. I tried to appease him over a defection I had foreseen and predicted to him. I knew that the effects of eloquence are lively but momentary. Men who let themselves be moved so easily calm themselves with the same ease: a cold and strong argument does not cause so much effervescence, but when it takes hold it penetrates and the effect that it produces is no longer erased.

The weakness of these poor people produced another effect that I had not expected and that I attribute to national rivalry rather than to the example of our firmness. Those of my compatriots who had not imitated me at all, seeing them returning to labor, hooted at them, left them in their turn, and as if to insult their cowardice, they came to line up around me; this example led to others and soon the revolt became so general that the master, drawn by the noise and the shouts, came himself so as to put order into things.

You understand what our inspector was able to tell him in order to excuse himself and to arouse him against us. He did not fail to designate me as the author of the riot, as a leader of mutineers who was seeking to make himself feared by means of the disturbance he wanted to stir up. The Master looked at me and said to me: "You are the one, then, who is inciting my slaves to cease working? You have just heard the accusation. If you have something to answer, speak." I was struck by this moderation in the first fit of anger of a man greedy for gain threatened with his ruin; at a moment when every European master, touched to the quick for his interest would have begun, without wanting to hear me, by condemning me to a thousand torments. "Boss," I said to him in lingua franca, "you cannot hate us; you do not even know us; we do not hate you either; you are not the author of our ills, you are unaware of them. We know how to bear the yoke of necessity that has subjected us to you. We do not at all refuse to use our strength for your service as fate condemns us to it; but by exceeding it your slave has deprived us of it and is going to ruin you by our loss. Believe me, transfer to a wiser man the authority he is abusing to your harm. Better distributed, your work will not be done any less and you will preserve laborious slaves from whom in time you will draw a much greater profit than the one that he wants to procure for you by overburdening us. Our complaints are just; our demands are moderate. If you do not listen to them, our choice is made; your man has just experienced it; you can do so in your turn."

I stopped talking; the overseer wanted to reply. The boss imposed silence on him. He ran his eyes over my comrades, whose sunken complexion and thinness attested to the truth of my complaints, but whose countenance moreover did not at all proclaim intimidated people. Afterward, having considered me once again: "You appear," he said, "to be a sensible man: I want to know what the situation is. You reprove this slave's behavior; let us see yours in his position; I give it to you and put him into yours." Right away he ordered them to remove my chains and to put them on our overseer; that was done instantly.

I do not need to tell you how I conducted myself in this new post and that is not what is at issue here. My adventure caused a commotion; the care that he took to spread it around drew me the esteem of all of Algiers. Even the Dey heard me spoken of and wanted to see me. My boss, having led me to him and believing that I pleased him, made him a gift of my person. Behold your Emile a slave of the Dey of Algiers.

The rules based on which I had to conduct myself in this new post followed from principles that were not at all unknown to me. We had discussed them during our travels.[17] And their application, although imperfect and very much miniaturized in the case in which I found myself, was certain and infallible moreover in its effects. I shall not speak to you about these tiny details; that is not what is in question between you and me. My success drew my boss's consideration to me.

Assem Oglou had reached the supreme power by means of the most honorable route that can lead to it: for from a simple sailor, passing through all the ranks of the navy and the army, he had successively raised himself to the premier positions of the State and, after the death of his predecessor, he was elected to succeed him by the unanimous vote of the Turks and the Moors, the Men of war, and the men of the law. For twelve years he had filled this difficult post with honor, having to govern an indocile and barbarous people, a restless and mutinous rabble of an army, greedy for disorder and disturbance, and that, not knowing what it desired itself, wanted only to stir things up and cared little whether things went well provided that they went in a different way. One could not complain about his administration, although it did not answer to what was hoped for. He had always maintained a rather calm regency: everything was in better condition than before, commerce and agriculture went along well, the navy was up to strength, the people had bread. But there were not any of those dazzling operations[18]

[*There are several sources of information about how Rousseau intended to complete this story.[19] They are agreed on the fact that Emile would eventually be released by the Dey and would continue his travels. Eventually he would settle on a desert island where he discovers a Spaniard and his young daughter. In one version Emile marries the daughter and then is joined on the island by Sophie, who has been looking for him. Thus, he lives with two wives. In another version, Sophie joins him before his marriage and the young Spanish woman marries someone else. Sophie becomes pregnant and drowns while attempting to detach some oysters from a rock. Emile then reads a letter in which the events leading to her seduction are revealed.*]

Editors' Notes

Abbreviations

Emile
Jean-Jacques Rousseau, *Emile; or, On Education,* trans. Allan Bloom. New York: Basic Books, 1979.

Collected Writings
Jean-Jacques Rousseau, *Collected Writings of Rousseau,* Volumes I–XII. Edited by Roger D. Masters and Christopher Kelly. Hanover, N.H.: University Press of New England, 1991–

Leigh
Jean-Jacques Rousseau, *Correspondance complètes.* Volumes 1–52. Edited by R. A. Leigh. Geneva: Institute et Musée Voltaire, 1965–1998.

Pléiade
Jean-Jacques Rousseau. *Oeuvres complètes,* Volumes 1–5. Paris. NRF–Editions de la Pléiade, 1959–1995.

Introduction

1. Mary Wollstonecraft, *A Vindication of the Rights of Woman,* ed. Ulrich H. Hardt (New York: Whitston Publishing, 1982; originally published in 1792), e.g., 65–67, 90–118, 171–202.

2. See 70–74 below. See, e.g., Sarah Kofman, "Rousseau's Phallocratic Ends," *Hypatia* 3, no. 3 (Fall 1988): 123–136; Carole Pateman, *The Sexual Contract* (Stanford, Calif.: Stanford University Press, 1988), 98–102.

3. E.g., Zillah R. Eisenstein, *The Radical Future of Liberal Feminism* (New York: Longman, 1981), 55–56; Joan B. Landes, *Women and the Public Sphere in the Age of the French Revolution* (Ithaca, N.Y.: Cornell University Press, 1988), 67–69, 85–89; Paul Thomas, "Jean-Jacques Rousseau, Sexist?" *Feminist Studies* 17, no. 2 (Summer 1991): 195–217.

4. E.g., Eva Figes, *Patriarchal Attitudes: Women in Society* (London: Macmillan, 1986), 97–101; Nannerl Keohane, "'But for Her Sex . . .': the Domestication of Sophie," *Revue de l'Université d'Ottawa* 49, nos. 3–4 (1979): 390–400; Susan Moller Okin, *Women in Western Political Thought* (Princeton, N.J.: Princeton University Press, 1979), 99–194.

5. For such discussions by men during this general period, see, e.g., François Poulain de La Barre, *De l'égalité des deux sexes* (1673); Joseph-Antoine Dinouart, *Le Triomphe du sexe, ouvrage dans lequel on démontre que les femmes sont en tout égales aux hommes* (1749); Philippe Joseph Caffiaux, *Défenses du beau sexe* (1753); Diderot, *Essai sur les Femmes* (1772); Claude-Adrien Helvétius, *De l'homme* (1773); Riballier, *De l'Education physique et morale des femmes* (1779).

6. See 63–64 and 269 below.

7. See 39–51 below.

8. E.g., *Preface to Narcissus, Collected Writings* II, 193; *First Discourse, Collected Writings* II, 4–5; *Discourse on the Origin and Foundations of Inequality Among Men*, or *Second Discourse, Collected Writings* III, 15.

9. Among the most prominent of these Enlightenment thinkers are Locke and Hobbes, to whom Rousseau repeatedly refers as among his principal adversaries. See Hobbes, *On the Citizen*, I–IV; Hobbes, *Leviathan*, VI–VIII, XI–XV; Locke, *Second Treatise of Government*, I–V, VII–VIII, XI. On Hobbes as one of Rousseau's principal interlocutors, see, e.g., Robert Derathé, *Jean-Jacques Rousseau et la science politique de son temps* (Paris: Librairie Philosophique J. Vrin, 1970), 110; Pierre Manent, *An Intellectual History of Liberalism*, trans. Rebecca Balinski (Princeton, N.J.: Princeton University Press, 1994), 68.

10. See, e.g., Hobbes, XX, 4–7; Locke, *Second Treatise of Government*, VII, 78–81.

11. *Second Discourse, Collected Writings* III, 20–43. Cf. Hobbes, *Leviathan*, VIII: "For the thoughts are to the desires as scouts and spies, to range abroad and find the way to the things desired."

12. Letter to Mirabeau, July 26, 1767.

13. *Geneva Manuscript, Collected Writings* IV, 79.

14. E.g., *Preface to Narcissus, Collected Writings* II, 2, 193n; *First Discourse, Collected Writings* II, 22; *Second Discourse, Collected Writings* III, 3–4.

15. *Federalist Papers*, no.10; *Social Contract, Collected Writings* IV, 166–172, 186–194; *Second Discourse, Collected Writings* III, 61–65; *Letters Written from the Mountain, Collected Writings* IX, 293, 298–302.

16. *Second Discourse, Collected Writings* III, 18–28, 40–42, 74–75.

17. See 236, 239–240 below.

18. The word "savage" or "sauvage" in French primarily means "wild." *Second Discourse, Collected Writings* III, 46–49; *Emile*, 42.

19. *Emile*, 212–215; *Second Discourse, Collected Writings* III, 36–37, 47–48, 91–92; *Dialogues, Collected Writings* I, 112–113.

20. *Social Contract, Collected Writings* IV, 131.

21. *Dialogues, Collected Writings* I, 130; *Letters to Malesherbes, Collected Writings* V, 575; *Second Discourse, Collected Writings* III, 49–54, 66, 74–75; *Emile*, 83–84; *Social Contract, Collected Writings* IV, 191–194; *Reveries, Collected Writings* VIII, 56.

22. *Emile*, 84–85; *Second Discourse, Collected Writings* III, 46.

23. *Emile*, 84.

24. *Second Discourse, Collected Writings* III, 49.

25. *Social Contract, Collected Writings* IV, 138–142; *Emile*, 445, 85.

26. *Social Contract, Collected Writings* IV, 155; *Political Economy, Collected Writings* III, 149–152; *Emile*, 39–40. The passage in *Emile* describes the Spartan "citoyen" and "citoyenne," the male and female Spartan citizen.

27. See 159–174 and 178–193 below.

28. *Social Contract, Collected Writings* IV, 154–157.

29. On the great popularity and influence of these two novels, particularly

on women readers, see, e.g., Anna Attridge, "The Reception of *La Nouvelle Héloïse*," *Studies on Voltaire and the Eighteenth Century* 120 (1974): 227–267; Ruth Graham, "Rousseau's Sexism Revolutionized," in *Woman in the 18th Century and Other Essays*, ed. Paul Fritz and Richard Morton (Toronto: Hakkert, 1976), 127–139; Gita May, "Rousseau's '*Antifeminism*' Reconsidered," in *French Women and the Age of Enlightenment*, ed. Samia A. Spencer (Bloomington: Indiana University Press, 1984), 309–317; Colette Piau-Gillot, "Le Discours de Jean-Jacques Rousseau sur les Femmes, et sa Réception Critique," *Dix-Huitième Siècle*, 13 (1981): 317–333; Barbara Corrado Pope, "The Influence of Rousseau's Ideology of Domesticity," in *Connecting Spheres: Women in the Western Wrold, 1500 to the Present*, ed. Marilyn J. Boxer and Jean H. Quataert, with a foreword by Joan W. Scott (New York: Oxford University Press, 1987), 136–145.

30. *Emile*, 214–215, 235, 243.

31. See 53 below.

32. *First Discourse, Collected Writings* II, 15n. See also *Julie; or, The New Héloïse, Collected Writings* VI, 188, 600n and 247 below; *Emile* 107–108 below; *Second Discourse, Collected Writings* III, 38–39.

33. Rousseau at times describes sexual desire as a true natural need; that is, a physical urge that we feel regardless of opinion. *Second Discourse, Collected Writings* III, 27, 39, 43. Yet sexual desire is not strictly speaking a true need; while the continuation of the species suggests that sex must be an "instinct," it is also true that, unlike hunger, we could potentially pass our lives without ever acting on it. At other times, Rousseau stresses that sexual desire is a need born more of opinion or imagination: "[T]he senses are awakened by the imagination alone. Their need is not properly a physical need . . . [or] a true need. If no lewd object had ever struck our eyes, if no indecent idea had ever entered our minds, perhaps this alleged need would never have made itself felt to us, and we would have remained chaste without temptation, without effort, and with out merit." *Emile*, 333; cf. "The Influence of Climates on Civilization," *Political Fragments, Collected Writings* IV, 53–54. Rousseau's detailed description of his own example serves to indicate how profoundly tastes are shaped by imagination and early childhood experiences. See, e.g., *Confessions, Collected Writings* V, 13–15, 23–24, 74–75.

34. See 211 and 225–226 below.

35. See 239–240 below; *Second Discourse, Collected Writings* III, 38–39; Cf. *Social Contract, Collected Writings* IV, 132; *Essay on the Origin of Languages* VII, 305.

36. See 67 below. The remainder of this paragraph draws on Patrick Hochart, "'Le plus libre et le plus doux de tous les actes:' Lecture du livre V de *Emile*," *Esprit* August–September 1997, 61–76; and Claude Habib, *Le Consentement amoureux: Rousseau, les femmes et la cité* (Paris: Hachette, 1998).

37. E.g., see 235–236 below.

38. On this point see Christopher Kelly, *Rousseau as Author: Consecrating One's Life to the Truth* (Chicago: University of Chicago Press, 2003) 109–112.

39. See 131–142 below.

40. *Second Discourse, Collected Writings* III, 65.

41. See 101 below.

42. See 69 below. It is necessary to keep in mind that Rousseau is writing before the invention of cheap and effective birth control.

43. See 73 below.

44. See 237 below.

45. *Emile* manuscrit Favre, Pléiade, I, 232.

46. See 73 below.

47. See 107 below.

48. See 147–148 and 107 below.

49. See 130 and 247 below. "The grave Emile is a child's plaything!" *Emile*, 431; *Julie; or, The New Heloise, Collected Writings* VI, 336, 457.

50. See 243 below.

51. Cf. 243 below with *Emile*, 213–214.

52. Judith Shklar, *Men and Citizens: A Study of Rousseau's Social Theory* (Cambridge: Cambridge University Press, 1969), 24.

53. See 71 below.

54. See 243 below.

55. Ibid.

56. See 241 below.

57. See 216 below.

58. "At the salt mines of Salzburg, they throw a leafless wintry bough into one of the abandoned workings. Two or three months later they haul it out covered with a shining deposit of crystals. The smallest twig . . . is studded with a galaxy of scintillating diamonds. The original branch is no longer recognizable. What I have called crystallization is a mental process which draws from everything that happens new proofs of the perfection of the loved one." Stendhal, *Love*, trans. Gilbert Sale and Suzanne Sale (London: Penguin Group, 1975), 45.

59. See 54 below.

60. Cf. e.g., Judith Still, "'La Nouvelle Héloïse': Passion, Reserve, and the Gift," *Modern Language Review* 91, no. 1 (January 1996): 40–52.

61. For an excellent survey of views of *Emile and Sophie* and a defense of the view that it is comic rather than tragic, see Michel Launay, *Une grève d'esclaves à Alger au XVIIIᵉ siècle avec Emile et Sophie; ou, les Solitaires de Jean-Jacques Rousseau* (Paris: Jean-Paul Rocher, 1998).

62. See 273 below.

63. See 215 below.

64. *Second Discourse, Collected Writings* III, 46.

65. See 72 below.

66. Cf. 69, 72–73, 102–103 with, e.g., 236 below. Cf. *Social Contract, Collected Writings* IV, 147–148, 152–153.

1. *Narcissus; or, The Lover of Himself*

1. The important preface to this play can be found in *Collected Writings* II, 186–198.

2. The term is "portrait ainsi travesti." A "rôle travesti" in the theater is a female part played by a man or vice versa.

3. Passy is now a part of Paris. Rousseau often visited a relative there when it was a sort of suburban retreat.

4. This is a verse from act 1, scene 6, of the opera *Atys* by Philippe Quinault and Jean-Baptiste Lully. In the opera, Atys is a devotee of the goddess Cybèle and believes himself, and is believed to be, immune to love. Nevertheless, he falls in love with Sangaride, is driven mad by Cybèle, kills Sangaride, and is turned into a tree before he can kill himself. Valére evidently enters singing, identifying with Atys at the point of the opera when he is still thought to be immune to love.

5. The expression "pris sans verd," literally, "caught without a green one," is from a game. Here it means "without a response."

6. The expression "courrir les champs," (to run through the fields) had the sense of going mad.

7. The key to this scene is that the word "personne" is a feminine word that can be applied to a male or a female person. For the rest of the scene Angélique replies using a feminine pronoun, but this has been authorized, as it were, by Valére's reference to a "person" rather than a woman. To convey this the pronoun is replaced by "person" in the translation.

8. These were all real taverns.

9. Reading "faut-il" rather than "fait-il" (as in Pléiade).

2. *Queen Whimsical*

1. Rousseau probably completed this work in the spring of 1756. It was printed without his permission in 1758. In the preface to this edition it was denounced as a dangerous work attacking laws, morals, and religion. The publication of such a work was justified by the desire to unmask the false philosophy of the author. Rousseau later gave permission for it to be published in a collection of his writings, although he then said that he regretted having done so.

2. This foreword was written by Rousseau.

3. At the top of the manuscript Rousseau wrote, "N.B. have this recopied by someone who knows how to follow and who is very attentive."

4. At this point the manuscript adds, "I say six months, not in succession; that would have been so much rest for her husband; but taken in the intervals suited to annoy him."

5. Literally, "not knowing which saint to devote himself to."

6. The Divan was the Turkish council of state presided over by the grand vizier.

7. Pierre d'Ortigues de Vaumorière (1610–1690) wrote novels and *Harangues on All Sorts of Subjects, with the Art of Composing Them.*

8. Diogenes the Cynic, who lived in a barrel, rolled it around upon noticing the furious activity of his fellow citizens when their city was under siege.

9. The manuscript reads, "Ladies of the palace." The point here and below in the discussion of nursing the infants is that the king and queen defy the court's contempt for lower-class practices.

10. In the eighteenth century, Vaugirard was a small village outside of Paris. Now it is a part of Paris.

11. This is a reference to the argument of Rousseau's "Letter on French Music," which denies that there is any French music. See *Collected Writings* VII, 141–174. Schah-baham is a character in two novels by Claude Jolyot de Crébillon fils. He frequently asks foolish questions.

12. In other words, saints. The reference is to the practice of naming children after saints to obtain their intercession with God.

13. These two fairy tales were put into verse by Charles Perrault (1628–1703). Perrault was a participant in the "quarrel between the ancients and the moderns." It should be noted that the two fairy tales referred to here are notable for involving murder and incest. The contrast with Machiavelli made in the text is not based on the innocence of the fairy tales.

14. Rousseau originally wrote, "tale: for," and then continued with the following couplet:

I tell you Lord, and you will acknowledge
The more you believe you foresee, the more you go astray.

3. The Two Sexes

1. Louis Béat de Muralt published *Letters on the English and the French* in 1725.

2. Richardson's *Clarissa Harlowe* was translated into French by the abbé Prévost.

3. The word translated as "chasteness" is *pudeur*. It carries the connotations of modesty or decency.

4. The line is from Voltaire's *Discourse in Verse on the Nature of Men.*

5. Herodotus III.12.

4. "On Women"

1. Most editors have suggested that this was probably written around 1735, but it is quite possibly from the 1740s, when Rousseau was working for the Dupin family.

2. Zenobia was the queen of Palmyra in the third century A.D. Lucretia committed suicide in 510 B.C. after being raped by Sextus Tarquin. Rousseau began a play devoted to her. Cornelia (second century B.C.) was the mother of the Gracchi brothers. Arria was the wife of Caccena Paetus and committed suicide under the reign of the emperor Claudius. Artemisia (fourth century B.C.) built the famous Mausoleum as the tomb of her husband. Fulvia denounced the Catiline conspiracy. Elisabeth was the queen of Hungary and the regent of Poland. The Countess of Thököly was a leader of Hungarian resistance to Austria in the seventeenth century.

3. This is from the preliminary discourse of Voltaire's *Charles XII.*

5. "Sophie; or, The Woman"

1. Brantôme (1540–1614) reports that when Julia, daughter of Augustus, was asked whether she was concerned about becoming pregnant by her many "friends" and thereby having her activities discovered, replied: "I provide for

this, for I never receive anyone or passenger in my ship, except when it is loaded and full." Pierre de Bourdeille, Seigneur de Brantôme, *Dames galantes, Oeuvres Complètes*, ed. Ludovic Lalanne (Paris: Renouard, 1876), 10:170.

2. "Supplément" can mean either supplement or substitute.

3. Deuteronomy 22:23–27.

4. Hercules, or Herakles, son of Zeus and Alcmene, was a hero renowned for his courage, strength, and prowess. Hera, Zeus's wife, drove him mad, and in a fit of frenzy he killed his wife and daughter. His famous labors were undertaken as expiation for this crime. When Hercules was hunting the Lion of Cithearon, King Thespius of Thespiae, wanting his fifty virgin daughters to bear the young hero's children, either tricked him into sleeping with one of his daughters every night, by giving him the impression that he was sleeping with the same woman (Apollodorus, *Library* 2.4.10), or offered that he bed them all in a single night, which Heracles did (Pausanias, *Description of Greece* 9.27.6). The sources, unlike Rousseau, do not speak of this as a rape. Omphale was a Lydian queen or princess to whom Hercules was enslaved for a year. Ovid describes how Hercules was utterly subjected to his fair mistress, who wore Hercules' lionskin and weapons while he wore her clothing and did women's work, even holding her basket of wool as she wove. Ovid, *Heroides* IX.55–118; *Fasti* II.305–358. Samson, an Old Testament figure also remarkable for his strength and prowess, fought to deliver the Israelites from the Philistines. The strength God promised him was maintained on the condition that he abstain from certain actions, including cutting his hair. He fell in love with Delilah, a Philistine, who took money to discover the secret of his strength, and cut his hair while he slept. He was then imprisoned and his eyes burnt out. Judges 13–16.

5. See pages 238–240 below and *Discourse on the Origin and Foundations of Inequality Among Men, Collected Writings* III, 20–21, 24–25, 71–73, 88–90, 92–93.

6. In the *Republic*, Socrates is asked by his interlocutors to examine what justice is and whether it is good; that is, worthy of the devotion it demands. In the course of this examination, Socrates and his interlocutors construct a just society "in speech," in order to see more clearly both what such a society would demand from its citizens, and whether citizens devoted to justice would be happy. In book V, the question is raised whether a just society would require the abolition of the private family, which would include freeing women from childbearing and child-rearing to do the same tasks as men. Both the family and romantic love are presented there as in tension with justice, because they lead to profound private joys and griefs that we do not share with others, and that can be in deep tension with the demands of the "common good." Plato, *Republic* 449a–466e.

7. See *Emile, Pléiade*, 4:668: "When one loves, one wants to be loved. Emile loves men; he therefore wants to please them. All the more does he want to please women. His age, his morals, his project—all unite in nourishing this desire in him."

8. Plutarch, *Lives of Illustrious Men: Lycurgus* XIV–XV; Xenophon, *Constitution of the Lacedaemonians* I.2–10.

9. Cf. e.g., Aristotle, *Politics* 1269b20–23.

10. Ovid tells how Minerva, the virgin goddess of wisdom and warriors, recounts how she invented the flute, but then threw it away when she caught sight of a reflection of herself playing it. Ovid, *Fasti* VI.693–703.

11. François de Salignac de la Mothe Fénelon, *Traité de l'éducation des filles,* chapter 5. Fénelon (1651–1715), a theologian and archbishop, was also director of a college for converted Protestant girls, called Nouvelles Catholiques.

12. See, e.g., Homer, *Iliad* XIV.153–223.

13. Apelles (fourth century B.C.), court painter to Philip II of Macedonia and Alexander the Great, was often named during the Renaissance as one of, or indeed as, the pinnacle of the art of classical antiquity. His works are known only through descriptions, as none survive. Pliny, *Natural History* VII.38. The saying is reported by Clement of Alexandria in *The Pedagogue* II.12.125.

14. La Duchapt was a famous milliner. Rousseau refers to her shop, which was near the Opéra, in *The Confessions, Collected Writings* V, 288.

15. In the eighteenth century, dress was very elaborate, and among the upper classes, the ceremony of dressing, or of performing one's *toilette,* occupied a great deal of time and effort. It was also a social gathering, as women gathered circles of friends and admirers who would attend them at their dressing tables, spending the hours while the women dressed discussing matters both frivolous and weighty.

16. Ispahan (also known as Esfahān or Isfahan) was a city so great that according to an old Persian proverb "Esfahān is half the world." The golden age of Esfahān occurred under the Safavid dynasty in the sixteenth to eighteenth centuries. The harem to which Rousseau probably refers was the very large one attached to the royal court. The often powerful mothers, wives, and favorites of a harem, as well as a harem's chief attendants, at times exercised significant political influence in the affairs of various courts. Albania was part of the Ottoman Empire at the time that Rousseau wrote. One of his sources for information about Persia was Jean Chardin's *Voyages en Perse,* 4 vols. (Amsterdam, 1735).

17. As a child, Emile is not permitted to ask indiscreet questions either, because restraining and channeling his imagination, particularly with regard to sex, is a critical part of his education. *Emile, Pléiade,* 4:490–501.

18. See statements made by Rousseau's character the "Savoyard Vicar" in one of Rousseau's central religious writings, the "Profession of Faith of the Savoyard Vicar." The Vicar argues that, lacking "certain and manifest signs" from God regarding which is the true religion, "all religions are good and pleasing to God." "I consider all particular religions as so many salutary institutions that prescribe in each country a uniform manner of honoring God through a public cult"; "the essential cult is that of the heart." Thus, despite his own "skepticism" regarding the gospels, the Vicar scrupulously performs all the rites prescribed him as a vicar. *Emile, Pléiade,* 4:609, 627. See also the relation between Julie and her husband Wolmar, who is an atheist and does not share her faith. The end of Julie suggests that Wolmar may be converting to Julie's faith. *Julie, Collected Writings* VI, 611.

19. Matthew 6:7. This is one of the instructions that precedes the Lord's Prayer in the Sermon on the Mount.

20. *The Death of Abel*, by Salomon Gessner, was published in German in 1758 and first translated into French in 1786. Gessner (1730–1788), a painter and poet, was admired by, among others, Herder, Goethe, and Lessing. *The Death of Abel*, an epic poem, gives a biblical account of the first encounter of human beings with death, sweetened by descriptions of the beautiful world that human beings owe to a benevolent Deity, and the promise of eternal life hereafter.

21. This refers to the "Profession of Faith of the Savoyard Vicar." The "Profession" is offered as an example of "how to reason with one's pupil" in order to show him that he has a genuine interest in being just. The relation between reason and the inner sentiment in the "Profession" is complex. In the end, however, Rousseau's Vicar claims that the "inner sentiment" that we will find our happiness in being good to others, and that justice must have force in the world, are decisive proofs that prevail against the uncertainty we are led into by our reason. The natural religion of the "Profession" is therefore grounded upon sentiment. *Emile*, Pléiade, 4, 558–636.

22. "To catch every new lover in her net, the lady uses all the craft she can, not keeping always the same face for each; she fits her looks and actions to the man." Torquato Tasso, *Jerusalem Delivered*, trans. Anthony M. Esolen (Baltimore, Md.: Johns Hopkins University Press, 2000), 4:87.

23. Virgil, *Eclogues* 3. 64–75.

24. The adversary in question is Charles Bordes, who wrote a critique of Rousseau's *First Discourse*. See *Final Reply, Collected Writings* II, 127.

25. "Once her modesty is lost, a woman will refuse no other disgraceful act." Tacitus, *Annals* IV.3.

26. Ninon (Anne) de Lenclos (1620–1705), a prominent figure in the literary and political Parisian circles of her time, which included Molière and Racine, was celebrated for being as relaxed regarding love affairs as she was staunch in friendship. She was the "decent man" whom Rousseau insists mothers should not attempt to make of their daughters. Later in *Emile*, Rousseau discusses women brought up to be "learned and brilliant" and to be "president[s] of a tribunal of literature." He claims that a woman brought up in this way, disdaining "all the duties of women, always begins by making herself a man after the fashion of Mademoiselle de l'Enclos." *Emile*, Pléiade, 4:768.

27. Rousseau's doubts regarding both the possibility of reaching "abstract and speculative truths," and regarding their usefulness for the happiness of human life, should be considered here. See, e.g., *Emile*, Pléiade, 4:551; *First Discourse, Collected Writings* II, 19–21; *Moral Letters, Collected Writings* XII, 179–189; *Reveries of the Solitary Walker, Collected Writings* VIII, 17–27.

28. For an account of convent education, see, e.g., Albert Marie-Pierre de Luppé, *Les Jeunes Filles dans l'Aristocracie et la Bourgeoisie à la Fin du XVIIIe Siècle* (Paris: Edouard Champion, 1924).

29. "She who devoured, and wiping her mouth, says: I have brought forth no evil."

30. In the French it is clear here that Rousseau is addressing a woman reader.

31. On Sparta, see Plutarch, *Lives of Illustrious Men: Lycurgus* XIV–XVI; on Germany, Tacitus, *Germania* VII–VIII, XV, XVII–XIX. The revolutions in Rome to which Rousseau refers and as Livy recounts them, are as follows. Lucretia, famous for her beauty and chastity, was raped by Sextus Tarquinius. Her plea that her dishonor be punished and her subsequent suicide are presented as pivotal to the downfall of the Tarquin monarchy and the establishment of the Roman Republic. In the second incident to which Rousseau refers, the plebeians gained the right to stand for the prominent consular office after prolonged efforts by two tribunes, Licinius and Sextius. They were first moved to undertake this difficult reform by Ambustus, who was in turn moved by the complaints of his daughter that she was treated with less respect than her sister because she was married to Licinius, a plebeian. The third incident is the downfall of Appius, which heralded the end of the tyranny of the Decemvirs. In order to satisfy his lust for a beautiful young girl, Virginia, Appius had her legally declared a slave belonging to one of his dependents. Her desperate father killed her rather than let her be dragged away, and the enraged crowd followed him and others in overthrowing Appius. The last incident occurred when Rome was under imminent threat of attack by Coriolanus, a Roman exile. He called off the attack because of the entreaties of his mother, Veturia, and his wife, Volumnia. Livy, *The History of Rome from its Foundation* I.58–60; VI.34–42; III.44–48; II.34–40. On Coriolanus, see also Plutarch, *Lives of Illustrious Men: Coriolanus* XXX–XXXVII.

32. The term "paladins" refers to the (usually) twelve knights who followed Charlemagne, described in famous medieval romances such as the *Matter of France* and the *Song of Roland*.

33. Laïs (fourth century B.C.), said to be of Corinth, was a courtesan renowned for both her beauty and her price. She consorted with such famous men as Aristippus, Demosthenes, and Diogenes. Athenaeus, *Deipnosophists* XII.544; XIII.588–589; Diogenes Laertius, *Lives of Eminent Philosophers* II.74–75, 84; IV.7. Cleopatra was celebrated not only for her beauty—or rather, her charm—but for her lavish and decadent way of life, and for having Julius Caesar and Mark Antony as lovers. Plutarch, *Lives of Illustrious Men, Caesar* XLVIII–XLIX; Plutarch, *Lives of Illustrious Men, Antony* XXV–LXXVII.

34. "She who does not act because it is not permitted, acts." Ovid, *Amores* 3.4.4.

35. Plutarch, *Lycurgus* XIV; Plutarch, *Moralia, The Sayings of Spartan Women*, 240–242. See *Second Discourse, Collected Writings* III, 10; Aristotle, *Politics* 1269b12–1270b5.

36. Pythagoras (sixth century B.C.) was a pre-Socratic philosopher and mathematician. I cannot find the story in Brantôme's works. In his edition of *Emile*, Allan Bloom provides the following useful speculation: "Matteo Bandello (1480–1562) tells in his *Novelle* (III, 17), the story of Madonna Zilia who made a similar demand on a lover. Given the enormous popularity of Bandello and the number of writers who used his stories (e.g., Shakespeare for *Romeo and Juliet*), the tale Rousseau tells here probably goes back in one way or another to Bandello." *Emile*, 493 n. 29. Brantôme does speak of women wanting men

to keep silent about their affairs, a desire opposed to men's desire to tell about their exploits. Brantôme, *Dames Galantes*, 9:501–529.

37. The second to last sentence in this footnote is missing from the Pléiade edition.

38. "The severe temper of the son of Peleus, who does not know how to yield." Horace, *Odes* I.6.5–6. Horace refers to Achilles, the hero of Homer's *Iliad*, whose first lines read: "Sing, goddess, the anger of Peleus' son Achilleus and its devastation, which put pains thousandfold upon the Achaians." Homer, *Iliad*, trans. Richmond Lattimore (Chicago: University of Chicago Press, 1951), I.1–3. The epigraph Rousseau chose for *Emile* is drawn from Seneca's *On Anger*. Anger, or the spirited resistance we feel to what crosses our wills, is according to Rousseau part of the fundamental psychological phenomenon of amour-propre, the character of which is the pivot upon which human happiness or unhappiness turns.

39. This is a summary of the practical teaching of the "Profession of Faith of the Savoyard Vicar."

40. A "Phoebus" was a smooth, seductive talker.

41. This Sophie is in love with Telemachus, the hero of Fénelon's *The Adventures of Telemachus* (1694), written for the instruction of his pupil the duke of Burgundy, second in line of succession to Louis XIV's throne. Earlier in *Emile*, Rousseau had described how Emile's tastes are in part formed by reading only one book: *Robinson Crusoe*. Sophie's tastes are similarly formed by reading the heroic poem, *The Adventures of Telemachus*, considered an important work of French political thought at the beginning of the eighteenth century. It describes the lessons learned in his wanderings by Telemachus, son of Ulysses. During his travels, Telemachus is tutored in the guise of Mentor by Minerva, the goddess of wisdom, in order that he may one day become a wise ruler of Ithaca. In book 6, Fénelon tells how Telemachus falls utterly in love with Eucharis, a nymph on Calypso's isle; only when Minerva succeeds in taking him away from her does Telemachus's love of virtue reawaken.

42. Cicero (106–43 B.C.) wrote the *De Officiis* in 44. Cicero's perhaps most practical work on ethics, addressed to his son, treats virtue in three books: in the first, virtue is treated in light of our true end; in the second, in relation to what is naturally useful; and in the third, possible conflicts between virtue and what is useful are addressed.

43. See *Pléiade*, 4:491–493.

44. *Discourse on the Origin and Foundations of Inequality, Collected Writings* III, 38–40. Rousseau there argues that one must distinguish "between the moral and the Physical in the feeling of love. The Physical is the general desire which inclines one sex to unite with the other. The moral is that which determines this desire and fixes it exclusively on a single object, or which at least gives it a greater degree of energy for this preferred object . . . the moral element of love is an artificial feeling born of the usage of society, and extolled with much skill and care by women to establish their empire and make dominant the sex that [must] obey. This feeling [is] founded on certain notions of merit or beauty that [a human being prior to development in society] is not

capable of having." In the state of nature "[l]imited solely to that which is Physical in love . . . Everyone peaceably waits for the impulsion of Nature, yields to it without choice with more pleasure than frenzy; and the need satisfied, all desire is extinguished."

6. Women of Paris

1. "Nonchalance": Rousseau uses the Italian word because the noun *désinvolture* did not yet exist in French, although the adjective *désinvolte* did.

2. The "Gascon philosopher" means Montaigne: "And although the women of the great kingdom of Pegu, who have nothing to cover them below the waist, but a cloth slit in front and so narrow that whatever ceremonious modesty they seek to preserve, at each step they can be seen whole, may say that this is a device thought up in order to attract the men to them and divert them from their fondness for other males, to which that nation is altogether addicted, it might be said that they lose by it more than they gain and that a complete hunger is sharper than one that has been satisfied at least by the eyes" *(Essays*, III, 5, *The Complete Essays of Montaigne*, trans. Donald Frame (Stanford: Stanford University Press, 1958), 654.

3. Rousseau evokes here a skill on which he prided himself; not only was he a patient and neat copyist of his own works (he made several copies by hand of *Julie*), he often sustained himself during his life by working as a copyist of music: this shows for example in the detailed article "Copyist" for the *Dictionary of Music (Collected Writings* VII, 383–384).

4. *Ni galons ni taches* at first appears anomolous, since the ordinary sense of *galon* is galloon or fancy trim; but the real meaning here is etymological: "The word *galon* comes from pieces added to clothing, to cover its holes or stains: thus *galons* have become the ornament and decoration of the rich, after having been one of the signs of poverty" *(Encyclopédie* VII, 452).

5. The word *fard* properly means only white grease (or paint), but is used here for any kind of makeup; it also connotes cover-up and falsification.

6. That is, to a depth equivalent to four fingers' width.

7. The word *demoiselle* could be used for any unmarried girl of relatively high station, but in a narrow sense it properly designated only a noble daughter.

8. This passage is reminiscent of the tone of Montesquieu's *Lettres persanes*, for example this one from a letter from Usbek to Roxanne: "in this country . . . women have lost all restraint; they go before men with their faces uncovered, as if to request their own defeat; they seek them out with their gazes" (letter XXVI).

9. This expression comes from the stanza of Tasso already quoted in letter I, XXIII, 67. See *Collected Writings* V, 67.

10. Saint-Germain was still called a *faubourg* (suburb) because it had been outside the city when there were still walls. Les Halles was the central market place, next to the Marais.

11. Women of the Pays de Vaud.

12. "Their air is so modest . . . that a man is sometimes under a tempta-

tion of telling a woman that she is handsome, to have the pleasure of letting her know it" (*Letters Describing the Character and Customs of the English and French Nations* [London: Edlin and Prevost, 1726], 35).

13. *Grande loge* is not a customary term for the theater, where "first loge" would seem closer to the intended meaning; Rousseau may have accidentally borrowed it from the Freemasons, who had established their first *grande loge* in France in 1728.

14. These are clichés (*chaîne* and *flamme*) of conventional love rhetoric which to him, however, possess a true and authentic meaning but are no longer persuasive in Parisian society.

15. This passage recalls once again Montesquieu's satire of French morals in *Lettres persanes* (1721): "Here husbands accept their lot graciously and regard infidelities as the blows of an inevitable fate. A husband who wished to possess his wife all by himself would be regarded as a perturber of public joy and as a madman who wanted to enjoy the sun's rays to the exclusion of all other men" (letter LV). Julie's lover places himself in the role of Montesquieu's Persian, describing foreign customs with humor and detachment.

16. He imitates here the style of the libertine novelists such as Claude Crébillon or Charles Duclos: "Chance forms these sorts of liaisons; lovers take each other because they please each other, and leave each other because they cease to please each other, and because everything must end" (Duclos, *Les Confessions du comte de* ***, in *Romanciers du XVIIIᵉ siècle* [Paris: Pléiade, 1965], II, 224).

17. By insisting on the complete *interchangeability* of love objects, Julie's lover is characterizing in extremely schematic form a position that is the antithesis of the romantic notion of love, which admits of but a single, irreplaceable loved one: "Love is not love / Which alters when it alteration finds" (Shakespeare, Sonnet 116).

18. That is, the "others" (or new lovers) enumerated in the previous paragraph.

19. This metaphor is based on the word *traits*, here translated as "quips"; but which also means "arrows."

20. "Grimaces" are here analogous to a comic mask.

21. The word is *tailles*, the basic capitation tax in France, which fell almost entirely on the third estate.

22. "This war" appears to mean the Seven Years' War of 1755–1762, the "other war" then being the War of Austrian Succession (1741–1748). The writer of the letter could not himself, circa 1736, be alluding to either of these wars; but the notes' author is the "editor," who refers here to his own time frame and not the novel's.

23. The provincial governance being invoked here placed great administrative and even judicial powers in the hands of noble landholders.

24. This is likely an allusion to Isaac Joseph Berruyer's *Histoire du peuple de Dieu* (History of God's people), 1727.

25. This programmatic passage, which is in effect a restatement of *Julie*'s own strategy, was reproduced word for word in Jaucourt's article *Roman* (Novel) in the *Encyclopédie*. Many of Rousseau's contemporary critics found

morally reprehensible the idea of working toward virtue in literature by speaking from "the bosom of vice." That was, of course, the basic schema of confessional literature (more common in England than in France), to which tradition *Moll Flanders*, for example, is closely related.

7. Women of Geneva

1. The last sentence of this note was added for the edition of 1782. One of the "intelligent people" referred to was d'Alembert himself. See *Collected Writings* X, 354.

2. Herodotus III.12.

3. The *Lettres portugaises* published in 1669, is now attributed to Gabriel-Joseph de Lavergne, vicomte de Guilleragues.

4. The last sentence of this note was added for the edition of 1782. For some of the discussion referred to, see 244–265 below.

8. Letters to "Henriette"

1. A wound from the lance of Achilles could be cured only by a touch from the lance.

9. The Death of Lucretia

1. The edition of 1792 adds the following passage: "(*Aside*). Gods who see my heart, illuminate my reason: act so that I do not cease to be virtuous. You know well that I want to be so, and I will always be so if you wish as I do."

2. In the edition of 1792, Pauline's speech begins as follows: "We ought to seek our advantages in the weaknesses of those whom we serve. I feel that all the more as, our union having been subjected to this price, my happiness depends on success." Then, as a new sentence, it continues, "But the interest . . ."

3. In the edition of 1792, the scene ends with the following passage:

Ah, Sire, might it please the heavens! but . . . Forgive me, if my anxious zeal gives me a lack of confidence that your courage disdains, but is useful for your security and perhaps for that of the state.

SEXTUS.

Friend, what vain cares! But if I might only see Lucretia, I am content to die at her feet; and let the whole universe perish!

SULPITIUS.

She uses all her wiles to avoid you. . . . However, you will see her. The moment has just been settled upon. In the name of the gods, go wait for her, and let me see to everything else.

Then the edition of 1792 has two scenes that represent the dramatic continuation of this one, but are not found in the Neuchâtel manuscript.

SCENE [Ib].

SULPITIUS, *alone.*

Young fool! no one but you has lost his reason; and it is my misfortune to have my outcome depend upon yours. I absolutely must find out Brutus's intentions. A secret meeting to which Collatinus has been admitted gives me some hope of learning everything by means of this facile and limited man. I have already been able to gain his confidence. May he be the blind instrument of my plans; may I get wind of the plots I suspect by means of him; may he assist me in climbing to the highest degree of favor; may he unwittingly deliver his wife to the prince; may, finally, love—fatigued by possession—facilitate my pushing the husband aside, remaining alone master and favorite of Sextus, and subjecting one day in his name all the Romans to my rule.

SCENE [Ic].
PAULINE, SULPITIUS.

PAULINE.

No, Sulpitius, to no avail would I have spoken; she does not want to see the prince at all; and what she refused to Collatinus's argument, she would not have accorded to the pretexts you suggested to me. Besides, each time I wanted to open my mouth, her presence inspired an invincible resistance. Far from her eyes, I want all that pleases you; but before her I can want nothing more than what is honest.

SULPITIUS.

Since a futile timidity carries the day, since neither my arguments nor your interest have been able to bring you to speak, all we can do is arrange between them a meeting that appears unplanned.

4. Rousseau devotes the second longest chapter of the *Social Contract* (book 4, chap. 4) to a discussion of the Comitia, or popular assemblies, in order to discover "how the freest and most powerful people on earth exercised its supreme power" (*Collected Writings* IV, 203). The Roman Republic was divided into three classes of Tribes, each of which was further subdivided into ten Curiae, and each of these into Decuriae. Moreover, a body of a hundred horsemen or knights was formed from each of the tribes and denoted as a Century. Popular assemblies of the Roman people gathered according to the division into tribes, curiae, or centuries could be convoked; it is to such assemblies that Brutus refers here.

5. Additional fragments can be found in *Collected Writings* X, 176–180.

10. *Essay on the Important Events of Which Women Have Been the Secret Cause*

1. Although some editors have suggested that this was written in the 1730s, the editors of Pléiade reasonably suggest that it dates from the 1740s, when Rousseau was working for the Dupin family.

2. Rousseau is referring to *Roman History* by Catrou and Rouillé, published in 1731. The passage in question involves the two daughters of Fabius Ambustus, one of whom married a plebian and the other, a patrician. The former complained that she was being shown too little consideration. As a result, her father worked to have certain offices opened to plebians. The authors conclude, "It

seems that it was the destiny of Rome, that the great events always were begun by women."

11. *The Levite of Ephraïm*

1. Rousseau intended to publish the *Levite of Ephraïm* along with *On Theatrical Imitation* and the *Essay on the Origin of Languages*. The manuscript of this draft preface is found between two letters from February and July 1763, suggesting that Rousseau intended to publish the work at about that time.

2. See Judges 19–21.

3. Rousseau refers to his flight from France after the condemnation of his *Emile* by the Parlement of Paris and the warrant for his arrest. The order for his arrest was issued June 9, 1762. That afternoon, warned of these actions, Rousseau fled Paris for Geneva, but Rousseau's native city burned both the *Emile* and *Social Contract* and ordered his arrest. In his *Confessions*, Rousseau relates that it was on the morning after his departure from Paris that he thought of composing the *Levite of Ephraïm*, which he wrote during his voyage and completed afterward at Môtiers. Rousseau relates the circumstances of the composition of the work in his *Confessions*, XI (*Collected Writings* V, 485–491).

4. See the previous note.

5. Rousseau explains in the *Confessions* (XI; *Collected Writings* V, 4–91) that the style of his *Levite* is taken from the *Idylles et poëmes champêtres* by Salomon Gessner (1730–1788), a poet from Zurich who wrote idylls in prose that praised the simple life, as translated by Jean-Jacques Hubner, a Genevan Calvinist who converted to Catholicism. Hubner sent his translation of Gessner's *Idylles* to Rousseau at the end of 1761 (Leigh, IX, 347–348).

6. See Genesis 35:17–19. Benjamin was the son of Jacob and Rebecca.

7. This paragraph and the last one have no analogue in Judges. The scriptural version of the story begins simply: "And it came to pass in those days, when there was no king in Israel, that there was a certain Levite . . ." (Judges 19:1 [KJV]). Rousseau substantially embellishes the scriptural account. For a treatment of Rousseau's departures from Scripture, see Thomas M. Kavanaugh, *Writing the Truth: Authority and Desire in Rousseau* (Berkeley and Los Angeles: University of California Press, 1987), chap. 5.

8. Numbers 36:8 (KJV): "And every daughter, that possesseth an inheritance in any tribe of the children of Israel, shall be wife unto one of the family of the tribe of the father, that the children of Israel may enjoy every man the inheritance of his fathers."

9. Jebus is another name for Jerusalem.

10. Priests were drawn from the tribe of Levi.

11. Rousseau appears to have invented the term "sons of Jemini," which he uses here and below instead of the term "Benjaminites" found in the scriptural version.

12. See Deuteronomy 13:13 (KJV): "Certain men, the children of Belial, are gone out from among you, and have withdrawn the inhabitants of their city, saying, Let us go and serve other gods, which ye have not known?"

13. Genesis 49:27 (KJV): "Benjamin shall ravin as a wolf: in the morning he shall devour the prey, and at night he shall divide the spoil."

14. The scriptural version of the story concludes here, so the continuation is Rousseau's own embellishment.

12. *The Loves of Milord Edward Bomston*

1. According to the *Confessions*, Rousseau considered incorporating this narrative of Edward's adventures into the text of *Julie* but "finally decided to cut them out altogether because they would have spoiled its touching simplicity since they did not have the same tone as all the rest" *(Collected Writings* V, 439). The only source for it is the handwritten copy of *Julie* he made for the Maréchale de Luxembourg, to which he appended it; it was first published in the Dupeyrou (Geneva) edition of 1780, after Rousseau's death.

2. Letter IV, XVII, 428.

3. On the subject of "mercenary love," cf. letter VI, VI, *Collected Writings* VI, 549.

4. The convent was in the eighteenth century a place of refuge as well as a home for the religious.

5. The formulation is similar to what St. Preux says to Julie in part I: "when I cease to love virtue, I will no longer love you" (letter I, V, *Collected Writings* VI, 34).

6. Austria was considered part of Germany in the eighteenth century, with Vienna as its capital.

7. "Ministrations" (*soins*) is an extreme euphemism for the sex act which, instead of propagating the race, would in this way be serving to extinguish it.

8. This strange shift from singular to plural is in the original; the elliptical sentence goes almost without transition from the general to the particular.

15. On Love

1. The term *honnête homme* originally applied only to members of the nobility, but Rousseau uses it in an extended sense as part of an effort to call into question standards about what it means to be a decent man.

2. Constance is the heroine of Diderot's *Natural Son*. Cénie is the heroine of Mme. de Graffigny's play of the same name. Mme. de Graffigny (1695–1758) had spread the rumor that Rousseau had broken off relations with Diderot at a time when they had, in fact, temporarily reconciled. See *Confessions* in *Collected Writings* V, 386.

3. "Unaware of the treacherous breeze." The quotation is from Horace, *Odes*, I.5.5.

4. *Aeneid* V, 654. The Trojan woman had set fire to Aeneas's ships in order to force him to settle in Sicily.

5. *Le Petit Jehan de Saintré* by Antoine de La Sale was originally published in the fifteenth century and republished in 1724.

6. "Unsightly is an old soldier." The quotation is from Ovid, *Amores* I.ix.4.

7. These are characters is Voltaire's *Zaïre* and *Nanine.*

8. *Rüelle* is the part of the bedroom where women received visitors while doing their toilette.

9. "Against his will, against hers." The quotation is from Suetonius, *Titus* vii.2. Rousseau adds, "against the spectator's will."

10. This note was added in the edition of 1782. Rousseau is referring to the French translation of Richardson's novel.

11. This note was added in the edition of 1782. *The London Merchant; or, The History of George Barnwell* by George Lillo premiered in London in 1731.

16. Letters to Sara

1. It is thought that Rousseau wrote this when he was approximately fifty, as the presumed author of the letters is. That would place the composition around 1762. The text of the first four letters is from the final draft done by Rousseau. The fifth is from the earlier draft. The final draft has the title, "The Greybeard in Love," which is crossed out. Only the final version has the epigraph and introductory notice.

2. "Neither the credulous hope for a soul that responds to me" (Horace, *Odes*, IV.1.30).

3. This statement has led some readers to believe that these letters were not written as a dare, but were intended by Rousseau as love letters from himself to a younger woman.

4. The writer uses the second person familiar to address Sara here and below.

5. In this part of the letter the writer uses the formal second person.

6. At this point the writer reverts to the familiar second person.

7. The gender makes it clear that the writer is referring to himself here.

8. In this sentence the writer uses the formal second person, but the letter continues with the informal.

9. The writer reverts to the formal second person.

10. The writer resumes the informal second person here.

11. The writer reverts to the formal second person.

12. The writer resumes the familiar second person.

13. This letter exists only in the draft.

17. The Naturalness of the Family

1. Victor Gourevitch has pointed out that Rousseau used and modified slightly a translation of Locke done by David Mazel, published in 1691. See *The Discourses and Other Early Political Writings*, ed. Victor Gourevitch (Cambridge: Cambridge University Press, 1997), 376–377. In the text we have altered the quotation to correspond with Mazel's translation as changed by Rousseau. Locke's original from chapter 7 of *The Second Treatise of Government* reads as follows:

79. For the end of *conjunction between Male and Female*, being not barely

Procreation, but the continuation of the Species, this conjunction betwixt Male and Female ought to last, even after Procreation, so long as is necessary to the nourishment and support of the young Ones, who are to be sustained by those that got them, till they are able to shift and provide for themselves. This Rule, which the infinite wise Maker hath set to the Works of his hands, we find the inferiour Creatures steadily obey. In those viviparous Animals which feed on Grass, the *conjunction between Male and Female* lasts no longer than the very Act of Copulation: because the Teat of the Dam being sufficient to nourish the Young, till it be able to feed on Grass, the Male only begets, but concerns not himself for the Female or Young, to whose Sustenance he can contribute nothing. But in Beasts of Prey the *conjunction* lasts longer: because the Dam not being able well to subsist her self, and nourish her numerous Off-spring by her own Prey alone, a more laborious, as well as more dangerous way of living, than by feeding on Grass, the Assistance of the Male is necessary to the Maintenance of their common Family, which cannot subsist till they are able to prey for themselves, but by the joint Care of Male and Female. The same is to be observed in all Birds (except some domestick ones, where plenty of food excuses the Cock from feeding, and taking care of the young Brood) whose Young needing Food in the Nest, the Cock and Hen continue Mates, till the Young are able to use their wing, and provide for themselves.

80. And herein I think lies the chief, if not the only reason *why the Male and Female in Mankind are tyed to a longer conjunction* than other Creatures, *viz.* because the Female is capable of conceiving, and *de facto* is commonly with Child again, and Brings forth too a new Birth long before the former is out of a dependency for support on his Parents help, and able to shift for himself, and has all the assistance is due to him from his Parents: whereby the Father, who is bound to take care for those he hath begot, is under an Obligation to continue in Conjugal Society with the same Woman longer than other Creatures, whose Young being able to subsist of themselves, before the time of procreation returns again, the Conjugal Bond dissolves of it self, and they are at liberty, till *Hymen*, at his usual Anniversary Season, summons them again to chuse new Mates. Wherein one cannot but admire the Wisdom of the great Creatour, who having given to Man foresight and an Ability to lay up for the future, as well as to supply the present necessity, hath made it necessary, that *Society of Man and Wife should be more lasting*, than of Male and Female amongst other Creatures; that so their Industry might be encouraged, and their Interest better united, to make Provision, and lay up Goods for their common Issue, which uncertain mixture, or easie and frequent Solutions of Conjugal Society would mightily disturb. (John Locke, *Two Treatises of Government* [Cambridge: Cambridge University Press, 1988], 319–320).

2. For this note, see *Collected Writings* III, 73–74.

3. *Ibid.*, 38–40. In this context Rousseau discusses the distinction between "the moral and the Physical in the feeling of love." He says that the latter is "that general desire which inclines one sex to unite with the other." The former

is "that which determines this desire and fixes it exclusively on a single object." Thus, the moral in love depends on the development of an ability to make subtle comparisons.

18. Mothers and Infants

1. The word "moeurs" is translated as "morals." In the *Social Contract*, Rousseau describes "moeurs" as that form of law that is "the most important of all; which is not engraved on marble or bronze, but in the hearts of the citizens; which is the genuine constitution of the State, . . . preserves a people in the spirit of its institution, and imperceptibly substitute the force of habit for that of authority." What we commonly understand as laws are only the sides of the arch, of which "moeurs" are the "unshakable Keystone." *Collected Writings* IV, 164–165. For a discussion of how this term is used by Rousseau and his contemporaries, see *Collected Writings* II, 203–204 n.7.

19. Domestic Life

1. The island was alluded to earlier without being named; see letter IV, III, *Collected Writings* VI, 339, and note.

2. He refers to the manner of constructing consecutive rooms (*enfilade*) without a separate corridor, so that one had to pass through all of them to reach the end.

3. Cf. letter III, xx, *Collected Writings* VI, 305: this domestic aesthetics is echoed in a passage from book III of the *Confessions* describing the house of Mme de Warens, characterized by "a patriarchal abundance with which ostentation is never united" *(Collected Writings* V, 88).

4. These are ideas that Rousseau shares with the Physiocrats, for whom land, essentially inexhaustible, was the source of all true wealth. They thus complement the theory of the city (letter II, xvi, *Collected Writings* VI, 198–199) where the same mechanism works exactly in reverse: the greater the concentration of population, the more things decline.

5. Thirty *batz* make a *thaler*, the monetary unit of Bern, in the jurisdiction of which Clarens is located.

6. "People can resist anything, except kindness, and there is no surer means of acquiring the affection of others than to give them one's own" (II, v, *Collected Writings* VI, 166).

7. L.L.E.E. = *Leurs Excellences*, the Bern senate, which governed the Pays de Vaud.

8. Ancient name of Sparta, the legislation of which, promulgated by Lycurgus and described by Plutarch, was much admired by Rousseau: spouses there had to contrive, according to Plutarch, "means and occasions how they might meet together, and not be seen" (Thomas North trans., Blackwell edition, 1928, I, 131).

9. The *parterre*, or ground level, in the French theater had no seating.

10. St. Preux's wish to be admitted to favors refused to Wolmar has, of

course, great symbolic importance. Equally striking here is the unexpected way he compares his prerogatives to those of a lackey, an echo of his earlier station in Julie's father's house, which he finally seems to have outgrown.

11. *Céracée* is curds, and *gru* curds mixed with cream. The Salève referred to in the note is just southeast of Geneva (in Savoie), therefore at the other end of the lake from Clarens. The Jura is the mountainous area to the north and west of Geneva.

12. Allusion to letter I, xxiii, *Collected Writings* VI, 66.

13. In picking up on Julie's allusion (see previous note), St. Preux has slightly shifted the subject to make one of his own. Instead of contrasting the Valaisans and the women of Clarens, he pairs the symbolism of the chalet, which connotes dairy products (cf. letter I, xxxvi, *Collected Writings* VI, 92. and Rousseau's note) and the cellar, which connotes wine; but he thereby also alludes to their tryst for which the chalet stood, and the drunkenness for which she reproached him.

14. The possible relationship between aspects of the English character and red meat is also suggested in *Emile*, where Rousseau asserts that in England "great villains harden themselves to murder by drinking blood." *Emile*, 153.

15. Pythagoras abstained from wine and flesh of all kinds; Plutarch is quoted at length on this subject in book II of *Emile*, 152–153.

16. Cf. note 161 to letter II, xxiii, *Collected Writings* VI, 332.

17. Fifty *écus* in Geneva or France are 150 *livres* (pounds); but in fact *écus* were not in use in the Vaud.

18. This comment reflects deep Calvinist suspicions about dance, which was forbidden in Geneva at the time of Rousseau's youth.

19. Whichever text was actually composed first, most of this paragraph and all of the next one are indeed repeated in the *Letter to M. d'Alembert on the Theater*, 1758 (*Collected Writings* X, 344–345). Any reader who recognized the argument from having read the *Letter to M. d'Alembert* would have to conclude either that Rousseau "plagiarized" St. Preux in the *Letter* or that St. Preux is a fiction of Rousseau's, which would demolish the novel's carefully maintained ambiguous status. Thus this explanation after the fact that he earlier was "quoting" St. Preux is intricately tied up with *Julie's* possible claim to authentic status.

20. Although this "infusion" is of course metaphorical, it is also almost literally what St. Preux imagines: that a kind of spiritual fluid flows out from Julie to fill others: cf. letter II, vi, *Collected Writings* VI, 166.

21. The terminology of this phrase is significant, for although Rousseau never assumes (as the *Discourse on Inequality* shows) that human society can revert in time to its more innocent state, there is always a sense in which it can hope to recapture some of the unspoiled qualities that the state of nature evokes.

22. See note 79 to letter I, xxxvi, *Collected Writings* VI, 91.

23. There is no known printed source for this maxim, but it has more than one attributed source and he may well have heard it quoted. In essence, it is similar to Montaigne's "Few men have been admired by their domestics" (*Essays* III, 2), and the English version, "No one is a hero to his valet."

24. *Grands jours* refers to an assize or assembly of judges who come to the outlying provinces to hear cases.

25. The plural is in the French, and probably indicates a passage from the singular to a generalization: the whole paragraph passes here into the plural.

26. The *Roman de la rose* had been revived by an adaptation in modern French in 1735 by Lenglet-Dufresnoy, of which the text is:

Car Richesse ne fait pas riche

Celui qui en tresor la fiche,

Mais suffisance seulement

Fait homme vivre richement.

(vv. 5191–5194)

One could translate: "Wealth does not enrich the one who puts it in money; for self-sufficiency alone makes men live richly."

27. The origin and status of property are important subjects treated in part II of the *Discourse on Inequality* (see *Collected Writings* III, 48–55) and in the *Social Contract* (book I, chap. IX, *Collected Writings* IV, 142–144). *Propriété* also meant property.

28. He will return to these subjects in letter V, II.

29. At the beginning of the letter, St. Preux said it had something to do with a future project of Edward's, perhaps concerning him. If that project were to have St. Preux oversee his own properties in England, then the length and ostentatious systematicity of this letter might be taken as St. Preux's attempt to persuade Edward that he has acquired all the wisdom necessary for the undertaking of managerial responsibilities in the master's name.

20. "A Household on Rue Saint-Denis"

1. This fragment is said to have been written around 1735, although it could have been ten years later. Rousseau's first visit to Paris had been several years before the earlier date.

21. *Emile and Sophie, or the Solitaries*

1. See *Emile*, 477.

2. Rousseau wrote a note summarizing this passage, "After a long cooling off that produced a domestic separation, Emile, touched by a somber melancholy of his wife whose cause he does not know, is softened, returns to her, seeks to penetrate her fatal secret, to bring her back to him, to take back his former neglected rights. One day, more ardent than ordinary, he throws himself at the feet of his young wife and presses her with such vivacity that Sophie, moved and feeling herself ready to give way, suddenly gets up impetuously, teaches him with effort, with fright, a horrible secret that separates them forever, then throwing herself rapidly into a dressing room that she closes upon herself, leaves him, on his knees as he was, immobile, crushed, stupid, and outside of himself. It is this moment of the impetuous flight of the wife and the annihilation of the husband that it is necessary to grasp well."

3. See *Emile*, 83.

4. In one of the manuscripts this paragraph is followed by this incomplete passage: "The more necessary it is to wait the more difficult it is. How to stop the impetuosity of the passion that agitates us? With what to feed the devouring fire that consumes us or how to suspend its activity, upon what to distract the attention that one is giving to one's own torments? One does not put off the scent the pains of the soul any more than the sufferings of the body. On the contrary, it is necessary to abandon oneself to them so that they exhaust us and, weakened by them, we soon have less force for feeling them. By letting the rage of an angry man exhale, by letting a man cry in his torments."

5. Emile is trained as a carpenter.

6. The word translated as "proud" here is *fière*, whereas the word translated as "prideful" earlier in the sentence is "orgueilleuse." Both can be distinguished from vanity, but Rousseau always uses *fier* (*fière*) positively. He sometimes uses *orgueil* more neutrally, or even negatively.

7. The word translated as "pride" is *orgueil*.

8. As the editors of the Pléiade note (p. 1721 n. 2) the word "Monsieur," translated here as "Sir," would not have been used for an artisan.

9. Sophie had visited Emile in a workshop in *Emile*, 437–438.

10. See *Emile*, 181, where Emile, lost in the forest, finds his way home by determining which way is south by the direction of a shadow at noon.

11. See Descartes, *Discourse on Method*, V, where reason is identified as the "universal instrument."

12. In this case a renegade is a Christian who has converted to Islam.

13. This is a sort of small cannon on a pivot that shoots stones or nails instead of cannonballs.

14. One of the manuscripts reads, "I was ceaselessly at the wheel." At this point the same manuscript has a note, apparently indicating events that occur after the story breaks off: "I saw the vessel leave with a thrill of joy mixed, nevertheless, with a regret, more tender than sad. I was in the condition of a man weary with living who is reaching his final rest, but who, renouncing life without pain and recalling the sweet moments he tasted in it, bids it farewell, and then sighs while leaving it voluntarily. As the vessel went away all my former affections seemed to flee along with it. Ready to lose it from sight I brought my sight back upon the objects that surrounded me and exclaimed to myself while contemplating them: 'All is forgotten: henceforth this Island is the universe for me.' Then addressing myself to the good Old Man, I said to him while embracing him: 'We shall be the entire human race for each other. May I be able to make life as sweet for you as I hope to find it near you.' He smiled, then embracing me in his turn: 'Come,' he said, 'become acquainted with your universe; perhaps you will find there an abode less sad than its aspect has promised you.'" On another sheet of paper, the description of the island begins, "we were as if buried in a sort of sunken path that, forming branches lost itself at the foot of the rocks and had no other exit than the path by which we had come. If I had believed in magic I would have regarded myself at that moment like Aladdin's nephew in the *Thousand and One Nights*." On another sheet is a

description of a woman: "two large dark eyes that were shining, piercing, impossible to bear. I doubt that any European woman had any like them. Nothing is so lively and so quick as their language. But I do not conceive what such eyes can say when they are not speaking of love. Their gaze must be frightening in old age."

15. During his education Emile had had the experience of being tricked when a stronger magnet was used to counter the influence of a weaker one. See *Emile*, 173–175. One of the results of this experience was his discovery of how to make and use a compass.

16. The Knights Hospitalers were founded in Jerusalem in the eleventh century. They were established in Malta in the sixteenth century. They frequently fought against the Barbary pirates.

17. For these discussions and the principles see *Emile*, 458–467.

18. The principal manuscript ends here.

19. The most complete account of these alternative endings can be found in *Une Grève d'esclaves à Alger au XVIIIe siècle* by Michel Launay (Paris: Jean-Paul Rocher, 1998), 84–89. This volume contains a wealth of information about *Emile and Sophie*.

Index